SUSTAINABLE GOOD GOVERNANCE, DEVELOPMENT AND DEMOCRACY

SUSTAINABLE GOOD GOVERNANCE, DEVELOPMENT AND DEMOCRACY

N. BHASKARA RAO

Los Angeles | London | New Delhi
Singapore | Washington DC | Melbourne

First published in 2019 by

 SAGE Publications India Pvt Ltd
B1/I-1 Mohan Cooperative Industrial Area
Mathura Road, New Delhi 110 044, India
www.sagepub.in

SAGE Publications Inc
2455 Teller Road
Thousand Oaks, California 91320, USA

SAGE Publications Ltd
1 Oliver's Yard, 55 City Road
London EC1Y 1SP, United Kingdom

SAGE Publications Asia-Pacific Pte Ltd
18 Cross Street #10-10/11/12
China Square Central
Singapore 048423

Published by Vivek Mehra for SAGE Publications India Pvt Ltd, typeset in 10.5/13 pts Adobe Caslon Pro by Zaza Eunice, Hosur, Tamil Nadu, India and printed at Chaman Enterprises, New Delhi.

Library of Congress Cataloging-in-Publication Data Available

ISBN: 978-93-528-0811-3 (HB)

SAGE Team: Rajesh Dey, Alekha Chandra Jena, Suhagchandra Dave and Ritu Chopra

Dedicated...

*To my late parents, Freedom Fighters Nagulapalli
Seetaraamiah and Somidevamma, and to my village,
Mudunuru, Krishna District, Andhra Pradesh.*

*Responsible for my imbibing social concerns with national
outlook and for my pursuing development, democracy and
governance issues since my high school days.*

Thank you for choosing a SAGE product!
If you have any comment, observation or feedback,
I would like to personally hear from you.

Please write to me at **contactceo@sagepub.in**

Vivek Mehra, Managing Director and CEO, SAGE India.

Bulk Sales

SAGE India offers special discounts
for purchase of books in bulk.
We also make available special imprints
and excerpts from our books on demand.

For orders and enquiries, write to us at

Marketing Department
SAGE Publications India Pvt Ltd
B1/I-1, Mohan Cooperative Industrial Area
Mathura Road, Post Bag 7
New Delhi 110044, India

E-mail us at **marketing@sagepub.in**

Subscribe to our mailing list
Write to **marketing@sagepub.in**

This book is also available as an e-book.

Contents

List of Abbreviations

AAP	Aam Aadmi Party
ACB	Anti Corruption Bureau
ADR	Alternate Dispute Resolution
ASCI	Advertising Standards Council of India
BAIF	Bharat Agro Industry Foundation
BJP	Bharatiya Janata Party
BPL	Below Poverty Line
BSP	Bahujan Samaj Party
CAG	Controller & Auditor General of India
CBEC	Central Board of Excise and Customs
CBI	Central Bureau of Investigation
CHRI	Commonwealth Human Rights Initiative
CIC	Central Information Commission
CPR	Centre for Policy Research
CSO	Central Statistics Office
DGCIS	Directorate General of Commercial Intelligence and Statistics
ECI	Election Commission of India
EIU	Economist Intelligence Unit
GG	Good Governance
GRAAM	Grassroots Research and Advocacy Movement
GST	Goods and Services Tax
HQ	Headquarters
HRD	Human Resource Development
IAC	India Against Corruption
IAS	Indian Administrative Services
ICCR	Indian Council of Cultural Relations
ICSSR	Indian Council of Social Science Research
ICT	Information and Communications Technology
IICA	Indian Institute of Corporate Affairs

IIMC	Indian Institute of Mass Communication
IOT	Internet of Things
KV	Kendriya Vidyalaya
MGNREGS	Mahatma Gandhi National Rural Employment Generation Scheme
MKSS	Mazdoor Kisan Shakti Sangathan
MP	Members of Parliament
MSSRF	MS Swaminathan Research Foundation
NABARD	National Bank for Agriculture and Rural Development
NBA	News Broadcasters Association
NBSA	News Broadcasting Standards Authority
NCAER	National Council of Applied Economic Research
NDA	National Democratic Alliance
NES	National Extension Scheme
NOTA	None of the Above
NSS	National Sample Surveys
ORG	Operations Research Group
OSD	Officer on Special Duty
PCI	Press Council of India
PDS	Public Distribution System
PEO	Programme Evaluation Organisation
PIB	Press Information Bureau
PIL	Public Interest Litigation
PLS	Parliamentary legislative studies
PRAGATI	Proactive Government and Timely Implementation
PSBs	Public Sector Banks
RBI	Reserve Bank of India
RDO	Revenue Division Officer
RJS	Rastra Jagriti Samithi
RSS	Rashtriya Swayamsevak Sangh
RTE	Right to Education
RTI	Right to Information
SA	Social Audit
SDG	Service Delivery Guarantee
SEWA	Self Employed Women's Association
SWAN	State-Wide Area Networks

TIFAC	Technology Information Forecasting Assessment Council
TRAI	Telecom Regulatory Authority of India
UPA	United Progressive Alliance
VLW	Village-Level Worker
VRO	Village Revenue Officers

Foreword

It is always a pleasure to read whatever comes from the facile pen of Dr Bhaskara Rao. His path-breaking studies have been based on in-depth research and authentic empirical data. He has been a pioneer in many fields—opinion polls, public awareness campaigns, election poll surveys, RTI, ICT, etc. As a media researcher with immaculate credentials, he is widely respected. His voice has been one of sanity and sobriety. Any senior political leader or high dignitary should have been happy to write a foreword to his latest work but he picked up an humble student for the job. I feel honoured.

This excellent study is on a theme of great contemporary relevance for all of us. Legislature, Executive and Judiciary are the three well-established organs of the State. Dr Rao flags the role of three other what he calls the pillars of the Republic—media, civil society (NGOs/CSOs) and political parties. All the six are bound by the Constitution and have got to be transparent, responsible and accountable to the seventh—the ultimate masters—'we, the people of India'. Also, all of them have to be motivated, above everything else, by the impera-tives of participatory democracy, all-inclusive development and good governance.

As recently as in 2017, in all humility, I came out with a study titled 'Democracy and Good Governance'. I am glad that Dr Rao's title provides a corrective by adding the third essential dimension of development and drawing pointed attention to the dilemmas faced by the trinity. There are multiple linkages between democracy, development and governance. Democracy is hardly amenable to any precise definition. Also, it has many variants. But, our conception of democracy is of a participatory system in which the people govern themselves through their elected representatives. The end purpose is development and to be meaningful it should not be measured merely in economic—GDP/GNP—terms and on the anvil of the prosperity of the few. What is important is effective human development, fulfilment of basic civic and social rights and freedom, dignity and quality of life for all including the poorest of the poor. And, this calls for good quality governance—for less government and more governance.

The journey from government to governance is a long, arduous and never ending one. Governance is for doing good to everyone equally and assuring the development of all without sacrificing the basic tenets and framework of democracy. Good governance has to be wedded to development and democracy with transparency and accountability as essential ingredients. Governance has to be responsive and responsible, citizen friendly and sensitive to the urges, aspirations and needs of the people. Even though late, realisation seems to have at last dawned upon us that even economic reforms for faster development cannot succeed without first ensuring good quality, clean governance. The problem assumes systemic dimensions and calls for a multi-pronged response. With politics and politicians in the driving seat, everything ultimately depends upon our so-called representatives selected by political parties and formally elected by the people under a very divisive and faulty system.

What Dr Rao hints at and says mildly with his characteristic civility, I would put bluntly with a hammer. In past decades, there has been a steep erosion in the credibility and respect of political parties and politicians. The cost of democracy is getting too prohibitive and entirely disproportionate to the service to society rendered by the political class. Somewhere or the other elections are going on almost all the year round. Apart from the high costs in terms of human resources, many, many thousands of crores are spent by the Election Commission, Union and state governments, political parties, candidates and others. Incidentally, much of it is black money. Even when Houses of Parliament are not allowed to function or transact any business day after day, the expenditure on them is estimated to be 14.5 crores per day.

In a sense, the widening gulf between the politicians and the people is a global phenomenon today. But we as a nation cannot afford it. Speaking on the concluding day of the Constituent Assembly, Dr Ambedkar made a very pertinent remark. He said that times were changing fast. People, 'including our own', were being moved by new ideologies. They were getting tired of a government by the people. They would rather have a government for the people and could not care less whether it was of the people or by the people.

Traditionally, public life for us was for service and sacrifice. Honourable exceptions apart, it is no more so. By and large, it has become a profession or business and is looked upon as a lucrative career option for getting rich quick and wielding power. Our people are still prepared to make sacrifices for the nation and for fellow citizens provided the sacrifices began from the top and the political class and the senior bureaucracy agreed to cut their highly luxurious perks and emoluments. Unfortunately, our political parties have been functioning only as transmission belts to power. While reforming our democracy and bringing about all-inclusive development through good governance will involve action on several fronts and involve a wide range of political, parliamentary, administrative, educational and judicial reforms, electoral and political party reforms deserve the highest priority. As pointed out by Dr Rao, 'Without political parties coming under a democratic regime (with genuinely free and fair inner party elections) and a regulatory framework, there cannot be distinct change in the country for good governance.' The earlier the parties themselves realise it, the better. 'This is in their own long term interest ... and that of the country's democracy, development and governance.' Dr Rao goes on to say that Gandhiji was among the first few 'to visualise and even warn about [the] likely ill effects of political parties'. In 1948, a little before his assassination, he wrote in his diary:

> The Congress has gained the trust of the people on account of its sacrifices and penances but if at this moment it were to let the people down by becoming their overlord and, instead of remaining their servant, arrogate to itself a position of master, I venture to prophesy on the strength of my experience of long years that though I may be alive or not, a revolution will sweep the country and that the people will pick out the white-capped ones (*neta*s) individually and finish them.

Indian polity continues to face serious challenges. The present situation with regard to the state of the nation and democracy is indeed very grim. Not only the institutions of legislature and executive manned by politicians but also the judiciary—until now considered the last sheet anchor of democracy—are under dark shadows. There has been a sharp decline in the credibility of other pillars of our republic. With some exceptions, the media tends to become an extension of business and the civil society institutions represented by NGOs and CSOs also have lost much of their shine and potential to emerge as citizens' movements.

Immediate remedial action is called for. Howsoever idealistic and utopian it may seem, the most urgent need seems to be to bring politics and public life back to being for sacrifice and service and to restore faith in the quality, integrity and efficiency of democratic institutions and those who run them.

If we resolve to convert every challenge into an opportunity and keep democracy, development and good governance on the top of our national agenda, there need be no cause for despair. A massive churning is on. In the vastness of the desert, we must not lose sight of the oases of hope.

Dr Bhaskara Rao's excellent work covers a wide spectrum, raises many pertinent questions and suggests viable mechanisms for resolving conflicts and ways out from difficulties. I hope this dispassionate voice of sanity would be heard and the book would be widely read. It should serve as a clarion call to all of us to wake up, introspect and act.

Subhash C. Kashyap
Constitutional Expert
Former Secretary General, Parliament
New Delhi

Preface

In 2050, 30 years from now, Indian Republic completes 100 years. What we have achieved in the last 70 years has not been mean. A hundred years should be good for a country, with even India's complexities, to accomplish its goals as envisaged by the constitution makers. Will India be able to achieve its goals in the next 30 years? Will democracy deepen and take deeper roots? Will development be encompassing and fulfilling the basic needs? Will governance assure the rule of law and be inclusive and participative? What are the measures and correctives that need to be pursued for that? Will we accomplish what we envisioned, assuming we continue doing what we have been doing for the last 70 years, even if we do in a better way?

The country will have had six national elections by 2050 assuming a normal course of elections (after 2020). Unless we make concerted efforts now for the next 10 to 15 years and also make a breakthrough, we will not be consolidating the democratic model so wisely adopted to accomplish a truly welfare state, with happier and creative people. If a mere change in the party in the government could achieve what we had envisaged, we could have achieved everything by now, with as many as 16 national elections to Lok Sabha and over a hundred elections to state assemblies already conducted. Clearly, a mere change in political parties or having election-centric governments is not sufficient to rejuvenate and accomplish our bigger goals.

This very issue is what this book is all about. It introspects in detail how India will fare any better and accomplish more than an incremental growth in GDP and such other quantitative measures, while retaining the virtues of democracy, and political party driven governments. Is this not a dilemma? Can we do so by going bit by bit, certainly not even by taking to one change at a time approach? We have been talking of reforms for two decades now. Although we have taken initiatives on the economic front, we have hardly done so in other sectors. We have been talking about electoral reforms, for example, for more than two decades now. Similarly, we have been talking about administrative reforms as well as about the results of legislations like anti-defection amendments. Despite constituting committees and commissions, there is no evidence that a big difference has been achieved.

For over five decades, I have been working in New Delhi as an analyst, advisor and evaluator of policies and programmes in various capacities, without losing my moorings and rural origins and upbringing in a Gandhian family. I was also personally acquainted with the push and pulls in power corridors of Delhi, including the concerns and compulsions of mass media in the country. In my first book published in 1967, *Politics of Leadership in an Indian State, Andhra Pradesh*, I described how democratic traditions were deep rooted in the society, much beyond the realm of parliament and assemblies. That book was based on my own involvement as a student activist in electoral campaigns and in civil society initiatives. I wrote that book in response to Selig S. Harrison's book *India: The Most Dangerous Decades*, published in 1960, which threw doubts on India's democratic foundations.

In writing this book now, I have benefited mostly from the writings of and discussions I have had with Dr Subhash C. Kashyap in the last couple of years. Apart from being one of the leading constitutional experts in the country, Kashyap has written extensively on the functioning of the pillars of the republic, in the background of the constitution and the spirit with which it was drafted. That made me recall my acquaintance and association during my youth with a heavyweight leader of Andhra Pradesh, Kakani Venkata Ratnam (1950–1970), who inspired me to write this book. Uneducated himself, Kakani was responsible for the establishment of schools in every village of the Krishna district and the spread of professional education in the Krishna district, in particular, all in less than a decade. He held every elected position from village upwards and set an example while showing what the democracy–development–governance axis was all about, all without much of *bhashan* and sermonising and irrespective of whether he had won or lost an election or was in power or not. Fifty years after his sudden death, while leading a youth agitation, he is still remembered in the villages and by many accomplished medical doctors and engineers even in the USA.

This book is not a continuation of my earlier book, *Good Governance: Delivering Corruption-free Public Services* (SAGE, 2013). I have tried to outline what good governance should be and in what respects governance is much beyond government. It discusses a holistic view and proposes interventions needed for rejuvenating democracy–development–governance trajectory. Going beyond the conventional view of the four pillars of the State, a six-pronged pursuit of governance is proposed. The other two pillars suggested are society and political parties, and these two should do their job with accountability and transparency under the framework of 'checks and balances'.

N. Bhaskara Rao

CHAPTER 1

Seven Decades of Republic

In the seven decades as a parliamentary democracy,[1] what we in India have achieved is commendable, but more significant are the things we could not or ought to have achieved and the areas where we have lagged behind, and we need to catch up with these faster. For this to happen, we need to take a critical view of key differentiating sectors and explore options, alternatives and correctives. There is an increased realisation and craving for better governance, and claims have also been made about offering good governance, of course without realising the fact that such development cannot be guaranteed merely after forming a government and cannot also be claimed by promises of political leaders however grand and populistic they may be. Unless we take a holistic view and interlinked initiatives, not in bits and pieces but as a package of interventions, we will not be able to catch up. Equally critical is the understanding of what constitutes good governance. Unless such a holistic understanding is widely accepted, we will continue to tinker around and end up with marginal change, thus losing out on some more decades of opportunities.

Whither Seven Decades of Planned Development?

If after seven decades of planned development efforts, one per cent of the population owns much more than half of national wealth and their share is on the rise at the expense of the rest of the population, is it not time for a forthright introspection of what went wrong and how we should correct them and make a headway in the model of governance, development and democracy?

In his address on the eve of 67th Republic Day in January 2016, the then president of India Pranab Mukherjee reminded the nation that 'our finest inheritance, the institute of democracy, ensures to all citizens justice, equality and gender and economic equity', which is at the core of our nationhood. He further said, 'The spirit of accommodation, cooperation and consensus building should be the preferred mode of decision making.'[2] Have we achieved that stature in our democratic system and movement in our development endeavours? Can quantitative terms of income and wealth indicators tellingly reflect the status of a nation? An Oxfam report[3], released mid-January 2017, states that 'India's richest one percent now hold a huge 58 percent of the country's total wealth'.[4] The *World Inequality Report 2018*,[5] released in mid-December 2017 by World Wealth & Income Database, observers that India's record on inequality (in incomes) is the worst. It concluded that not only does this pose a challenge to public policy—particularly in figuring out a redistribution of wealth—it could also potentially trigger social unrest.

According to Credit Suisse Global Wealth Report, 2016, the top one per cent of Indian population owns 58.4 per cent of the country's total wealth[6] and this was an increase from 49 per cent in the year 2014. This reveals the fact that with each passing year, the top one per cent is grabbing more and more of the wealth share from the bottom 99 per cent. An analysis of Credit Suisse for 15 years, between 2000 and 2016, shows that the share of the top 10 per cent of India's population in the total wealth of the country has increased from 68.8 per cent to 80.7 per cent and the share of other groups has declined remarkably. The bottom half own a mere 2.1 per cent of the country's wealth. Moreover, according to the same report, out of the newly created wealth in the Indian economy, the top one per cent appropriated 61 per cent and the bottom 99 per cent are left with the rest. The report reiterates the support data that even within this one per cent of more than 125 crore people of India, only a handful at the top were benefited.

The policies followed by various governments have also contributed to growing inequalities. The Credit Swiss numbers confirm that India is one of the most unequal societies. This is also what the World Inequality Report noted about India in December 2017.[7] It projects that in a decade the share of the rich in India's wealth is likely to go up to 75 per cent, which means that it has been a 'trickle up' effect instead of 'trickle down', which we were promised at the onset of the Five Year Plans. This is how the number of billionaires in India have gone up from 13 in 2004 to 69 in 2010.[8] Interestingly, 15 of them are from the real estate sector. In 2015–2016, 27 new billionaires were added, making India home for 111 billionaires by early 2016 whose assets had also increased by 20 per cent during the period.[9] According to Oxfam, 57 billionaires in India have the same amount of wealth as that of the bottom 70 per cent of the population. An ICRIER[10] study by Radhicka Kapoor brought to light how capital augmenting technological progress has increased income and wage inequalities. The share of total emoluments paid to labour fell from 34.5 to 22.4 per cent of gross value added between 2000–2001 and 2011–2012 and that of wage workers declined from 26.9 to 18.5 per cent during the period. The situation in 2018 has again marginally declined.

If democracy in vogue does not enable the poor and achieve basic needs core objective of people and the constitutional priorities even in 70 years, then the growth model need to be questioned, corrected and repositioned. This, however, does not mean democracy per se be reconsidered; but the institutions and the policies, procedures and practices and the structures built over the decades need to be relooked. It is because parliamentary democracy cannot sustain unless social democracy and development is assured. This is what Babasaheb Ambedkar had warned at the onset of the Constitution of India.[11]

As the Indian government keeps claiming that the country's growth was the fastest ever before with the highest growth achieved in the year 2015 at 8.7, the World Bank downgraded India's status and shifted to that of a 'lower middle income country'. The tag of India being a 'developing country' was under a threat of change of its status globally. Even after 70 years of democracy, 15 general elections, 12 Five Year Plans, and 7.4 per cent GDP, if political and economic power remains the privilege of a few, should we continue with the same assumptions of our development paradigm?

Creating wealth is good for a society. How it is distributed or shared and reaches its people are even more important. It is certainly a desirable first step towards poverty eradication. But is it sufficient? Continued inequality is bad in realising growth potential and also a threat to political independence. Growth without equity is not durable and sustainable. Growth without distribution is no guarantee for equity and democracy. Democracy implies equal and level playing opportunity for people, which in turn reduces inequalities.

In the last 70 years, President's Rule was imposed in states by the Union government for more than 130 times. The parliament has also been revoked on many occasions on the pretext of 'instability' of an elected government or by initiating the anti-defection law. Such situations have arisen irrespective of whichever party's government has been at the Centre. Too many amendments have happened in many existing laws and many of the laws are even outdated; about 1,000 laws were declared outdated in 2015 by the 'Modi government' based on a review by a committee.[12] It took 58 years for the Supreme Court to conclude that ordinances should be revoked in exceptional circumstances and that they should not be extended without going through the legislative process. We have more than 1,000 ordinances issued so far and there were instances of issuing some of them a few days before a session of the parliament or immediately thereafter. What does that mean? By bypassing the democratic processes, are we lessening the significance of the parliament?

All this, however, does not mean that we give up democracy. Rather it implies that we streamline the functioning of democratic institutions, processes of governance and the governance mechanisms, procedures and practices. Democracy is not positively correlated with redistribution without special efforts and relook at the political structures.

Has the 73rd Amendment to decentralise resources and responsibilities (1992) made any difference either in efficiency in the delivery of anti-poverty programmes or in reversing centralisation of political power? On the contrary, corruption has been decentralised to grassroots, to panchayat level. That is why, huge money is being spent now to get elected to gram panchayats, too.

Right to employment, by means of implementing the Mahatma Gandhi National Rural Employment Generation Scheme (MGNREGS), is not strictly meant for unemployment eradication; rather it is only a guarantee for work for certain days in a year as a part of the poverty relief initiative. This programme was meant for rural people, especially for those engaged in the farm sector since work is not available for certain days in a year because of seasonality of agriculture. First, the guarantee at the outset was for hundred days and that is for certain type of work, which is decided by the local panchayat or a government agency from time to time. Despite the talk and hype, hardly half of that many days work was provided in any of the year in the last ten years (2008–2018).

Drinking water is not guaranteed for many, although schemes after schemes were introduced over the decades with many promises. Even by 2016, more than half of the villages in India were without clean drinking water. Poor households spend more to buy drinking water than what some spend for a glass of milk for their children. This is despite the fact that today we have advanced technologies for treating water.

Lack of potable water leads to several health hazards as almost half of health problems of people are water born, arising out of drinking water from polluted sources of all kinds. But the health sector has also not made good progress. It took 70 years for India to make at least some generic drugs available on prescription. Spurious drugs vitiate the right to health for certain basic facilities.

Housing for all is yet another slogan with new schemes every time there is a change in Government, or even of the Minister. Even in

2018, the target for a roof to every need is far away. Basic needs—*roti, kapada aur makan*—was a poll time slogan decades ago. Lack of an all season connecting road is another problem that villagers often complain about. These basic needs still, in 2018, remain far-fetched. And yet, promises of the politicians continue to lure people.

Concentration of power has been on the rise over the years both in the states and at the Centre. Certain 'high command culture' is attributed for the increasing disconnect of political leaders and ministers with local people and organisations. Even within states such a trend is blatant despite the rhetoric of decentralisation. Unequal distribution of power at every level is what determines the quality of governance. Democracy is not just about holding elections. It is more about voice that individual citizen hold as and when he or she needs to avail public services. Hierarchy of power is continuing despite the prevalence of policies for decentralisation and the spread of newer communication technologies. No good governance could be expected in an atmosphere where concentration of power and wealth are with only a few people.

Economic reforms are meant to accelerate growth with equity. But reforms should not end up in facilitating the creation of more special zones and big infrastructure projects, opening up of foreign capital and even privatisation of what has been built over seven decades as part of public welfare and social justice responsibility of the State (irrespective of the government). These measures have their relevance but they cannot operate with guaranteed privileges, profit margins and such other advantages. Social reforms with regard to discrimination, gender inequalities, prejudices, stigma about certain communities or professions, deprivation of people from education, and so on, are critical for development and good governance.

According to a recent UNESCO[13] report, India will be half-a-century late in achieving its global educational commitments and the country needs fundamental changes in its education system. According to this review, India is expected to achieve universal primary education in 2050 and universal lower secondary education by 2060.[14] In spite of realising the criticality of education, the percentage of illiterate is reasonably even after 70 years of independence. Although there is the desirability to allocate at least 6 per cent of the GDP for education, not even half of that is budgeted.

After infrastructure of primary education has been made a state responsibility, there is now a growing trend to even privatize primary education, which is opening up business opportunities for many private players. This is happening in a big way across the states without any regulatory mechanism in place, and this has hardly been debated in public. Although education was placed as a fundamental responsibility of the state in the constitution, it took more than four decades to declare it as a fundamental right, only with the passing of the Right to Education Act of 2009. And, since then, the states seem to be competing in ignoring the Act rather than implementing!

It is quite appalling to notice the outright promotion of private schools, which are mushrooming everywhere, not only at the levels of higher and professional education but even at primary and secondary levels, when the country invested for so many decades in establishing public schools with reasonable infrastructure providing free school uniform, mid-day meal and books to children. The mere argument that supervision of these public schools or even community participation was missing should not necessarily lead to bypassing these schools in favour of private schools, whose primary outlook in most cases is profit making.[15]

More formal education and universal access to education will reduce inequalities sooner or later. However, this notion should not hold true only at the macro level nor should it remain merely a theoretical proposition. Social realities with regard to caste, religion or region need to be moderated if cannot be neutralised. For example, the suicide of a Dalit student at Central University, Hyderabad in January 2016 has revived an old issue. As many as 12 postgraduate students from the university had committed suicide in a decade and, surprisingly, 10 of them were from Dalit households of mostly agriculture labourers. The Andhra Pradesh High Court took a suo motu public interest litigation (PIL) on suicide cases of students in university campuses of Hyderabad over a period of 12 months.[16] Can we expect the minimum sensitivity required for handling such situations when neither the head nor the members of the senior faculty of the university/institution represent the Dalit community?

Quality of education is yet another aspect that needs introspection. The findings of a Stanford University and World Bank study indicate that the overall learning outcome of undergraduate engineering students of India in terms of 'overall higher order thinking skills' is 'substantially low' compared to Chinese and Russian counterparts.[17] Eighty per cent of the graduates in engineering were found to be unfit to pass proficiency tests as they lack skills and knowledge for proactive role and initiatives. The British used education as a tool to build a workforce to meet the demands of various jobs for their own benefit. We are still continuing that very job-centric education system without any sensitivity to the socio-economic conditions of India at present and without giving much heed to the realities and the challenges facing the nation.

Some mindboggling reports surfaced in 2016 when, after a re-examination, the topper in XII Board examination in Bihar could not even recollect the subjects she was taught in school. Bihar Government had no option but to cancel the results of examination after of the case was exposed by a TV channel.[18]

Census of India 2011 recorded that 120 million (i.e., 11%) of the youth under 25 years of age are either without work or are on the lookout for work, and most of them are educated and skilled. Nearly one-fourth of the youth of 20–24 years of age are on the lookout for work.[19]

Regular droughts in about half of the districts in the country, more so in some of the states, add to the problem of poverty of the disadvantaged people, which leads to another perennial problem among this section of the society, that is, of suicides. The number of suicides in recent times at various levels calls for a serious appraisal. Such cases were even recorded among students at the high school level in 2015 in Telangana, which were on account of humiliation and failure to pay fees of one kind or another. There were more than a dozen cases of student suicides in Kota, Rajasthan, where failure in internal examinations led to the commitment of suicides of the high number of students who were otherwise preparing to appear in competitive examinations after their internal examinations.

Empowering Local Governments

India has been placed by various external and internal agencies in a strange way as far as social development indicators are concerned. Many studies, including some empirical ones,[20] have analysed this phenomena and yet we do not seem to have taken corrective measures to ward off the lapses in policies. It is obvious because social sector allocations over the decades have been low and inadequate to meet up the challenging tasks. These allocations are still on the decline; as against 3.4 per cent in 2010–2011, such allocations including food subsidies reduced to 2.84 per cent of the GDP in 2014–2015. It was not expected much beyond 3 per cent of the GDP even in 2016–2017. And not all that was allocated was actually spent on the intended purpose. This is despite the correctives measures prescribed after the analysis of many international agencies.

Modern form of slavery is another problem that has contributed in destabilising the Indian economy and society. As per the Global Slavery Index, brought out by Walk Free Foundation, a human rights organisation, India has the largest population of modern slaves in the world with more than 18 million bonded labourers, forced beggars and sex workers. It accounts for 1.4 per cent of India's population.[21]

Despite the 73rd and 74th Amendments to the constitution in 1992, indicating a list of functions that can be transferred to local governments, there is no evidence that local panchayats have been empowered. Even state financial commissions have not devolved required finance to districts in some states for the proper functioning of the panchayats.

The Andhra Pradesh High Court expressed its dislike (January 2016) for the practice of selecting candidates for welfare schemes, including old age pension and scholarships, by some nominated individuals only when it is the responsibility of the locally elected people's representatives. Such tactics are obviously meant to deprive or deny certain sections otherwise eligible for such benefits.

In 2015–2016, zilla parishads in the two states of Andhra Pradesh and Telangana, for example, languished for lack of funds as central funds were either cut or stopped for some reasons. As a result, some key projects had to be deferred or wound up. Each district of these states lost 20 to 30 crores of rupees on account of changes in the central accounting system. Several welfare schemes had to be deferred, which included schemes meant for protected water supply, construction of rural roads and repair of school buildings.

Since more than one-third of the budgets of zilla parishads and a much higher percentage of revenue of municipalities are spent on establishment and maintenance, these government bodies have practically become ineffective. The number of meetings of elected representatives were reduced to discussion or advisory points only. This is also because zilla parishads do not have their own sources to generate revenue and set their own priorities. The 14th Finance Commission notionally increased allocations but they are being sent to gram panchayats directly. But we need to see whether this new system will make any difference in empowering local communities after 2020.

In practice, it is the administrative officers in New Delhi who pre-scribe effective implementation of various services to states, including those of health and education, and even where states actually have the responsibility. Many of the schemes continue to be driven by the Union government, while they should be rather need-based, locally driven and citizen-centric.

Farmer Suicides

Farmers enjoy no security of reliable kind and continue to live in uncertain condition and risks. The number of deaths of farmers and village artisans from the states has been increasing every year. The situation now is such that it looks like local officials and elected rep-resentatives have lost touch with the realities and governments have failed to tackle the chronic and widespread distress. This is despite the many initiatives that Reserve Bank of India (RBI) undertook including the setting up of National Bank for Agriculture and Rural Development (NABARD), some 50 years ago, after surveying the rural credit scenario for the first time in the mid-1950s identifying the existence of an agrarian crisis and realising the seriousness of farmers' debts. Some pertinent questions still hold good, for example, what has been the net outcome or result of all those efforts and why do farmer suicides continue to alarm. A 2015 official report (on crimes in India)[22] showed a marginal decline in the number of farmer suicides in official records, that is, to less than 15,000. However, in the same report, another nearly 5,000 cases of suicide of farm labours were shown separately for the same year. Moreover, about one-fifth of those farmers who committed suicides were in debt. Crop insurance is still being experimented. Regular and reliable availability of pesticides, seeds, fertilizers and irrigation are still far from a reality. Farmers in some parts of the country are even giving up cultivation for want of timely supply of water and, in some cases, lack of good monetary returns for the produce. Remote sensing technologies are not yet availed to prevent farmer suicides. Indian technologists have not been motivated enough to take on the issue of farmer suicide. As farmers are being harassed by banks for outstanding loans of even a couple of thousands, it was revealed in parliament on 4 April 2018 that an amount of 2.4 lakh crore was written off by public sector banks (PSBs) as bad loans.

Child Marriages: Is the Girl a Liability?

The practice of child marriages is not a thing of the past. It is not only prevalent in the present society but is also spreading. As an example, in the slightly better developed Guntur district in Andhra Pradesh which has a relatively high literacy rate, government agencies prevented 90 child marriages between April 2014 and November 2015. Legislations such as Prohibition of Child Marriage Act 2006 have failed to heal the fundamental evil practices of society.[23] Even after 70 years of independence, people continue to think that a girl is a liability. Three sisters of 3 to 10 years died of starvation on July 2018, hardly a couple of kilometres from the Parliament House in New Delhi. Then there have been horrifying happenings of girls being raped including in shelter homes, as if girl child is uncared. As many as 70 deaths of children were reported in Gorakhpur's government hospital alone for want of oxygen cylinders, as India celebrated its 70th year of Independence on 15 August 2017. In August 2017, reports came in about the death of 88 new born babies in a government hospital in Rajasthan. The Gorakhpur case was not the first time, nor would it be the last time, that such incidents of infant and child mortality in government hospitals have been reported. Such deaths continue to be reported in high numbers from across the country as if the neglect has not been an exception or as if it happens by default. An analysis of the Gorakhpur case indicates that the system collapsed under financial strain.[24]

A study conducted on 900 school-going girls in six states by an independent agency, Break Through, revealed that half of the girls are sexually harassed on their way to school and 32 per cent are stalked. Despite having laws on the rights of the child, efforts on the ground have been disappointing. Kailash Satyarthi estimated that 43 lakh children toil in conditions of exploitation and forced labour. Another 98 lac are out of school. He states, 'Every eight minutes, a child goes missing and 8.5 lakh children die before their birthday.'[25]

High Consumption of Tobacco in Children

A global survey indicated that 10 per cent of children in the age group of 15–17 years consume tobacco in some or the other form daily, and this amounts to over 4.5 million children. The figure in India is also very high, despite the presence of 'Cigarettes and Other Tobacco Products Act of 2003'. This shows how companies are allowed to entice children into using tobacco at a very early age.

Women Rights

Seven decades after independence, men and women are still not viewed and privileged equally. Although legal provisions were made for equal wages between men and women in 1976, it was not implemented until 1996. However, even after implementation, equal wages for both men and women are still not provided in many sectors despite all other things like qualification, age, skills, etc. being equal. In some cases, women are taken on contract basis to avoid equal wages.

It is an irony that women who are known for upholding rituals and traditions are denied entry and *puja* at the Siva temple in Shinga Nagar near Shirdi in Ahmednagar district, Maharashtra. In 2015, the local panchayat elected a woman for the first time as its Sarpanch. But the temple in the village was not opened for women even after a march of 1,000 women on the occasion of the 67th Republic Day. Instead of welcoming them, the women were stopped and taken into custody by the police. The state government remained silent initially and yielded only when pressure built up. Even decades after the entry of Harijans into temples was made legal, women are continued to be discriminated till now. Even Muslim women have to take the legal route to enter mosques and *dargahs*, as evident in the case of Haji Ali in Mumbai, ironically the most cosmopolitan metro of India.

Bribe

According to a study by CMS Research House,[26] an analysis of data for over a decade reveals that it is the poor and the underprivileged communities who suffer while availing basic public services because of corruption in the form of bribes, whereas the better off section of the society finds the bribe amount manageable or often are likely to have 'a contact' or a middle person to cope with the situation.

Six months after taking charge of the country's Chief Vigilance Commissioner in 2016, after retiring as an Income Tax officer, K.V. Chowdary, observed that corruption in the country cannot be brought down by Lokayukta, Lokpal or anti-corruption bureaus and it is possible only when people themselves are determined to eliminate it by keeping away from paying and seeking bribes.[27]

Around 14 per cent of GDP is spent in the name of subsidies so that the poor could avail of the benefits. However, the poor can avail of only some, that too after paying a bribe. In fact, nearly 4 per cent of seekers of public services are deprived of such public service as they are often not able to pay the bribe or they do not have any 'contact' person in the respective department.

R.K. Raghavan, a former CBI Director, stated that 'the levels of integrity of public servants [were] plummeting rapidly'[28] at a time when the Union government was in the process of increasing their salaries by 15–20 per cent as recommended by Seventh Pay Commission. He wrote that 'we should worry about lack of integrity in the whole civil service', and 'what is depressing is higher echelons are not setting an example to those below'.

Dissent and Dialogue Is the Essence of Democracy

In his address on the Republic Day Eve in 2017, President Pranab Mukherjee called upon the citizens to 'complain, demand and rebel'. Why did he say that? Perhaps he wanted to remind the citizen that they have remained passive and that the best safeguard for a democracy is to have active citizens.[29] With the growing use of communication technologies, citizen can now be far more active and interactive. In an earlier speech made in West Bengal, President Mukherjee expressed his anguish that 'differences between people are on increase, tolerance in people is on decline and that capacity to locally solve conflicts is on decline as mutual respect between people is on decline … as news media reports more of such trends'.[30] Of course, the president did not accuse the media for that, but as he expressed these views only a few days before his Republic Day address to the nation indicated how serious he was with his observations?

G. Philomena, a senior journalist, while writing in *New Indian Express*, observed that government today is not so much 'By' the people but 'Buy' the people the way elections are won using money power; 'For' the people has become 'Far' from the people; and instead of 'Of' the people, governments have become 'Off' the people as to the powers. Coupled with neglect of social development, these threats stare at the republic.[31]

Spread of Technology

Klaus Schwab of World Economic Forum[32] had mentioned in January 2016 to have met two economists of MIT Sloan School of Management, cautioning that technological revolution increases inequality in the world as the spread of machines increases unemployment and disrupts labour markets. He concluded that an increase in inequality remains the biggest social concern surrounding the current technological revolution which he calls as 'fourth industrial revolution'. He cautioned that India will face social tensions in particular because of low skill, low pay and high skill, high pay segments.

A recent report by the Swiss Bank UBS said that spread of artificial intelligence and robots will harm economies like India by cutting its cheap labour edge. What does it mean? Why is it being discussed? e-Pragati (2015),[33] for example, in Andhra Pradesh, is for delivering government services online in a coordinated manner by integrating all departments for the convenience of citizens and business. A state government typically will have about 33 departments and over 300 agencies extending around 700 services to citizen across departments. e-Pragati is expected to integrate all of them in a two-year period. But despite proliferation of information and communications technology (ICT) in the country, there has not been scaling up of e-services to citizens nor are there any means to assess the extent to which these services are availed. e-Pragati has potential to prevent farmer suicides, but there is no indication either that suicides have declined.

Analysing the rise and fall of political dynasties, even in democracies, Ajit Balakrishnan observed certain factors which contribute to fall of dynasties, such as the weakness in the institutional structure of political parties, absence of rules and procedures fostering internal democracy within political parties and centralisation of collection and distribution of funds, often illegal.[34] This is evident not only in India but also in some other democracies. Can we expect good governance without addressing and correcting these inherent trends? Certainly not. Focusing merely on the government of the day and its structure, and only of its efficiencies, will not result in good governance.

Decline in Party Politics

Preoccupation with 'party line politics' in everything, every time has neutralised or nullified the instruments created for governance. Conflict of interest of the representatives in legislatures is the other phenomenon hindering the processes of governance. The fact that the Speaker of Lok Sabha[35] on the concluding session of Winter 2015 had to observe that MPs were 'not bothered of national interests as they are in their own vested interests', indicates the kind of desperation speaker felt in running the House. That the Speaker was made to expunge these remarks on her own is a different matter, but the impression that was so widely felt across the country after these remarks by the Speaker did not get wiped out from the minds of people easily.

Political parties do not want to come under the ambit of Right to Information (RTI) Act when it is in their own interest to do so. Anti-Defection Act to prevent horse trading on the floor of the House did not make much of a difference in criss-crossing between parties of elected representatives. Disclosing assets and criminal background at the time of filing nominations to contest legislative positions, even after a decade of such disclosures by contesting candidates was made obligatory, did not make any difference, either to the extent the elected representatives accumulate wealth or in the number of elected representatives with criminal records, both in the parliament and state assemblies.[36]

Law-making at a Fit of Frenzy

The 2018 budget was passed in the parliament with hardly 14.5 hours of discussion against 58 hours of discussion on the budget in 2000.[37] Most of the bills that got passed in the parliament in recent years have hardly been deliberated on the floor. In fact, many have become Acts without even the members being conscious of them. Forty-seven per cent of the bills in last 10 years have been passed without a debate. RTI has become a legislation in 2005 with no discussion whatsoever on the floor of the House.[38] However, in 2016–2017, several members of parliament criticised how such an Act could came into being. It is evident that there is lack of seriousness and sincerity in implementing the legislations and in accomplishing what we promised ourselves. Yet we continue to claim accomplishing these tasks in a rather deceptive way. Right to Education (2009) is yet another such example.

Challenges of Governance

This book is about how and why we are nowhere near achieving the ideals, in spirit and in numbers, of what our founding fathers envisioned seven decades ago, and also the objectives outlined in the five year plans. Why good governance remain more as a political slogan and a mere rhetoric? It is either because either concerns for the actual reasons behind the governance issues is missing or our leaders and administrators have not been good enough, or both. It could also be because of a possible mismatch between the methodology adapted for good governance and the priorities of the pillars of the State. It is also possible that perhaps that the idea of 'governance' has not even been fully appreciated.

Times have changed and, as they say, change is permanent. And that disruptive change is even better. The problem at national level arises from the fact that efforts for change have to be simultaneous across the institutes of the State and the republic. Some pillars lag behind, others do not, and few march further ahead. Yet, in an electoral democracy, taking along everyone is essential to achieve and accomplish the goals. Good governance is a good case example. Such a State is being talked about and claimed by leaders in government for more than a decade now. Yet, we are nowhere near to say that good governance is being felt by people, be it any part of the country. How come? Why so? Our very perceptions about the notion of good governance are perhaps constrained or animated. What successive governments are doing in the name of good governance is contradictory, as if the course is of one step forward and two steps backward.

Country of Contradictions

India is known as a county of contradictions. On any dimension of development, one could say either way of that process such a trend with equal claim as to the direction. But more often analysis tends to be in a negative way and, more importantly, are done by using criteria or yardsticks that are foreign or are not in alignment with Indian culture and ethos. India cannot be objectively understood or analysed in good–bad terms or in a black-and-white frame or in a yes–no manner. This is because every human dimension and endeavour goes through a process with different implications at different time contexts. Efforts to measure such a process and quantity are bound to have limitations depending on with what perspective or perception one approaches the phenomena of change. Notwithstanding the rigidities of concepts and measurement methodologies used, research findings could go either direction of a good–bad continuum. Shifts in the very paradigm are evident in every sector and estate of the republic.

Pillars of the Republic

Legislative, judiciary, executive and media are often described as the four estates of the State. I have been advocating that civil society should be considered as an essential 'fifth estate' (not 'fifth column'!) of the State. They are expected to work in a 'checks and balances' mode for ensuring governance a reality. I now consider political parties as the sixth pillar of the State.

Fundamental changes in the very paradigm of public systems and public policies, and the processes in a democratic set up, as in India, are not comparable with other political systems (as in the case of communist China). Compulsions of a democratic system, and in a country of India's plurality, complexity and push-and-pull factors, matter as much as the outcomes and impacts. Electoral system and participatory process involved is at the root of change in the functioning of various pillars of the State.

Seeing Shyam Benegal's TV serial (in Rajya Sabha TV), *Samvad— Making of Our Constitution* (2010), one gets an exposure to the kind of concerns, insights and expectations that our constitution makers had about India and an emerging India. The 70 years of (the lengthiest) the Constitution with all complexities is increasingly under pressure for a relook. Our constitution has even seen more than a hundred amendments, pushed through with a two-thirds majority in the parliament, and many more such efforts have not stopped yet. An analysis of the amendments and their relevance may, however, not reveal much as in the case of, for example, devolution of powers to panchayats and municipalities under 63rd and 64th Amendments, the Right to Education (2009) and others. Fundamental rights, a unique feature of Indian Constitution, guarantees civil liberties, including individual rights, and yet, a rights regime has unfolded only recently, that too without much seriousness about implementation of those provisions, despite violation of these fundamental rights attracting penal code enforceable by the courts. Besides the Right to Information, the other six fundamental rights are (a) Right to Equality, (b) Right to Freedom, (c) Right against Exploitation, (d) Right to Freedom of Religion, (e) Cultural and Educational Rights and (f) Right to Constitutional Remedies. Then there are other rights under special Acts as in the case of Right to Information, Right to Education, Right to Employment, etc.

The Fifth Estate

The fifth estate is the civil society, which includes organised unions and bodies (different from the fifth column used to describe subversive or insurgent elements). Now, bloggers could also be included within the idea of fifth estate. The idea of 'fifth column' is just opposite to that of the fifth estate or the fifth pillar. Civil society, in its various manifestations, is the core of the State, next only to the apparatus of empowered agencies. However, because of unorganised character and diffused nature of the civil society, it has not acquired the significance it deserves, including in the priorities of news media. This could be cited as one of the factors for hitherto passive character of citizenry. There is increasing recognition that active citizenry is the best bet for governance and even a prerequisite for public service delivery and development process. As Subhash Kashyap[39] had put it, '[The] source of many of our maladies is in the disregard of the interests of the citizen....'

There has been widespread feeling in the country that concerns of political parties (and leaders) and the legislatures have declined, as basic needs and expectations of people are not being attended promptly. Even judiciary has come under criticism increasingly for delays in taking up cases, for their judgments, in the appointment of judges and for corruption in the judicial system. Mass media, more so the news media, have come under increasing public scrutiny and questioning for their coverage, conflict of interest and priorities. All these aspects have come under questioning by one or the other estates in a 'checks and balances' way as provided for in the constitution. The premise is that each of these estates or pillars of the State maintain a vigil and see that they operate in the best interest of the larger public and with future concerns. Instead, the tendency often has been that each estate is trying to dictate terms with the other, whereas the idea of checks and balances is to see that there is certain equilibrium between the estates which is maintained such a way that each estate tries to do the best of its expected or assigned role. With transparency in the regime around (with Acts such as RTI Act 2005), there is yet another opportunity for the political parties, legislatures, media and the executive to gear up and be more transparent, responsive to the larger clientele, that is, the citizenry and be community-centric.

Checks and Balances

Inaugurating an international meet on judicial reforms in New Delhi on 12 January 2013, President of India Shri Pranab Mukherjee reminded legal luminaries of the need for a semi-balance between the pillars of the State.[40] He suggested that each of the pillars should do its job well without intruding upon the functioning of other pillars and adversely affecting their roles. He felt that of late the feeling of judicial interference and intrusion is increasing in the country and, as a result, the balance between the pillars of the State is getting disturbed. He, however, acknowledged that good comes out of such judicial 'interference' at times. He was specific about legislature and executive and their specific roles. He even lamented delays in legal process resulting in piling up of cases in courts.

Cost of Parliamentary Democracy

The quality of governance in India eventually depends on the representatives who get elected to the three tiers of the parliamentary system—Lok Sabha, state assemblies and panchayats. How free and fair are the elections in these various levels in turn indicates the vibrancy of democracy.[41]

While the duration of Lok Sabha and state assemblies is five years and the elections are conducted by the Election Commission of India, the elections for municipalities, zilla parishads and panchayats are decided by the concerned state authorities and are also expected to be held every five years.

Overall, a voter could end up voting in five different elections in a five-year period, assuming that there would be no by-elections and none of the elections is deferred (as it usually happens in the case of panchayat elections). Some of these elections may even take place together. In an unprecedented way, in 2014 Andhra Pradesh experienced elections for four of these different bodies—Lok Sabha, state assembly, corporations/municipalities, zilla parishads and mandals. While the Lok Sabha and assembly elections were held at the same time, elections for the other two levels were held one after another before the Lok Sabha/assembly poll. But all these elections were held within a two-month period, between April and May 2014.

The expenditure for conducting these elections is incurred not only by the Election Commission of India, but by political parties, candidates and others, including the state governments and local administrations. In each of these elections, there is a ceiling on what a candidate could spend to reach out to voters. The expenditure ceiling in 2014 for Lok Sabha was INR 70 lakh, while for assembly it was INR 28 lakh and 2 lakh and 1 lakh for the other two levels, respectively. However, in order to woo voters, candidates spend much more than the ceiling on their own in addition to what their political parties and concerned government agencies spend. Even political parties spend much more than what is indicated from their filings with the Election Commission of India. Never before an estimate of total expenditure involved in these various elections in the country, individually or together, was made nor did any such idea surfaced until a series of studies were conducted at various levels from 2005 to 2010. The attention has been more on corporate funding of elections than on total expenditure and its larger implications.

What does these elections at different levels cost the country over a five-year period? The cost is of course much more than the expenditure formally incurred by different players in an election. Based on an estimate of expenditure by CMS for Lok Sabha, two assemblies and by-elections in between over the last couple of elections for Lok Sabha and state assemblies (of 2014), an overall estimate of expenditure in the elections for the three tiers in Andhra Pradesh in 2014 was made. The CMS study across the states in 2007 and 2008 on the percentage of voters who claimed receiving money for vote in a quid pro quo way was used for this national estimate. An expenditure of over INR 150,000 crore was found involved in a five-year period to uphold electoral democracy in the country (as far as 2014 elections are concerned). And, this was a conservative estimate. This analysis in 2014 also indicated that the expenditure is significantly increasing with every election. Only one-fifth of the total expenditure was on account of the Lok Sabha elections. This was a preliminary estimate for the elections to primary legislative bodies, with constitutional provision to have polling with a fixed periodicity. About one-third of the total expenditure was on account of elections for the state assemblies. The

Table 1.1 *An Estimate of Expenditure Involved in Elections over a Five-Year Period, Assuming These Different Elections Are Held Separately (Estimation of 2014 Elections)*

Level	Number of Seats	Expenditure (₹ in Crore)
Lok Sabha	540	30,000
Assemblies	4,500	45,000
Municipal Corporations/ Municipalities	465	15,000
Zilla Parishads (direct/indirect)	590	10,000
Mandals (direct/indirect)	6,500	20,000
Panchayats (direct/indirect)	253,000	30,000
Total estimate for all these polls over a 5-year period		**150,000**

Source: CMS.

rest was all for keeping up the ritual of periodic elections for local governments comprising corporations/municipalities and panchayats at the district, mandal and village levels.

The expenditure by political parties is considerably less in the local elections, less than 10 per cent against 20 per cent in the case of Lok Sabha. On the other hand, the percentage of expenditure by aspiring candidates to get nomination of a party to contest in local elections is much higher than in the case of Lok Sabha. Also, the percentage of expenditure that goes into 'note-for-vote' is higher in the local elections, as a much higher percentage of voters are distributed cash and a relatively higher percentage of voters receive such offerings from more than one candidate. Anywhere from INR 2000 to 5000 was distributed per vote in some municipality elections in Andhra Pradesh in April 2014.

Additionally, India spends on account of elections for several other bodies, like cooperatives and local bodies involving periodic elections as a matter of institutional (legally backed) requirement; for instance, cooperative societies as in the case of sugar mills, credit or housing societies, and unions and associations of all kinds, especially of larger bodies holding vote banks or funds or providing services (like credit). The frequency of these elections is less than five years and there have been several instances of deferring and delaying in these elections. These include. Wherever such periodic elections are conducted, 'quid pro quo expenditure' is involved in lieu of vote. Wherever there is involvement of politicians of political parties, the phenomena of note-for-vote is more rampant. The difference is in the extent and nature of expenditure. Such expenditure in elections in the states of South India is much higher. A preliminary estimate indicates that the expenditure involved in such functional elections at the national level could be as high as that of the elections of the constitutional bodies at national, state and district levels.

Why do elections at different levels have to be based on inducement? Lure of all kinds has become a phenomenon of elections at all levels in the country and is a key feature of competitive politics. I doubt whether there are any elections anywhere in the country that is devoid of cash inducement involving black money. Elections are expected to bring out the best of talents, ideas and better governance, and strengthen institutions that are the pillars of democracy. Can we expect all that with the kind of expenditure that is being incurred in the elections? And, that very expenditure is increasing year after year, election after election.

Unless we are able to hold these various elections with minimum expenditure and without luring the voters by candidates and parties through spending much beyond the ceiling level as prescribed by the Election Commission of India, we cannot ensure representative legislatures and good governance. In fact, this expenditure in elections is the source and origin of all corruption in the country. Moreover, without addressing the basic issues involved in this process, we cannot expect to curb corruption at any level in the country, including black money.

Is India a 'Flawed Democracy'?

Certainly not. One can say such only at after a superficial review at a given point in time. Some isolated incidents, often hyped in news media, can lead to such an assessment. In its Global Democracy Index, the Economist Intelligence Unit (EIU), a London-based organisation that brings out *The Economist*,[42] had ranked India in January 2018 at 42nd place with 7.23 score against 9.87 of Norway and even 9.22 of Denmark at the 5th rank. Neither can be strictly compared with India. It is, indeed, interesting that EIU had taken five categories for this ranking: (a) electoral process, (b) pluralism, (c) civil liberties, (d) functioning of the government and (e) political participation and culture. These five criteria, nevertheless, help guide the destinies of democracy in India by way of radical adjustments.

As outlined in this chapter, unfulfilled tasks are all around and correctives are called for on several fronts. All this cannot be accomplished by any one government and in one tenure and by any one or more combination of political parties. Complexities, being governance issues, cannot be tackled in isolation or with reforms in one or two sectors of the republic. Foundations of the republic have to be consolidated and strengthened. Unless we take a multipronged initiative on six fronts (political Parties, Media, education and the three pillars of state) simultaneously, the idea of good governance cannot be a reality and parliamentary democracy cannot be sustained.

Notes and References

1. Parliamentary democracy implies power to the people, government by the people and for the people, and representative with checks and balances provision ensured among the pillars of the State.
2. *The Hindu*, 26 January 2016.
3. 'An Economy for the 99%', Oxfam, https://www.oxfam.org/sites/www.oxfam.org/files/file_attachments/bp-economy-for-99-percent-160117-en.pdf (Accessed 13 June 2018).
4. 'Richest 1% Own 58% of Total Wealth in India: Oxfam', *The Hindu*, 17 January 2017, http://www.thehindu.com/business/Economy/Richest-1-own-58-of-total-wealth-in-India-Oxfam/article17044486.ece (Accessed 13 June 2018).
5. *World Inequality Report 2018*, World Wealth & Income Database, http://wir2018.wid.world/files/download/wir2018-full-report-english.pdf (Accessed 13 June 2018).
6. 'The Richest 1% of Indians Now Own 58.4% of Wealth', *Live Mint*, 11 November 2016, https://www.livemint.com/Money/MML9OZRwaACyEhLzUNImnO/The-richest-1-of-Indians-now-own-584-of-wealth.html (Accessed 13 June 2018).
7. The *World Inequality Report 2018*, a World Wealth & Income Database's report, was prepared by economists Thomas Piketty and Lucas Chancel. 'Income Inequality in India Worsens, But Slower than Russia and China: Report', *Live Mint*, 15 December 2017. https://www.livemint.com/Politics/0W83vrWtlQBpJ4qR5zZYyI/Income-inequality-in-India-worsens-but-slower-than-Russia-a.html (Accessed 13 June 2018); 'High Growth Does Not Necessarily Mean High Inequality, Says Lucas Chancel', *The Hindu*, 14 December 2017. http://www.thehindu.com/business/Economy/high-growth-does-not-necessarily-mean-high-inequality-says-lucas-chancel/article21653028.ece (Accessed 13 June 2018); Arindam Banik, 'Oxfam Reports Growing Inequality in India, Quality Education is the Best Way to Reverse This Trend', *Times of India*, 1 February 2018.
8. Presentation on economic inequalities at New Delhi Habitat Centre by Professor Himanshu of Jawaharlal Nehru University, New Delhi and Tinku Muragai of World Bank, 22 January 2016, ICRIER-UN meet on Inequalities. See *The Hindu*, 17 January 2017.
9. 'India Adds 27 New Billionaires', *The Hindu*, 25 February 2016, http://www.thehindu.com/business/Economy/india-adds-27-new-billionaires/article8276674.ece (Accessed 13 June 2018). Also reported in *Times of India* and *Hindustan Times*.

10. Radhicka Kapoor, 'Technology, Jobs and Inequality Evidence from India's Manufacturing Sector', Working Paper 313, Indian Council for Research on International Economic Relations (ICRIER), January 2016. http://icrier.org/pdf/Working_Paper_313.pdf (Accessed 13 June 2018).

11. Babasaheb Ambedkar, in his writings, reiterated linkage between democracy and development and the idea of social democracy was reiterated.

12. One of the initiatives of Prime Minister Modi was to wind up outlived legislations. Senior officers were assigned to identify such laws. This has been a continuing endeavour of the Central government since 2014.

13. 'Education for All 2000–2015: Achievements and Challenges', 2015 Global Monitoring report of UNESCO, http://unesdoc.unesco.org/images/0023/002322/232205e.pdf (Accessed 13 June 2018).

14. 'India Will Be Late by 50 Years in Achieving Education Goals: UNESCO', *Live Mint*, 6 September 2016, https://www.livemint.com/Politics/hCN-ChishenJwWp3jC0iRCL/India-will-be-late-by-50-years-in-achieving-education-goals.html (Accessed 13 June 2018).

15. N. Bhaskara Rao, 'Desolate State of Primary Education', *Transparency Review* 10, no. 2, October 2017; *Idem.*, 'Children's Libraries Deserve Serious Reposition', *Transparency Review* 4, no. 5, December 2011; *Idem.*, 'Is Privatizing Primary Education a National Pursuit?' *Transparency Review* 3, no. 2, June 2011.

16. 'Discrimination on the Campus', *The Hindu*, Hyderabad, 26 January 2016, http://www.thehindu.com/opinion/lead/Discrimination-on-the-campus/article14019816.ece (Accessed 13 June 2018).

17. '"Indian Engineering Students Gain in First Two Years, High-order Thinking is Poor": Study', *Indian Express*, 4 April 2018, http://indianexpress.com/article/education/indian-engineering-students-gain-in-first-two-years-high-order-thinking-is-poor-study-5122475/ (Accessed 13 June 2018).

18. 'Bihar "Topper" Fails Retest, Arrested', *Times of India*, 26 June 2016, https://timesofindia.indiatimes.com/india/Bihar-topper-fails-retest-arrested/articleshow/52921045.cms (Accessed 18 June 2018).

19. censusindia.gov.in

20. https://www.tribuneindia.com/2006/20060923/saturday/main1.htm

21. 'India Leads World in "Slavery"', *Hindustan Times*, 31 May 2016, https://www.hindustantimes.com/delhi-news/india-leads-world-in-slavery/story-yDsLeHIku0MO5DBsdQ38hL.html (Accessed 18 June 2018).

22. http://ncrb.gov.in/StatPublications/CII/CII2016/pdfs/NEWPDFs/Crime%20in%20India%20-%202016%20Complete%20PDF%20291117.pdf

23. *New Indian Express*, Hyderabad, 27 January 2016.

24. Abhay Shukla, Ravi Duggal and Richa Chintan, 'How Gorakhpur was choked', *Indian Express*, 1 September 2017, https://indianexpress.com/article/opinion/columns/gorakhpur-hospital-tragedy-gorakhpur-hospital-deaths-brd-hospital-uttar-pradesh-how-gorakhpur-was-choked-4823005/ (Accessed 21 June 2018).

25. Kailash Satyarthi, 'The Struggle for Childhood: Protecting and Educating Every Child is the Greatest Moral Struggle of Our Time', *Times of India*, 14 November 2016, https://blogs.timesofindia.indiatimes.com/toi-edit-page/the-struggle-for-childhood-protecting-and-educating-every-child-is-the-greatest-moral-struggle-of-our-time/ (Accessed 21 June 2018).

26. 'CMS-India Corruption Study 2017: Perception and Experience with Public Services & Snapshot View for 2005-17', CMS Research House, New Delhi, http://cmsindia.org/sites/default/files/Monograph_ICS_2017.pdf (Accessed 21 June 2018)

27. Central Vigilance Commissioner was quoted in *Eenadu*, 13 February 2016.

28. R.K. Raghavan, 'The Stained Steel Frame', *The Hindu*, 28 January 2016. R.K. Raghavan is a former director of CBI and a frequent writer in newspapers.

29. 'Continue to Complain, Rebel, Demand, President Pranab Mukherjee Tells Nation', *Indian Express*, 26 January 2016, https://indianexpress.com/article/india/india-news-india/peace-cannot-be-discussed-under-shower-of-bullets-president-pranab-mukherjee/ (Accessed 3 July 2018).

30. *Eenadu*, 20 January 2017.

31. 'Fourth Industrial Revolution: What It Means, Why It's Being Discussed', *Indian Express*, 22 January 2016, https://indianexpress.com/article/explained/fourth-industrial-revolution-what-it-means-why-its-being-discussed/ (Accessed 3 July 2018); see also, *New Indian Express*, Hyderabad, 27 January 2016; e-pragati (http://e-pragati.in/)

32. The Global Competitiveness Report 2017–2018 (http://www3.weforum.org/docs/GCR2017-2018/05FullReport/TheGlobalCompetitivenessReport2017%E2%80%932018.pdf)

33. http://e-pragati.ap.gov.in/

34. Ajit Balakrishnan, 'The Fall and Rise of Political Dynasties', *Business Standard*, 14 December 2015, https://www.business-standard.com/article/opinion/ajit-balakrishnan-the-fall-and-rise-of-political-dynas-ties-115121401155_1.html (Accessed 3 July 2018).

35. Smt. Sumitra Mahajan, Loksabha Speaker, 2015 (http://loksabha.nic.in/)

36. N. Bhaskara Rao, 'Social Audits Are Real Performance Indicators', *Transparency Review* 9, no. 2 (June 2016); see also the website of Association for Democratic Reforms (ADR; https://adrindia.org/).

37. 'Shortest Discussion on Budget since 2000', *The Times of India*, 4 March 2018, https://timesofindia.indiatimes.com/india/shortest-discussion-on-budget-since-2000/articleshow/63603440.cms (Accessed 3 July 2018).

38. N. Bhaskara Rao, 'Agenda for the Third Year of RTI', *Transparency Review* 1, no.1 (January 2008); see also *Times of India*, 11 December 2017.

39. See Section 'Stability and Good Governance' (pp. 375–380), in Subhash Kashyap's, *Our Constitution* (New Delhi: National Book Trust, 2015). This book has been reprinted several times since 1995 by the National Book Trust.

40. *Eenadu*, 13 January 2013. President Pranab Mukherjee tells that each pillar of State should do its job well in such a way that checks and balances are in vogue.

41. Based on two large scale surveys in 28 states in 2005 and 2007 and small simple surveys among voters in every subsequent election in the country, CMS had estimated the poll expenditure for Assembly and Lok Sabha elections in 2014 and subsequently till 2017. See 'Rs 30,000 Crore to be Spent on Lok Sabha Polls: Study', *NDTV*, Election News, Press Trust of India, 16 March 2014, https://www.ndtv.com/elections-news/rs-30-000-crore-to-be-spent-on-lok-sabha-polls-study-554110; 'Major Parties Spent ₹5,500 Crore on Uttar Pradesh Poll Campaign: Study', *The Economic Times*, Press Trust of India, 17 March 2017, https://economictimes.indiatimes.com/news/politics-and-nation/major-parties-spent-rs-5500-crore-on-uttar-pradesh-poll-campaign-study/articleshow/57686403.cms; 'Lok Sabha Elections: Black Money May Account for 1/3rd of ₹30,000 cr Poll Expenses', *Financial Express*, Press Trust of India, New Delhi, 1 April 2014, http://www.financialexpress.com/archive/lok-sabha-elections-black-money-may-account-for-13rd-of-rs-30000-cr-poll-expenses/1237428/

42. 'India Slips to 42nd place on EIU Democracy Index; US at 21st', *Live Mint*, 31 January 2018, https://www.livemint.com/Politics/SBf9tTUhoG29zuJ3rKrqoO/India-slips-to-42nd-place-on-EIU-Democracy-Index-US-at-21st.html

CHAPTER 2

Options and Alternatives

An understanding of the governance–development–democracy paradigm is not complete without being sensitive to the linkages among different critical variables of parliamentary democracy. Only in that context there would be a better understanding for the concept of 'power to people'. Without representative democracy, no good governance could be claimed by any government, however popular or populistic it is.

With seven decades of parliamentary democracy experience, we now need to see how representative and inclusive has been our democracy and how participative and development oriented have been our efforts. To this end, we need to explore options and alternatives so that good governance could be evoked, explored and sustained.

Understanding Linkages

The idea of good governance and its sensitivity could be expected only when the linkages among different functions, systems and pillars of the state are understood. Chief ministers claiming good governance simply because they intend to give honest or corruption-free government may be a limited and subjective perspective. But such an outlook is desirable, provided the linkages are not ignored and the feeling of complacency is not there. Equally important are citizen awareness and activist citizenry.

What is linkage? What is meant by linkage analysis? Why such a skill is determining and could be a differentiator? Linkage is implications, consequences and influence of an action or initiative or an intervention on other functions or systems, directly or indirectly and sooner or later. Concern for the consequences is the essence of idea of linkage. Let us look at some examples.

The first example is about a field study for the Ministry of Education, Government of India, on girls dropping out from school in Madhya Pradesh, which I did in 1982. In the report I prepared, I highlighted the status of toilet facility in schools as a factor for girls dropping out. The ministry was disappointed and shelved that report. It was for the UNICEF[1] a couple of years later to see the linkage between girls' dropout and the toilet facility, and that was how a policy for toilet facility in schools was prepared later. But the ministry did not see or was not sensitive to that linkage and the situation continued a decade after the report. The second example is about Vision 2020 for Andhra Pradesh which I piloted in 2001. I suggested that the draft I had prepared should be put to the public to invite open-house discussion so that the vision becomes that of the people, not the one by the chief minister. But the chief minister was more interested to rope in a foreign consultant (as he was more interested in attracting investments) and went ahead with that, not realising what it meant. The vision idea was never understood by any of the stakeholders and the vision 2020 became a ridicule soon.[2] Mahatma Gandhi saw the opportunity in salt satyagraha for galvanising the public for freedom movement. The emergence of Malaysia as a modern country was an early realisation by its leaders of the linkage between temperature and the productivity of the people. The success rate of most of the development programmes is disappointing because the government did not realise the need to involve the society in conceiving and implementing those programmes. Way back in the late 1950s, when Prime Minister Jawaharlal Nehru prompted Bharat Sevak Samaj and wanted it to take up building a bund to control floods out of the Kosi River in Bihar, many did not understand his foresight about public cooperation and their involvement in developmental endeavours.

An understanding of the linkages depends on our relations between pillars of the State, civil society, the media and educational stream. The makers of our constitution saw more clearly the interdependence among the different pillars and services of the State and provided for checks and balances in the constitution than the successive governments seem to have. Equilibrium between different services and pillars of the State is a critical dimension that governments have to keep in mind and until the linkages are understood, not possible. Such sensitivity will not come unless one is engaged in a linkage analysis involving the people. Concern for the consequences of actions is essential to provide good governance. If we do not see the essentiality of discipline in political parties for improved governance, how can we claim good governance? If we do not see the linkage of 'conflict of interest' of elected representatives and their representative character, how can we claim good governance? If we do not see the significance of civil society to ensure participative and inclusive development and government, how can we come up with good governance? If we are not sensitive about 'note-for-vote', how we could address corruption in delivery of public services and governance? Sustainability comes from the linkage.

Both sincerity and zero corruption in government are essential but not sufficient for good governance. Transparency, accountability, responsiveness, inclusiveness, participatory and decentralised nature in government operations are as critical for good governance. Skill for and sensitivity to linkages should be an essential feature among people, civil society groups; and that of every function of formal government agencies and political leaders even more. Eventually, the good/bad dilemma at any point in time or situation gets resolved on this understanding of linkage of one decision or initiative to the other. That is what wisdom is all about. Linkage analysis is a springboard for insights for future and sustainable development.

Such a skill was what our ancestors tried to impart to young ones by way of folk tales and simple stories. And that is what epics are full of and which continue to dictate or shape our lives, cultures and societies. With life today becoming far more complex and interrelated, significance of linkage and compulsion of understanding the dynamics involved is even more and inevitable. Today we have new tools too for such an analysis. Factor analysis to simulation to data analytics are some. Good governance depends on this undercurrent phenomenon and linkage processes and dynamics.

Power to People

The need today is a shift from top-down to bottom-up in the very paradigm. Top-down model of democracy and development has not worked. This requires citizen and community become active and governments more focussed, whereas, more and more, it is corporations, market institutions and consultants (middlemen) who are becoming powerful. Despair in people is increasing, leading to alienation of individual and nurturing of passivism. Even a discourse on governance is on the decline the same way as was in the case of local self-governance in earlier years of our independence. Concern for local issues is on decline in the people's representatives as is evident from what they do in the House they were elected to.

That Indian republic is 'union of states' is ignored (or forgotten). The 'Centre' (Union) has become the focus. The 'Centre' has become the focus, and idea of a centre has become the mindset of political leaders and media ignoring that it is a federal system. Over the years, Dr Subhash C. Kashyap,[3] as a constitutional expert, has been highlighting this anomaly in our public discourse and its implications for governance. The Union cannot be strong without local bodies being strong first. That states are 'subordinate' to the Union has imprinted on the minds of not just the national political parties but the media and the public too. Adding to that, states are expected to take up what is locally relevant or appropriate with the 'approval' (not *consultation*) of the 'Centre'. This trend is one of the contributing factors for increase in the number of local parties and divides in the polity, fragmentation in the society and slow progress and percolation of development schemes.

As far as federal–state relations are concerned, it may be worth exploring and adopting certain features of the USA model, of course with modifications for Indian specifics. This is for greater powers to the states than they now enjoy in India. So also for the local governments in turn: districts, municipalities and panchayats. Recent talk for devolution of power remains symbolic, discretionary and more as a rhetoric. The finance for election campaigns model of the USA (based on TV advertising) is something that India should avoid. We should come up with a model where poll campaigns will be less cost-based and not be a source for a quid pro quo–based politics, as they are now.

The unit of administration in terms of setting priorities and mobilising resources should be at the revenue division or district level. In Andhra Pradesh, the Revenue Division Officer (RDO) has been given the responsibilities recently similar to those of the District Collector, whereas in Telangana state, revenue divisions are being abolished.[4] The states must have greater autonomy and they in turn must devolve powers to the districts. A recent experiment is that of *mohalla sabhas* in Delhi. These sabhas decide their priorities and budget allocations in such a way that people take interest and participate in the implementation of development and welfare schemes.

Elections at gram panchayat, mandal and zilla parishad levels, that is, contests to various positions at these levels, should not be on party lines with a party symbol. Instead, the contest should be based on familiarity, needs and personalities of the contestants on their own credentials and proposals or agenda they put forward. The elections at each level should be direct and candidates should be local with their name in the local voter list. Vote bank politics, which is what party-based elections end up with, should be discouraged. Elections based on political parties in local panchayats divide people more, increase election time corruption and threaten the very implementation of public schemes in an inclusive way.

Such an 'alternative politics' need new tools and new methodology. The idea of *gram sabha* is good but how to make this happen? Unless gram panchayats have the power to decide on the resources and priorities, local committees do not become effective instruments. People's representation has to come from out of those local processes. Only then leadership can come from grassroots. Only then concerns about women and children get priority. And a people-centric and need-based approach is possible. Spread of government and dependency of citizens on government have eroded the fundamentals of freedom, independence, responsibility, decentralisation and citizenship. This affects the governance that prevails at any point.

Based on experiments in Nilokheri and Almora, National Extension Scheme (NES) was launched in mid-1950s with the basic understanding that new ideas and tools need to be spread across the country. One of the concerns focussed on was involvement and participation of people in developing need-based activities with only partial help from the government. In this model, initiated by Albert Mayor, people's contribution was anywhere upwards of 20 per cent including the labour component. It was based on this NES experiment that S.K. Dey (who was the first and the last union minister for community development in the Nehru cabinet) developed the idea of 'Community Development Programme'. The assumption was that if a team of experts in farming, entrepreneurship and extension of public participation and a village level worker (VLW) work together closer to the people, the development would be more equitable. This became the model that Jawaharlal Nehru adopted for the next decade (1960–1970). Thereafter, VLW became village development 'officer' and the extent of the local contribution and participation in local development works was converted into a special contribution by development agencies. With this, the discretionary role of the development officer has become a built-in feature of these functionaries. With political parties becoming the driving force of Panchayati Raj bodies by the late 1960s (in the wake of 1956 Balwantrai Mehta report on three-tier Panchayati Raj system), the idea of public contribution and participation lost enthusiasm. With discretionary dole-outs for development projects increasing, the role of the elected political representative became more subjective. This was when dependence of individuals on government went up higher and higher. With frequent elections at one or another level, vote bank politics set in and with every round of election, money power multiplied after 1980s and even more after 1990.

The idea of *shram-dan* (voluntary labour) by local people is a natural and assured way of citizens' taking interest in looking after what was created and in availing the benefits locally. Today this is a missing element. To correct the perception that idea of shram-dan is applicable only for small projects, Pandit Jawaharlal Nehru made Bharat Sevak Samaj take up Kosi river bund project in Bihar, which at that time was a major river rejuvenation project. Citizens from the area and elsewhere in the country were mobilised to offer their shram-dan and take back that idea to their communities. The fact that such a tradition was inherent in Indian ethos and lifestyle is forgotten. The Sikh community best exemplifies this culture. The Golden Temple at Amritsar was built by people themselves and to date is looked after meticulously. The idea of *langar* (free serving of food) by *gurudwaras* anywhere in the world is yet another such unique living example. One could imagine what would be the fate of such langars or such other community feeding programmes, should the government take over.

The idea of Grameen Bank[5] and the movement for credit to rural poor with an element of citizen involvement in Bangladesh, pioneered by Mohd Yunus, has left behind a more lasting example of changing living standards of nearly nine million poor women. In 25 years, this social development approach has acquired high credits and become a much sought-after model of empowering people the world over, including urban centres and wherever relatively poor population lives. While the Bangladesh model is based on 'do not wait for the government', India has gone the opposite way of depending on the government for everything that people otherwise could do on their own. Also, while the Grameen Bank model depends on citizen participation and active involvement, in India we have moved away from such an approach.

The Public Cooperation Division, with which the Indian Planning Commission started, was wound up 20 years ago as if the very idea of public participation has been given up to make people depend on government for everything! This meant 'more government'. A decade later, some states in India took to 'self-help groups' based on the successful Bangladesh Grameen Bank movement. And, in no time, renamed as Dwakra groups, they were adopted by many states, but without the essential feature of Grameen Bank, that is, 'least government' as to its support and supervision. That is, the flow of money and assigning work activities to Dwakra groups is at the courtesy of the chief minister; if it is not there, their very prospects become doubtful even if they have existed over a decade. And political leaders seek their support during elections, hence the question, 'Where is the people-centric development?' Development should certainly not mean eternal dependence of people on the government.

There is a need to reassess development schemes and their sustainability beyond government's political patronage, support and supervision. Even more, lures of political parties, both the ones being talked in formal poll manifestos and the others being offered as welfare measures, need to be restrained instead of going all out without concern for their implementation and long-term consequences.

The present approach of the government is creating awareness about a development scheme or programme as if higher the awareness, the better the implementation. Involvement or participation of the local people in the process is given secondary or no importance. The national democratic alliance (NDA) government, for example, had launched well over 40 schemes or programmes (2015–2017). Only a couple of them were from earlier years. In first two years, it had spent well over a thousand crores of rupees to promote awareness of the schemes. But a CMS study[6] for the Ministry of Information and Broadcasting had indicated that hardly 5 per cent of people, even among stakeholders, were aware of those schemes even when they are with nomenclature 'Pradhan Mantri Yojana'. Event orientation or celebration approach is not enough to initiate change in the development paradigm. Political parties today often become insensitive after coming to power as if they had come to power to cater and serve the interests of the party rather than the people.

One-third of those in rural areas, who built a toilet in their house, go out and continue open defecation despite government spending so much for awareness. One reason for these people building a toilet is government's subsidy. Similar was in the case of subsidy the government gave for adopting solar heater in the earlier years. The focus in promoting should not be on subsidies but for the 'logics' and 'linkages' involved in adopting a toilet or taking to solar panels to the overall 'well-being' of the people.

The newly elected chief minister of Kerala[7] in his first press state-ment addressing the people of the state promised that his government works for all in the state irrespective of their political affiliation and voting record. Going by public utterances of other political leaders in government in many states, one does not get such a feeling of being inclusive of serving all people. In fact, activities indicate otherwise as partisan.

The newly constituted Telangana government (October 2016) took a logical step when it reorganised the state by increasing the number of district from 13 to 31 and increase mandals (from 459 to 584) and divisions (from 43 to 69).[8] This is a first step in taking the government closer to the people. But doing this without discouraging the dependence of the citizens on government and rejuvenating or enabling them for active participation in governance at the local level will not produce desired results. That is an essential first step towards shifting the paradigm of governance.

Gandhiji's idea of *gram swaraj* was endorsed by all sections of lead-ers and active people of pre-Independence time. In fact, many global leaders as well as development economists continue to refer to gram swaraj as an ideal political model for good governance based on decen-tralisation, holistic habitats, self-sustaining communities and living on what is affordable and locally available or produced. The model is based on the belief and respect for the five elements of nature (*panch bhutas*) and concern about not just oneself but also for the neighbours and successors (next generation). And their lifestyle is based on conserving and having minimum needs and in the realisation of the fact that happiness is not externally derived. This approach assumes governance where it is necessary, participative decision-making by people's representatives and trusteeship among those in positions of power and command of natural resources. How did we lose track of such a participative model?

Mahatma Gandhi was the foremost leader to visualise and even warn about the possible ill effects of political parties. Ignoring Gandhiji's foresight is what has cost the country successive govern-ments loosing direction by the 1970s and the rise of 'regime of political parties'. Political parties have come into being as an instrument of parliamentary democracy and participative development model, not to determine the very scope of democracy and as a substitute for civil society.

Realising how political parties are likely to be power hungry and what it meant for democracy, governance and equity, Gandhiji suggested soon after the independence that Congress party be converted into a social service outfit. The very idea of public service was the first casualty. Gandhiji and M.N. Roy were foremost to foresee that political parties are going to indulge in self-aggrandizement and will move away from ideology and people-centred issues. Babasaheb Ambedkar also cautioned about such a scenario. M.N. Roy,[9] a visionary in his own standards, visualised:

> … how there was going to be mad scramble for power by politicians winning elections using money and muscle power, and how they were going to neglect the people who would vote for them, how the party leaders were going to be dictatorial in their approach and how elected representatives of the people were going to be more responsible and accountable to their respective political parties and not to their electors.

Proliferation of political parties and their pursuit to power has made mockery of democracy. What was intended and expected of democracy is far different from what is being practised. With ideology no longer a creed of political parties, the ambiguity is all around as to the kind of governance. In the name of decentralisation, centralisation is being pursued. The result is proliferation and multiplication of the government, reducing the citizen to a voter. The despair of people is due to such a vacuum in governance and the decline in the representative nature of the elected legislators. Communist party took initiative, in the earlier years, with people's committees and mohalla committees. This approach of taking government closer to people, involving them in one way or other in sharing power is what kept the Left parties in power for long in West Bengal and Kerala. E.M.S. Namboodiripad and A.K. Gopalan in Kerala, Jyoti Basu in West Bengal and Manik Sarkar in Tripura deserve to be recalled for their initiatives to take power to people with their own approach to make difference in the kind of governance that was offered. With similar efforts by chief ministers N.T. Rama Rao in Andhra Pradesh (1983) and Bhairon Singh Shekhawat in Rajasthan deserve to be remembered. *Prajala Vaddaku Palana* (government at the doorsteps) of N.T. Rama Rao[10] and his structural reforms replacing centuries-old Tehsil (80–100 villages) with much smaller unit of governance at mandal (20–30 villages) level and strengthened as an administrative unit changed what was continuing as a British legacy until then. *Antyodaya* programme in Rajasthan (1977) was based on taking government to the most neglected, needy people at grassroots of the state. But this idea was not institutionalised. In the latter years, this approach has been reduced to vote bank politics. Rajiv Gandhi embarked on sending project funds directly to district collectors, not realising that it amounts to centralisation and adds to discretionary powers ignoring the state governments. To this effect, he made efforts to bring in 73rd and 74th Amendments for panchayat and nagar palika (1985–1986), which in later years lost the seriousness with which they were taken up as a movement. Even the idea of empowering women with 50 per cent reservation in local panchayats has remained a rhetoric.

Consider a revealing report with ministry-wise budgetary allocations for 2013–2014. For the actual disbursement of funds and actual expenditure (up to February 2014), this report gave two tables: one contained details about ministries spent much less than allocated fund (see Table 2.1) and the other listed ministries which spent more than allocated fund. The data so available brings out an interesting fact: where dole-outs to people are involved, they spend more than what was required. Also, where civil works were involved, a much higher percentage was spent. One can easily understand what this means— margins to middlemen? The ministries which spent less than what was allocated include health, education and drinking water. A four column story in the *Times of India* of 4 April 2018 says, based on a Controller & Auditor General of India (CAG) report on Delhi that 'substantial amount of ₹136.6 crores allotted for 2016–2017 were surrendered in projects related to the departments of education, health, development and public works and urban development'.

Table 2.1 *Ministry-wise Spend Analysis (2013–2014) at the National Level*

Ministry	Percentage Spent
Arogyashri, health and education	0.50
Tourism	0.96
Education college level	13.17
Technical education	33.20
Village drinking water	53.97
Panchayati Raj	59.84

Source: Eenadu, 22 February 2016, quoting official records.

Another glaring example is the allocations and disbursement for MGNREGS, floated with fanfare to alleviate poverty by providing work to the unemployed rural population. Responding to a PIL in the Supreme Court filed by Aruna Roy and others who were in charge of this very idea from its beginning, government conceded that INR 3,500 crore are not released to the states on account of MGNREGS since 2012. It further stated that 70 per cent of those who were engaged under MGNREGS were not paid wages within 15 days after work.[11] Successive presidents of India have been taking pride talking about MGNREGS while addressing the joint session of parliament as Pranab Mukherjee did on 24 February 2016 and so also the prime ministers from the Red Fort on 15 August every year since.

Who is responsible for this anomaly? Political leaders and bureaucrats are viewed by people as responsible. This reflects the lack of concern, seriousness and uniform attention of the elected leaders at the helm of affairs.

I remember a feature film that I saw, one depicting the grassroots realities of India and suggesting options available for people in an appealing way. It was a hit film of the time. But it seems to have made no difference on the emerging scene. *Naya Zamana* (1971), with Dharmendra as the hero, depicted the transition the country was in and, more pertinently, suggested a way forward from the dilemma. The film showed how inequalities exist in a village and how those with power exploit the poor. The film depicts how people could get together, settle disputes amicably locally on their own with a win–win outcome. The model suggested in the film was far more durable one for development. There were other films as well depicting citizens themselves resolving issues with conflict of interest locally with no involvement of a government agency and showing how villagers together could ensure government functionaries work for the local needs. What have we learned from all this? More and more awareness alone does not make centralised schemes work and remotely directed programmes do not yield desired results. In the earlier decades, regional films in Malayalam, Telugu and Bengali had reflected changing times with people-centric options as an alternative that could be explored by the people themselves. *Rojulu Marayi* (Changing Times), in which Waheeda Rehman—this was her first film—danced to the song 'Eruwaka Vachendoi' (Times are changing for better), was a remarkable film. It depicted how villagers could resolve conflicts locally and go forward. Another Telugu film, *Peddamaushulu* (Village Elders), depicts how village elders exploit the political power for amassing community wealth and how youngsters expose them.

Differentiating Parties

Veteran social activist and anti-corruption crusader Anna Hazare said in New Delhi recently (January 2018) that 'party-driven system fomented corruption, casteism and violence in the country'. More specifically, he felt that 'various parties have vitiated the atmosphere in colleges and universities by opening their wings and led the youth astray'. He suggested that since the constitution provides for a certain age to contest an election and says nothing about any party or the symbol of a party, we should do away with both, only then the democracy will be possible in the truest sense.

Clearly, it is high time that political parties and their role in a parliamentary democracy become more obvious and distinct. Is this possible in the present arrangement?

Today, people do not differentiate political parties on their ideological stands as much as they associate with individual leaders. It has been a decline of political parties and the rise of individual leaders. Proliferation of parties has added to this phenomenon. As a result, people do not see an alternative in the government model. Instead, it is the lures offered which differentiates the parties during elections. Election-time promises by political parties, leaders and candidates have lost their credibility and are forgotten soon after—and they vitiate the very process of democracy. Many agitations are result of this credibility crisis. The result is a certain political apathy and passive citizenry. Can we revive such a scenario and rejuvenate the political parties without correcting all of that accumulated malice in the system, much beyond which party has won or lost in an election?

The Case of a 135-year-old Party

On entering politics in 1983, Rajiv Gandhi called a meeting of nine people—six were secretaries of the Congress party. I do not know how I was invited but it was a surprise. I later came to know that it was to see what ails our political parties that attracted Rajiv and that was why he asked his aides George and Vijaya Dhar to invite me for that meet. Since I did not know most of those in the meeting personally nor I had any acquaintance with Rajiv, I kept quiet in the meeting while many of the secretaries present there were parroting virtues of the Congress party. Towards the end, Rajiv looked at me when I could not resist myself from saying that what was said by those leaders was different from what grassroots reality was. I told him that unless the party revives its Sevadal to its pride of place in the party, it was bound to lose its distinct identity and prime position as a national party. To serve, service and support had no longer been a priority in the functioning of that party for years.

Some political parties today are more poll-time parties or in vote bank pursuit and out of focus and out of range of people's expectations and aspirations. They hardly reflect and represent the grassroots realities. In this regard, all parties need a course correction. Conventional politics are unlikely to make a difference. Repositioning, not mere reshuffling, is the need for a different course of the parties. Not even change in leadership is enough. Repositioning should include three basic elements. First, advocacy for future, which means parties should have an agenda to pursue based on certain concerns and logics of beyond polls (whether call it ideology or not). Second, social service concern—and not poll-time interests—should not be denigrated. Third, empathy as to aspirations and expectations of people as they keep changing.

Big government, big business, big media, big corporates—it is this unholy dynamics, protecting one another in their own interest, that determines public policies, controls political parties and the very governance at any point of time. It is less of 'checks and balances' and more of *jugalbandi* phenomena. Should such trends go unchecked?

A Development Paradigm

'Development' has been chanted as an all-time mantra by governments and political leaders. Development has been a promise of those in power and of those who are aspiring to capture power. Development has been the theme of the 20th century. Most government campaigns are based on that goalpost. What this development is all about? Does it mean the same every time and for every country? And for every one? How it has become the part and parcel of the lexicon of every government? And irrespective of their growth path and political regime.

Until the Second World War, development was a term used more by biological and medical researchers to indicate the difference that an 'experiment' makes in the extent of growth or healing a wound. The term development could perhaps be traced to Harry S. Truman, President of the USA (1949)[12] as used for post-war happenings in a positive way across boarders and political systems. The plans and proposals for rebuilding war-torn countries were packaged as 'development plans'[13] of the USA, the donor. Alternatively, 'economic reconstruction' was also used to explain that phenomena. Both terms were used from an economic perspective and an 'aid or loan giver's point of view'. That was why perhaps 'social development' or 'social progress' or even behavioural change aspects of an individual or community were not a concern so much of the 'givers'. For the process was limited to 'giving' and 'taking' more at macro levels. In that context, quantifiable state of affairs in a relative context was what led to describe countries as developed and underdeveloped. For this, certain parameters or yard-sticks were advocated in quantitative terms from a giver's perspective.

What was then the idea of 'development'? It meant effect or gain or increase or growth or expansion (before and after). That such a gain or growth was not always without pain or erosion was not considered or realised. The idea of development was viewed in a measurable way or in relative terms (between different times or between countries). Development notion implied someone gives for some effect or outcome to someone (one country to another). Development neither had anything to do with the needs or expectations or aspirations of the local people or with the recognition of their potential capabilities. Such a concept of development did not imply involvement of local people; it meant more depending on an outside input or assistance for an outcome or result the giver would like to see. That was how, or in that context, the idea of development came into the political lexicon and modern politics and become an expression of governmental efforts to accomplish or derive certain outcomes based on given parameters. In the entire gamut of that term, quantification was the basis for viewing an outcome of an intervention as development.

In today's world, development means changing or improving the living conditions of people, bringing higher standards in living conditions, lifestyles and the infrastructure for that. Sustainable development goes beyond one-time effort or input and continuation of the course on its own with a drive from within and irrespective of outside input or assistance and expectations.

A decade later, by the early 1950s, with American aid and post-war driven politics, even the United Nations (and its affiliated organisations like UNESCO, UNDP and UNICEF, which came into being with certain 'desirables' for the nations as indicators of development) began to rely more on macro and quantitative variables. That frame was even used as the basis for aid agencies. This has become the indicator of the stage of development of countries. In this process, estimation of requirements of nations has become a criteria or a thumb rule in quantitative terms. For example, UNESCO has come up with desirables for democracy and development. One variable, for example, is the number of newspapers per hundred people that a country should have. It is an indication for the relative development of democracy. For a nation to be considered 'developed' should have 20 newspapers per 100 people. On similar lines, WHO came up with a number of nurses and hospitals a country should have to be considered developed. And of course the literacy level is there too. Such yardsticks were irrelevant for many nations like India with their own cultural and deep-rooted cultures.

It was evident to me during my PhD (1968–1970) at the University of Iowa, School of Communication. What UNESCO had come up with was pursued as a desirable global indicator and as a prescription for development of different countries. On my way back to India, I went to Paris headquarters of UNESCO (August, 1970). I had an argument with some officials there whether they were aware what it meant if countries like India had to follow the norm of 20 newspapers per hundred. I told them that it amounted to cutting more trees to achieve that goal, assuming people could afford to buy a newspaper. And if forests declined, there will be more severe implications. Also, I informed them, in India there was no need for every family to have a copy of its own as one copy was read by 10 to 20 people at that time at a given place. It was of course a decade later that UNESCO gave up such quantitative yardsticks for measuring development. So much for the idea of development!

The most reliable indicator of development, whatever that means, should be the coexistence of people (by dialogue and discussion) irrespective of their community, caste, occupations and affiliations. A second indicator should be no or the least exploitation of one by another. The third indicator could be how contended people and communities are about what they have access to. The fourth is governance, that is, how inclusive, participative and transparent is the governance process. The fifth is how much and how well citizens and communities do matter and how active they are in governance processes. All others criteria, which are otherwise viewed as 'development', are secondary to these. But many others also contribute as part of, they may be and are proof of development. Development without presence of those five elements is futile and cannot be sustainable.

Today development is quantitative as to growth rates at macro levels and consumer spending or purchase power. Development cannot be in terms of dependence of people on the government. It should not even be based on popularity packages and lures of political leaders or consumerism driven measures.

We have schools built by governments over the years but with shortage of teachers, textbooks, and without concern for values. Nevertheless, that is a development indicator. We have hospitals built by governments but with shortage of doctors and drugs. Today more infants die in hospitals than ever before if we go by news media. And now privatising these is what the governments are busy doing as symbol of development and project them as acts of good governance irrespective of whether it is affordable or not. The governments provide doles not only at election times but also as daily wages and claim such employment provided as development. Even women's self-help groups, a symbol of development, are not spared from being made as dependents of government and patronised by one or other political party leader. Television channels have proliferated in the country as nowhere else but it is to the consumer and market that they cater more than to citizens and community, thus making no difference. Successive governments have facilitated such a 'development'.

I remember a project of the World Bank in India that I was associated (1979–1980) with. That was on the 'cost of living index'. The study was designed, including the questionnaire, by the World Bank itself. I questioned certain fallacies in the research exercise so obviously development-centric. For example, some questions were whether a newspaper was being subscribed or not, how long the rice being eaten was, whether the shoe had laces or not, and so on.

This convinced me that measurements and prescriptions based on 'Western lifestyle' of development made least sense and that it only implied 'imposing' priorities of one country and one culture on to others. Many call it 'cultural imperialism'; I call it 'consumerism' at work. It was based on such research that the level of the development of a country and the extent of the 'assistance' to that country in a relative context was decided a few years ago. Such exercises were more to 'prescribe' countries in the name of standards and desirables.

A good old saying governments do not seem to bother about is that 'teaching how to catch a fish goes a long way than gifting a fish'. Skilling people should have become a development yardstick long before 2017. The basic premise is that skilling will spare people from the dependency syndrome. Which implies chances of the citizens getting out of the government's clutches!

More often, development is in numbers and percentages for some. For many, it is claims (and promises) of the political leaders in power. For some others, development is in mass media, and now also in social media. Claims of governments and their agencies at the macro levels and in an aggregate way often is different from the grassroots reality. We have now taken to ranking, indexes and such simplified number crunching exercise as yardsticks of our 'development'! No wonder, showcasing such a development has become a priority and preoccupation of many.

Every Five-Year Plan (before NITI Aayog) planned and targeted, and the governments claimed offering, basic public services to all. We did make considerable progress. But we have yet to accomplish targets and for most we have already shifted deadlines in the future. For example, even after 70 years of independence, more than a thousand villages in the country have no drinking water. Many children had never been to a school and many more have dropped out year after year at both primary and secondary levels. And yet the state governments are closing down some public schools for the presumed lack of enrolment! Monsoon continues to be the primary source for millions and millions of acres of cultivable land. Drought continues to cause hundreds of farmers' suicide year after year, and even in more numbers in the recent years. Public schools in two Telugu states during 2014–2017 were short of more than 13,000 teachers while there are many trained ones looking for a job. Most private schools in villages languish with untrained teachers and bare infrastructure. Such is the model of development that we have adopted and are pursuing! This reflects the gaps in the very notion of development that we are pursuing. This has not so much benefited from the democratic system that is being practised. For example, despite all the talk of decentralisation by the Union and the states for 70 years, we are heading for centralisation more and more. Accountability and representative character of the elected ones is not to the extent needed and proliferation of political parties, supremacy of individual leaders and the electoral practices are not sufficiently focussed on the basics, the citizens and the grassroots.

Development today has become an umbrella term for everything that a government does and for every political leader in power to dangle at polls, but only as long as they are in power. Once out of power, the same leaders take a totally different perspective of 'development'. Without any focus on governance, can we accomplish equity or active citizenry? But that term suits everyone!

Notes and References

1. An ORG study on girls dropout (1982), UNICEF (https://www.unicef.org/); N. Bhaskara Rao (ed.), *India 2021* (New Delhi: SAGE Publications, 1985).
2. The 'AP Vision 2020' was India's first state-specific study conducted in 2001. N. Bhaskara Rao was the chief coordinator of this project.
3. Subhash C. Kashyap, *History of Parliamentary Democracy: From the Earliest Times to the End of the Nehru Era* (Delhi: Shipra Publications, 1991).
4. *Eenadu*, 27 October 2016.
5. For more details on Bangladesh Grameen Bank, visit its website: http://www.grameen.com
6. *Indian Express*, 30 April 2016.
7. *Indian Express*, 24 May 2016.
8. *Sakshi*, 22 October 2016.
9. M.N. Roy, 'A New Approach to Political and Economic Problems', *The Radical Humanist*, Vol. 79 (January, 2016), Chapter XIV.
10. N.T. Rama Rao, former chief minister of undivided Andhra Pradesh and Bhairon Singh Shekhawat, former chief minister of Rajasthan, were the early leaders to come up with this idea of taking the government to the doorsteps of the people and to the last person in the field.
11. *Times of India*, 17 February 2016.
12. Janet Gilbert, '"Development": The Power of a Word to Define Our World' (2004), http://www.janegilbert.co.uk/unpublished%20papers/Development%20-%20the%20power%20of%20a%20word%20to%20define%20our%20world.pdf
13. Wolfgang Sachs, *The Development Dictionary: A Guide to Knowledge as Power* (London: Zed Books, 1992).

CHAPTER 3

Good Governance, Not Rhetoric

Good governance is a buzzing claim these days for leaders who are in power and also for those trying to get in power. What is good governance all about? Is it the same as what these political leaders mean? For most, it means government working against corruption or taking action against some corrupt officials or politicians. This is a limited perspective. For most of the leaders, governance is what the government is sized with. Governance is an outcome and sum total of what and how different pillars of the State perform and function. As GDP consists of product estimation by all sections of people, enterprises and production streams, governance includes what people, communities, institutes and enterprises are engaged in, outside and beyond the scope of government. What is not good governance could be outlined far more easily than what it is. There could, however, be some indispensable features. Good governance is a result of accumulated experiences in that it is an outcome of more than one tenure of a party in power. What are the distinguishing features of good governance, then?

Leaders of the country have looked at the idea of good governance from different perspectives at different stages of independent India. Soon after 1947, the immediate concern was food for every one and the criteria was poverty. The basic needs—*roti, kapada aur makan*—were the goals for development and considered as the outcomes of governance. Later it was irrigation, literacy, basic health and basic infrastructure (roads, electricity) and employment. Decentralised decision-making and people's participation and involvement in governance were also considered as crucial features of development.

For Mahatma Gandhi, decentralised governance, in which the citizens depended least on the government, was a concern. For Jawaharlal Nehru, people's participation and community development were a priority in which the school was viewed as a modern temple. Later, control of resources and appeasement of voters became the priority. More recently, corruption-free government and *Swaraj to Su-raj* and *Sab ke Sath, Sab ka Vikas* (or inclusive governance) have become the concern and criteria for good governance. A referendum in Switzerland, made in 2016, adds yet another dimension to good governance. Of late, 'happiness' (instead of GDP) is also being talked about as the ultimate goal of good governance.

Claims of good governance require to be qualified for the context of locale and the specific set of people, for it means different things to different sections of people. Outcomes of good governance cannot be in singular terms. A chief minister of a state claiming good govern-ance in his or her state simply because corruption is supposed to have been brought down or efforts are being made to that effect is a limited perspective about good governance. Even if crime and rape incidents are down, it does not imply that good governance has set in. One-time decline or increase in the performance statistics, as the case may be, of a government does not amount to good governance.

Processes, systems and institutes (and precedents) are far more important than one-time outcomes in quantitative terms. Only then good governance becomes the scene and stature of a country's political system, including the government, irrespective of the party in power. Sustainability features are far more dependable indicators for good governance. Only then good governance can take roots to such an extent that no leader or a party in power can fiddle with the funda-mentals of governance unilaterally. The eternal dilemma of 'means and ends' is what guides good governance, where means are not lost sight of in the pursuit of ends. The connection between means and ends need to be understood here. Mechanisms and systems of implementation of policies and programmes, as a part of government, determine the efficacy of governance. Good governance is not personality centric as much as process centric. This expects discipline, harmony, concern for future and good practices as a precedent.

Origins of Good Governance as a Concept

Although political leaders have been talking about good governance for much longer, the concept of 'good governance' was renewed for discourse in 1989 by the World Bank based on its experiments in the African countries with its structural adjustment policy. But that has not led to any difference in the functioning of government and has not brought in the much sought-after difference in the scope of economy and in the outcomes of interventions. Initially, good governance meant efficient implementation of policies (and fulfilling the electoral promises made to the people). But later, with adoption of more and more technologies in the functioning of government, the idea of e-governance and then the idea of mobile governance have come into circulation. Now some are even talking of real-time governance as if all of that amount to good governance.

As it happens, three international bodies have referred to the idea of 'governance': The World Development Report 1997, the Britton Woods Institute and International Monetary Fund. Their main concern was economic. They viewed governance as a prerequisite for the success of any economy as indicated by economic indicators of countries.[1]

A decade ago (in 2009), the United Nations came up with eight principles that a good government should follow:[2] Peoples participation and partnership; consultations with maximum of the population towards building consensus; accountability of political leaders in power; transparency in government departments; effective use of various technologies including mobile phone, social audit, responsive character; sensitivity of offices, and respect for rule of law.

Governance implies and encompasses much beyond the government of the day. What could be the specific distinguishing features of governance? What could be the principles and perspectives that governance involves? What are some of the functions that could be expected of governance? What is suggested here is only indicative.

Different Perspectives

Good governance could be looked from at least five different angles. First, how active and participative different pillars of democracy are; how well involved are the citizens, the political parties, the society and the education system of the country, as they all need to be sensitive and contribute in enabling the good governance features and consolidate the institutes in a checks and balances atmosphere. Second, how well the pyramid of economic structure is reversed in terms of access empowering enabling and the equity aspects. Third, in terms of intellectual freedom, civil liberties, social justice and plurality, how decentralised are the features, and how widely the outcomes or benefits of the governance are distributed to and availed by people. Fourth, how sensitive and self-controlled are the citizens about their dependence on the government. And fifth is the fact that concern and pursuit are beyond GDP parameters and, as such, how much focus is laid on social development aspects. ICT is changing the scope of governance as it is coming up with applications which would liberate citizens and stakeholders from the government's direct control.

The theme of 'good governance' attracted the attention of Indian scholars intermittently during the last two decades. Subhash Kashyap has been pursuing the theme for over 15 years now, mostly from a constitutional and parliamentary perspective. However, the Indian Council of Social Science Research (ICSSR)[3] did not follow up after sponsoring a monograph on the theme by Subhash Kashyap in 2003. Moreover, India International Centre did also not follow up its project called 'Towards Good Governance' in 1997[4] with L.S.K. Chopra as its prime mover. Pai Panandikar of the Centre for Policy Research (CPR)—with which Dr Subhash C. Kashyap was also associated—too pursued the theme in a larger context. The concerns of these initiatives were mostly efficiency of governments, functioning of the parliament, context of the constitution, corruption and reforms. Citizen, in these studies, was considered more as a user or a recipient of government services. None of them viewed citizen and society as a part of governance or inclusiveness as an essential element as much as corruption. None, except Subhash Kashyap, called for a holistic approach to set good governance in motion. Kashyap's Rastra Jagriti Samithi (RJS)[5] had even proposed for a campaign for good governance. As the result of a UNDP project on the theme, two collections (Ajit Banerjee and Chandrasekaran, 1996; R.S. Chikara, 2009)[6] were published. Indian analysts took to the idea of good governance more in the last decade and at the instance of one or other foreign funding agencies.

Distinguishing Features of Governance

First, the very idea of governance vis-à-vis the government is not static. There is no one definition which could be all inclusive. Second, as a phenomenon, governance is an ongoing process, beyond terms and tenures that government functions by. Third, governance implies and involves much beyond the government. It encompasses the pillars of democracy with the focus on the citizen and society. Fourth, governance expects some kind of equilibrium among the pillars of the State in a checks and balances atmosphere. Fifth, governance is much beyond GDP terms, where social development remains a core concern. Sixth, the poor, weak and minorities are viewed specifically with a trusteeship concern. Seventh, the dependence of citizens on the government cannot be a way of life. Eighth, quantitative yardsticks and approaches cannot remain key criteria for accountability and performance. Ninth, good governance implies limited government—limited to deliver essential primary services and making laws. Tenth, equality between regions and sections of people with level playing is a key concern.

Not any one or another of these ten features but in what combination most are in effect at any time determines the status of good governance. The status of governance at any point in time or context depends on them in a holistic way. But these cannot be conclusive parameters. In this process, public opinion and people's participation in formulating policies as well as in the implementation of government schemes and public policies, gains importance.

Good Governance: Compulsions and Characteristics

A quick overview of the seven decades of the journey of independent India indicates that we are nowhere near what our first leaders aspired for, nor have we accomplished what our constitution provided for and envisioned. The issue is not analogous to 'glass is half empty' but of critical appraisal of methodology and instruments and of exploring mid-course correctives. We of course have been tinkering with amendments, economic reforms and policy revisions and even U-turns in policies. We have been doing that most often in isolation as if government alone is responsible for all that and hence there have been frequent changes on the ruling political party. The government means cabinet of ministers, legislators and bureaucracy. Linkage and interconnectivity among these institutions and other pillars of democracy is either not fully explored or not analysed for insights and correctives. For example, 'note for vote' (that is, luring voters with money on the eve of elections) has devastating effect on the functioning of the government. This could happen as the advantages of parliamentary democracy was not grasped fully in the early years of electoral politics. Unless the practice of luring voters becomes all pervasive and detrimental to the functioning of the government, we cannot come up with appropriate measures even to tame this threat to democracy and development. A growing tendency of a feeling of 'great let down' is there in the country. Bureaucracy and political leaders are often accused of shortcomings and deficiencies. The focus has been on tinkering with administration, often described as reforms as if the effort is for 'incremental improvements' when the need is substantial, structural, and has to do with fundamentals, including certain practices of parliamentary democracy. Mere adjustments off and on, and in an isolated way, have not been good enough to cope with the accumulated malice within the system and with changing times and demographics.

That was the approach that the World Bank and its associates had taken with the idea of 'structural adjustments' for reviving economies of some declining African countries. But that concern and approach was mostly to do with economy, capital flows and governmental policies and governmental functioning as per the World Bank's perspective and prescription. That model did not reverse the pyramid of economy and development process. When that prescription did not yield or led to the desired revival and changes in the structure of economies, the World Bank came up with the idea of 'improving governance', but mostly by way of policies and efficiency of government. The impression was that a more efficient government would yield incremental improvements and make a quantitative difference in the living standards of people. In a nutshell, this model is what the World Bank described as 'good governance', in a similar way as Lux soap was upgraded by Lintas Advertising as 'New Lux' with change in odour or colour, pack and price, promoted by high-end actresses as models (when the priority should have been the larger issue to do with sanitation and hygiene). Also, that approach was government-centric and concerned more with GDP and per capita based development outcomes.[7]

A missing aspect in that process of the World Bank's prescription was the realisation that better governance is not possible without a 'good government'. They, however, missed the linkage aspect with grassroots realities. Good government in a parliamentary democracy is not possible without 'good politics', and good politics in turn is not feasible without good political parties. Good governance is not possible without good leaders with local concerns and determination to think of and change the future. And to get elected, a political party needs to win in a free and fair election to be able to give a good government. All this is not sustainable without active citizenry. That is why our Constitution starts with '*WE, The people*'. This can be a reality when the citizens are active and exposed to a more responsible mass media. If this linkage is not appreciated and structural correctives accordingly devised and implemented across, a government cannot distinguish itself as of good government and its governance described any better. These days, we of course talk of reforms but in isolation as if each reform is an end in itself. A government promotes itself these days going all out to manage its 'image' accordingly and more by expansion and proliferation. Today it is 'alliances' and 'partnerships' that determine the scope and nature of the governments. Today verbosity, rhetoric, self-claims and promises is what dominates our public discourse and politics as if ground realities can be managed or ignored or manipulated. Among all these, good governance has become a catchword for the leaders without meaning much. Political leaders in power continue to claim that they have ushered in good governance when in reality there is nothing new they could claim as achievement that can distinguish them from the previous governments.

What Is Beyond Governance?

In the overall assessment, beyond governance is the extent to which a government has become minimal, dependence of the citizen on government has become minimal and yet the outcomes are maximum. This could mean reversing the current trend of the citizen's dependence on government so that people can unleash their own potential and realise their ambitions. Where the role of government is at the best only as a facilitator and where the provision of checks and balances ensures equilibrium among the pillars of the State including the society. Conventionally, there were only three pillars, but over the decades, a lot has changed, including judiciary, legislature and executive. Later, the institution of mass media has come to be viewed as the fourth pillar. To this list, now should be included the 'society' as the fifth. The fifth pillar would include citizen-led groups and citizen-initiated functions and education system under public purview. All these together contribute to good governance. A concern for good governance has to be beyond the government and wider, among citizens and citizen groups, and not only with concerns of one election to the next but beyond.

The World Bank has come a long way in its perspective in this regard. In the World Development Report of 2017,[8] it highlighted the 'need for continued collaboration between Governments, Citizens, Civil Society and Private sector to improve governance and produce life-improving outcomes'. This needs to be followed to promote such a model.

Checks and balances is where every institution tries to do better within the scope of its functions without intruding upon the functional responsibility of other institutions. In that process, all are expected to perform better than before. This tussle between judiciary and legislative (judicial activism?) and between judiciary and media (trial by media) are two examples. To sustain good governance, this checks and balances provision is an important feature already envisioned in the Constitution. But it needs to be better understood and appreciated by the stakeholders.

Good governance–development paradigm expects and assumes that the citizen and the society are more sensitive and concerned about the rights and 'responsibilities' than about rights and 'privileges' and about freedom and 'duties'.

Good Governance Is an Ongoing Process

Good governance is an ongoing process. Good governance is not result of one-time initiatives or interventions or result of one term of a party in government. Outer boundaries of good governance cannot be specified. They could be only envisioned as good governance is still an evolving phenomenon, constantly shaping and sharpening the very scope of governance. Not merely what is envisaged as good governance but also what is reality and realised as the outcomes is what determines the scope of governance.

In my understanding, good governance means much more and beyond performance efficiencies in the existing systems of government and functioning of social and economic institutes. Without structural changes, expanding the very scope of policy formulation and reorienting mindset of people, good governance could not be expected. Good governance should not mean merely doing better than what is expected, but doing more and beyond. It should include equality, community and societal participation and partnership. Good governance is not limited to functioning and services of the government but much more and includes the pillars of the State apart from the civil society and political parties.

N. Vittal, a senior IAS officer of Gujarat Cadre (1960 batch) who has held senior positions like Chief Central Vigilance Commissioner, has written extensively on governance. In a yet to be published book, he writes that 'good governance would mean: rule of law, minimum corruption, chance for every citizen to rise to full potential and maximum productivity of systems'.[9]

Dr Subhash C. Kashyap has also discussed about good governance in a couple of his books.[10] He is perhaps the foremost scholar of distinct credentials, much beyond as a constitutional authority that he is known in the country. He did that in a serious and outside the context of politics. He reminded that although the Constitution of India has referred to 'governance' only once, in the Article 37 under the Directive Principles, what it signifies was not referred to. Article 37 indicates certain 'principles' being fundamental in the governance of the country (although not enforceable by any court). However, Dr Kashyap concluded in his book, *Indian Constitution—Conflicts and Controversies* that 'these fundamentals are defiled, defaced and debunked openly' as if no one can do anything about it. He concluded,

> There was little emphasis on the principles of governance or traditional values in Indian political thought' as [the] focus of the Constitutional Assembly was on organisation of the state apparatus, on a political system, on institutions of government, on division of powers, on functionaries and officers—their rights and jurisdictions.

Dr Kashyap sums up, 'The whole idea of good governance is that of giving, of serving, of doing good to the people, of solving their problems and making their lives more liveable, satisfying and enjoyable.' He observes, 'Good governance is limited governance'; it is a 'participative system'; and it is about 'citizen-friendly administration, economic growth and nation building'. As the World Bank indicated, the idea of good governance encompasses democracy, transparency and accountability.

Attributing the idea of good governance to Atal Bihari Vajpayee, Vice President of India M. Venkaiah Naidu (earlier a Union minister) explained what he thought of it,

> First, people should get what they are legally entitled without any wait or running around government offices, or having to pay any bribe, and without any discrimination. And government should

bring changes so that people could live happily, and government takes harsh measures against corruption, black money, and ensures transparency and accountability in government functioning.

He also talked of 'making people partners in development'.[11] He recalled what Prime Minister Vajpayee had said—that an individual, however great he/she may be, is not bigger than the country, and however capable a political party may be, it cannot be more important than the democracy.

Dr Pai Panandikar,[12] founder director of premier think tank, Centre for Policy Research (popularly known as CPR), has been a pioneer in public policy research and analysis on governance and development. Dr Pai Panandikar has led several series of debates based on CPR's studies by scholars over four decades. His latest was 'State of the Nation' symposium in September 2017, with Dr Subhash Kashyap as a key resource person. He contended that good governance involves performance of service delivery departments, public order and freedom of expression of the citizen within constitutional provisions and that it also advocates that citizens should be able to unleash their potential.

For Raman Singh, Chief Minister of Chhattisgarh State, good governance means 'providing citizens an efficient administration system which delivers effectively the responsibilities bestowed upon it'.[13]

N. Vittal[14] contended that governance is a rule of law, fairness in treating all citizen equally, corruption-less performance and delivery of services, decentralised mechanisms of state, freedom and participation of citizens in decision-making processes. It is generally believed that the criteria for a preferred state of affairs anytime, anywhere is governance by its functional features and service principles, and not by control or stability aspects of the government, not even by longevity of a head of the government in that post.

Jwala Narasimha Rao, an officer of Telangana chief minister's office, wrote in his Telugu book (2017)[15] that the idea of *suparipalana* is that security, equal opportunity, hassle-free availability of essential services and better living standards matter more. He also included 'promoting responsibility in individuals' as a desirable feature of governance.

Sustaining Development

The United Nations has identified 17 goals that nations should have to sustain development. Based on these goals, a Sustainable Development Solution Network[16] was launched. In 2016, this body ranked 149 countries in collaboration with a German agency, Bertelsmann Stiftung. India was ranked at 110. Interestingly, but not surprisingly, the countries in the top are European, smaller in size and the ones which stand out today as examples of countries with good governance.

Is sustainable development possible without good governance? What are these 17 goals of sustainable development which could determine the status of the governance of a country? The list available on the UN website is as follows:

1. End poverty in all its forms everywhere.
2. End hunger, achieve food security and improved nutrition, and promote sustainable agriculture.
3. Ensure healthy lives and promote wellbeing for all at all ages.
4. Ensure inclusive and equitable quality education and promote lifelong learning opportunities for all.
5. Achieve gender equality and empower all women and girls.
6. Ensure availability and sustainable management of water and sanitation for all.
7. Ensure access to affordable, reliable, sustainable and modern energy for all.
8. Promote sustained, inclusive and sustainable economic growth, full and productive employment, and decent work for all.
9. Build resilient infrastructure, promote inclusive and sustainable industrialisation, and foster innovation.
10. Reduce inequality within and among countries.
11. Make cities and human settlements inclusive, safe, resilient and sustainable.
12. Ensure sustainable consumption and production patterns.

13. Take urgent action to combat climate change and its impacts (taking note of agreements made by the UNFCCC forum).
14. Conserve and sustainably use the oceans, seas and marine resources for sustainable development.
15. Protect, restore and promote sustainable use of terrestrial ecosystems, sustainably manage forests, combat desertification and halt and reverse land degradation, and halt biodiversity loss.
16. Promote peaceful and inclusive societies for sustainable development, provide access to justice for all and build effective, accountable and inclusive institutions at all levels.
17. Strengthen the means of implementation and revitalise the global partnership for sustainable development.

The United Nations did not prescribe anywhere that the responsibility for realising or accomplishing these goals is primarily that of the government. But indications are that achieving these goals is the responsibility of both the government and the society. That is, all the pillars of the State have to work together to achieve these goals.

Swaraj to Su-raj? What Is It All About?

Prime Minister Narendra Modi gave a call from the historical Red Fort on the eve of the 70th anniversary of Independence for Su-raj instead of continue talking of Swaraj. What does this mean beyond sounding rhythmic? Earlier, the prime minister had claimed that his government is providing good governance. Some of his predecessors too have made such claims, may be less frequently. There was never any effort by any claimant to explain as to what this good governance was all about? What does it entail and when a government could claim good governance? What are the parameters on which one could weigh how well or how much a government is facilitating good governance? Does onetime good governance remains so forever? Is there a threshold?

Political leaders and people need to be sensitive to all such features and dimensions of good government so that the stakeholders could dissociate a government from its governance. The newly elected Assam chief minister, for example, claims, like other chief ministers, that he intends and plans to start good governance in the state. To him, it meant 'honest government and corruption free government'.[17] He claimed further that it was what Prime Minister Modi was trying for and wanted the chief ministers to ensure in their respective states. That is good. And that is the minimum any government is expected to ensure. But such a simplistic explanation of the intention does not distinguish a government from its predecessors. Even more importantly, such limited perspective does not enhance the very scope of government and does not help prepare the citizen and society to become active players in governance. Can a government remain honest if other stakeholders outside the government are not active? Such a view does not vitalize the society as the fifth pillar. Governance is not merely by and of the government of the day. Governance involves an active role played by political parties, mass media, citizens and society. For example, if schools under government are honest and the schools outside the government are not, can we claim the education system as good? Similarly about the health services; if the infrastructure is impressive but access to and the reliability of government hospitals is not there, can we say health services are good?

A country could not claim good governance merely because its GDP has increased recently or the crime rate has declined during a year or because instant polls in the mass media show that a higher percentage of the population is satisfied or happy with the current government or the prime minister? Such findings could be positive signs only when more important criteria and characteristics are also acknowledged. They include how well democratic traditions have taken roots in the polity or has the federal character provided in the Constitution been consolidated or does the government function in an inclusive way, in a spirit of participation of citizens and socioeconomic equity goal being pursued. Eventually what matters is the equilibrium between states and Union, between different political entities and cultural groups, among different pillars of democracy and between public and private sectors.

Use of statistics to manipulate the data—primary and secondary— has added to the complexity of public discourse on the outcomes of governmental efforts. What matters is how well matched are the proposals and performance and claims and achievement. How much of what government claims as 'achievement' is also 'performance' or is it that both are the same? These are different stages of the process towards realising intended goals. Vision without clarity is just an ambition. When the first-time chief minister of Assam, Sarbananda Sonowal, talks of good governance, he was referring to his intentions. That is good and is a much needed first step. He should not mix up statistical data to claim achievements and be contended with that. An analytical perspective can save a leader such mix-ups and 'achievement traps' from a statistical jugglery, as the Chief Minister of Andhra Pradesh did in 2016–2017.[18] In the process, the pursuit of good governance gets derailed and a temporal outlook takes over. The result is full page advertisements loaded with claims of achievements even on completion of hardly one year in office! Or even on completion of first hundred days! 'Su-raj' spells long-term concern and view of governance and is more reflective of the idea of governance. Prime Minister Modi should pursue the idea of Su-raj and sensitise the stakeholders and save people from getting lured to temporal benefits in the name of good governance.

Governance, Not Without Decentralisation

Dr Bibek Debroy is a full-time member of the NITI Aayog,[19] the think-tank advisory body to NDA government led by Narendra Modi. Speaking at a One Globe Forum on 'Transforming India's Governance Architectures', he noted,

> [Governance used to be centralised in pre 1947, it became even more centralised during post 1947. And one of the interesting things that has been happening in India, in terms of that institutional structure, is the greatest decentralisation and devolution and the empowerment of the local bodies. We are just witnessing the beginning of that transformation.

Since he was one of the pioneers to 'rank' the states of India for mass media, he understands the complexities.

If decentralisation alone is a feature of good governance, India would have entered such a phase as early as 1957. For that was when the Nehru government appointed a high power committee under the then chief minister of Gujarat, Balwant Rai Mehta. The Balwant Rai Committee report is a milestone in Indian democracy.[20] This report, for the first time, recommended a three-tier governance model—the governance structure comprising the village panchayat, the samiti and zilla parishad within a district at one level and the district, the state and the Union at the national level. It suggested popularly elected bodies for panchayat, samiti and zilla parishad. For a couple of years this model was followed. The report, however, did not talk of devolution of finances. The idea of popular election of *sarpanch*, block president and zilla parishad chair was given up after a couple of years and the indirect election practice was adopted. The logic is not known but that was the beginning of the spread of corruption in elections at the gross roots.

A second stunning turning point for decentralisation in governance was made by Rajiv Gandhi in 1992 with the 73rd and 74th Amendments to Panchayat and Nagar Palika Act. These constitutional amendments provided for financial devolution as well as devolution of responsibility for certain basic functions like health and education. In some states, more than 30 services were made the responsibility of the panchayats. The State Finance Commission is supposed to earmark certain percentage of revenue to gram panchayat. In some states, State Finance Commission has not even made notional demarcation for funding, even by raising it locally. What have we achieved in these three decades since these gram panchayat and nagar palika amendments were passed by the parliament?

Despite devolution of powers and resources, there is no evidence that the size of the Union or the state governments has declined. On the contrary, there is evidence of increase in the number of ministries, departments and functionaries. The only excuse for the increase could be that the number of development projects like MGNREGS and the number of pensioners have gone up over these 30 years. For example, at the village level, in place of *pattan–patwari* system of three decades ago, there are now four or five functionaries in a village operating from two different offices—one for the village development officer and the other for the panchayat office bearers. Earlier, panchayat affairs were maintained and operated by elected functionaries and development needs were looked after by a 'village level worker' who initially used to go to people more as a volunteer with an honorarium. Now, as the case is, there are more than one functionary in a village in the payroll of the government as employees of the state. As regards the position of 'development officer', by the very designation only, he or she expects that people seek his or her help. This very approach had tilted the scope of the government. There is no proactive orientation in their functioning.

Decentralisation without involvement of the local people is not going to help reduce government at any level. *Prajala Vaddaku Palana* (government at the doorsteps) was a popular scheme of the then Andhra Pradesh Government under Chief Minister N.T. Rama Rao. Under this scheme, the officials of various departments of government together went to a village and tried to solve pending as well as new issues villagers faced and to redress complaints there and then. Under this scheme (or that of *Antyodaya* in Rajasthan), only once in a while, may be once in a term of the government, such ideas were put to experimentation. But the takeaways from such experiments were never institutionalised nor have they enthused people to become active partners in governance in a continued way. Such opportunities and experiments should facilitate gradual reduction in the size of the government. Now with the new mass media based on broadband and Wi-Fi, and video conferencing more specifically, should come handy to reduce the size of a government. We also see municipal commissioners calling society groups for their cooperation once a year or when a massive campaign is taken up. But examples of society being viewed as a key partner in development and in attending to needs of people locally, without looking for government's 'sanction' or approval, are too few. Delhi government experimented when Sheila Dikshit was the chief minister with a *bhagidari* approach to involve resident associations was one that was formalised but lost its significance with the change in the political party in government. These civil society bodies were formed as independent groups but with government assigning them certain responsibilities and providing the money required for implementing the same. With change in the government, lessons from such experiments were never pursued, although the role and activism of society is an essential feature of good governance. Scuttling such initiatives with constraints adds to the apprehensions of self-motivated people. Participation and involvement of groups as registered societies or trusts and the like, as in the case of resident welfare societies, is a critical feature for governance. This is perhaps how NGOs have gained over CSOs.

A government which is huge and has expanded need not be viewed as better for governance. A well-structured government with systems can afford today to reduce its size even with an increase in the workload and increase in the population to be reached and serviced.

More than decentralisation of government closer to the people, it has been control and command methodologies that are gaining recently. Decentralisation over the years neither has led to significant moving of government closer to the people and increased its efficiency levels nor has it changed the scope and course of governance in terms of participation and involvement of the people at the grassroots.

In many ways, good governance sounds like Mahatma Gandhi's *Gram Swaraj* where gram sabha (village assembly) decides every aspect of public priorities. Recent (2015–2016) experiments with mohalla sabha in New Delhi helped the Aam Aadmi Party (AAP) government to claim good governance. But it did not take off elsewhere as it was an isolated initiative. *Mohalla Sabha* took initiatives about deciding how the available money could be used as well as in assessing required resources. Good governance expects such local initiatives and their institutionalisation.

In 2009, UNESCAP (a wing of the UN) Chief, Mr Yap Kioe Sheng of Poverty Reduction Section, listed[21] eight characteristics for good governance. In the Indian context, these eight characteristics could only be essential indicative attributes, not sufficient to distinguish a regime as good governance. Other desirable conditions for governance are parliamentary democracy, the obligatory provisions of the Constitution, social development and the extent of the involvement of corporates and communities. These conditions expected from government are relevant as much in the case of every other pillar of the republic, institutions—private or public—which have linkage with functioning of democracy, development process and the government of the day. A government led by a political party is there for a limited period—five years in India—but it could be shorter if it loses majority and may be longer if it gets re-elected. Also, the party in power changes its policies and priorities every time the composition of the support it has on the floor of the parliament change. As such, a good governance initiative during the tenure of a government may not remain so in future. Whether there is good governance at a given time need to be validated repeatedly. When the features or characteristics set roots and sustain irrespective of the party or its strength in the parliament, then one could say that a country is under good governance irrespective of the political composition of the government of the day.

New Instruments

There are certain new instruments today which facilitate realising or achieving these goals so that governance could take roots and get reinforced for good governance. Which are these? There are three types of instruments with potential to deepen and even change the scope of governance. These are: new legislations, new methodologies involving the citizens and new networks and interactive technologies.

First, there are a couple of recent legislations, which empower the citizens and bring in new awareness with implications to governance. These include right to information, right to education, right to employment, right to food, guarantee to delivery of public services, and so on. The Acts pertaining to these rights have ushered in new hope and opportunities. Under the Consumer Act, for example, a range of rights are included directly and indirectly, for instance, the right to fair treatment and the right to grievance redressal and compensation. What is not there as yet is the 'right to seek fulfilment of promises of parties to voters and even of the governments'.

Second, new methodologies to involve and engage the society. These include social audit, citizen charter, public hearing, PIL, disclosure provisions on a suo motto basis, and so on.

Third, social networks, new technology tools, social media or new mass media. These have brought in a new found voice, confidence and strength in people, society and stakeholders, who influence the governance. 'Hotspots of citizen activism' is a recent phenomenon quickly gaining ground in cities.

Together, these developments, features and provisions make it possible, as never before, to think of a good governance scenario as well as stature to work towards achieving such a status in government, development and democracy in such a way that the phenomenon is visible at micro levels.

Some Differentiating and Inhibiting Factors

What cannot be described as good governance is easier to say than what good governance could be. Good governance is an encompassing idea. It cannot be limited to the few features discussed so far. It is not merely an evolving idea, but it also has to be demonstrated and experienced by citizens—with no privileges attached or attributed. Some negative features in the name of good governance that may gain ground are indicated here as examples.

Uppala Gopala Rao,[22] a crusader and an RTI activist associate of mine for over a decade in Hyderabad, reiterates on every occasion certain desirable features that our predecessors had dreamt of about independent India. Together these features are indicative of the kind of state of affairs that the country needs to aspire for. Upon his entry into politics, N.T. Rama Rao espoused in Andhra Pradesh many of these principles which won him laurels and mandate to form government. Together with some of the features espoused by the United Nations forums and my own research over the years on governance, certain features are summed up here. Our elders who fought for free India and dreamt of a great India never wished to see a regime or live in a situation where certain desirables are not evident or available. I have identified some undesirable situations inhibitive of good governance. These include governance

- swayed by immoral earnings and practices of leaders and parties
- that thrives on image and manipulation in mass media
- in which minimum basic needs of people could not be met

- in which disparities between people are too glaring and not on decline
- in which creative ideas and initiatives are snubbed
- in which slavery of one kind or other is continued, including child labour
- in which exploiting others is a criterion for success
- in which ordinary and disadvantaged are neglected or ignored
- in which adulteration and duplicity has better chance to survive and scale
- in which questioning and criticism is not tolerated and curbed
- in which people are kept divided on caste, community and region basis
- in which fear of government or its functionaries haunts people at grassroots
- in which injustice and exploitation has better chance to thrive
- in which prompt and timely justice is an exception
- in which the citizen's immediate concerns are not responded but ignored
- in which more citizens have no civic sense and national concerns
- in which value of work and excellence is not encouraged
- in which illegal earnings and immoral behaviours have better chance
- in which interests of markets dictate policies instead of those of society
- in which greed and selfish pursuit rules and dictates public policies
- in which conflict of interest is not a botheration but a determiner of priorities
- in which women are not respected and not able to claim equal chance
- in which mass media has no concerns for the society and citizens, but has for markets and consumers
- in which the citizen's role is limited to and ends with voting in an election
- in which grievances of common people are neither promptly nor easily redressed
- in which rights of the citizens on basic needs and human dignity are not nurtured
- in which manipulation matters more than performance

- in which decision making is concentrated in a few individuals despite elections
- in which control and command continues to be the modus operandi of the government
- in which primary education and health are not a priority but allowed as profit making enterprises
- in which society is not part of process of governance
- in which the rule of law concerning common people in particular is not adhered to

From common people's perspective, these are differentiators of governments and one regime from another. The status of good governance is determined by a combination of these various features.

The Case of Switzerland

'Beyond good governance', for many, is a utopian idea, which means 'good, but not possible or feasible'. Unlike utopia, beyond good governance is not only desirable but possible and feasible. It is a process—a state or country does not reach or achieve good governance overnight or in one go; it is a gradual process. The time it might take could be a decade or more. (That governments in India, even one-year-old, claim 'good governance' is a different story.)

As regards a recent Swiss referendum for guaranteed basic income, the idea of guaranteed income for every family living in the country was rejected overwhelmingly by citizens. The idea of 'unconditional dole' by the State was viewed by citizens as 'unsustainable solution for society'. This confirms that the Swiss have reached the status of good governance and beyond. To put such an idea of a 'citizen' for a plebiscite in Switzerland, where its Constitution allows its 100,000 voters to seek a change in the Constitution, is an example of 'direct democracy'.

The fact that over two-thirds of voters rejected 'guaranteed basic income for everyone' living in Switzerland, after considerable debate, reflects 'least dependence on the government', concern for 'sustainable solutions' and recognition of the responsibilities of citizens. The government dole actually came from their belief that people would be even more productive and more creative if they are engaged themselves 'instead of being obliged to be productive'. The belief on the part of the citizens was that people do not feel responsible if they continue to depend on government doles and that such a culture does not promote human dignity, public service and active citizenry with concerns and GDP in real terms.

Finland and Netherlands, two of the other wealthy countries in the neighbourhood of Switzerland, also explored such an initiative as a part of going 'beyond good governance' and 'direct democracy' but gave up. The core philosophy is that of minimum role of the government and maximum role of the citizen and society in the governance of the country.

Another example of a beyond good governance situation comes from Italy. Despite a fragile political culture with frequent elections and changes in the ruling party, the governments continue to be as vibrant and sustained. That is governance is not government-centric or driven by or depends merely on the party in power. Also, another example is the resignation of Italian Prime Minister Matteo Renzi[23] for loosing on a referendum on Constitutional reform proposal taking 'full responsibility for the defeat', though he still had two years to complete his term as Prime Minister.

The scenario in India today is exactly the opposite of that in Switzerland. The dependency syndrome of citizens on government is all out and on increase. The expectations of voters from candidates and political parties during election times is also blatant and extensively vitiating the very free and fairness of electoral process. This trend has been on the increase in the country, not on decline for sure! How and when such a trend could get reversed to change the course for better governments and good governance in India? Hopefully the discussion in this book creates sensitivity to such possibilities!

Proof of Pudding Indicators

From a citizen's perspective, what determines the scope and structure of a government at any given time? No one aspect could be isolated. In the ultimate analysis, a combination of experiences and insights go into that process. Such accumulated sensitivities in different contexts determine how a government is viewed—at any given time. Governance is how different agencies, departments, institutes and directorates of a government function, fulfil their responsibilities and deliver basic services reliably during its tenure taking along the other pillars of the state, particularly the society.

The idea of good governance is continuation and consolidation of initiatives, despite changes in the government or the party in power and irrespective of who the head of the state is. This process obviously implies increased responsibility of the citizens and accountability of the political parties. Governance in this scenario is not limited to that of government machinery per se but maintaining an equilibrium among the pillars of the State. The immediate examples are some countries in Europe such as Netherlands, Italy, Switzerland and Sweden.

In the ultimate analysis, good governance involves any combination or all of the following essential elements.

1. **The ease and reliability of basic public services with which they are delivered.** *Roti, kapada aur makan* (food, clothing and shelter) is a decades old slogan used by leaders and parties. To these education and health has been added as the basic essential needs of people. More than two decades ago, Dewang Mehta[24] of NASSCOM added broadband connectivity for every house as a part of minimum needs. Today, some 15 to 20 services are considered as the basic public services, including occasional need-based services. The reliability of the availability and affordability of these services is expected from any government. In a good governance scenario, these services are ensured without any discrimination irrespective of the government or party in power or on account of shifts in policy priorities.

2. **Corruption free access, availability and delivery of public services.** Studies by CMS and many others, including those by governments, have indicated the extent and nature of corruption by the way of bribe as a quid pro quo arrangement in actually availing these basic public services or requiring a contact in the

office to get them delivered. About 5 per cent of those who seek these services could not avail them, as they could not afford to pay the bribe or know a contact. In a good governance scenario, the percentage of those who are deprived of basic services declines, not increases. Increase in transparency practices and use of technology, on the one hand, and citizen activism in ensuring access and delivery of services, on the other, makes it possible to dramatically bring down corruption in these basic public services.

3. **Employment or productive engagements and opportunities.** Conventionally, government was looked up on as the source for employment. With the rise of private sector and increase in self-entrepreneurship, job opportunities outside the government are far more now. But old perceptions continue. Two aspects are associated with a government job—privilege and permanence. Privilege of being part of the government and the associated social status. Permanence in that one can continue with likely retirement benefits and without any linkage to performance. Labour market and unemployment rate have become indicators of the economy. In a good governance state, employment are longer a yardstick but opportunities for self-employment, micro entrepreneurship and skills. Growth no longer remains job-centric. With adoption of newer technologies and digitalisation, job opportunities are bound to decline significantly in a matter of few years, particularly with the government. Labour laws no longer remain a tyranny in the market or a hindrance to growth. What kind of options and facilitations are available for productive engagement goes into kind of perceptions and experience of people about governance?

4. **Trust in and reliability of law and order mechanisms, instruments and security perceptions.** Police is viewed as one offering security locally. As such, its performance is a matter of significance in determining the stature of government and the nature of governance. For many people at the grassroots, government means local police. Good governance is where police is expected to behave more responsively. In a good governance scenario, police is hardly visible but the deterrence effect will be felt. Police will be known for ensuring peace and facilitator of rule of law. And, citizens and society will be involved in the functioning of police service at the

public level. Rule-based governance creates transparency in functioning and improves the trust between citizens and government.

5. **No discrimination in providing public services, without courtesies.** To what extent do government outlets and service delivery points operate by the rule of law? Uniform application of rules will be a hallmark for good governance. Citizens should experience equality in availing public services. A key variable is how well rules and procedures provided in law are known to people. How well guidance centres or help desks are relevant and responsive in that process will define the nature of governance.

6. **Responsive systems with redressal and such other mechanisms.** Citizens should be able to rely and get disputes resolved and the complaint redressal system has to be reliable and prompt. Citizen charter and similar instruments become obligatory to comply and facilitate the very need and scope for complaints and their redressal.

7. **Independent judicial system, prompt and easy access to justice.** Public trust in the Judiciary for its reliability, independence and affordability is not seen in an exceptional way. Such perceptions and experience are not in doubt in a good governance scenario. Access to the judicial system is not limited or a privilege. Awareness about laws and promotional aspect of judicial route like fast track tribunals, PIL, suo motu processes and proactive initiatives help expand the reach of judiciary among the needy. Transparency in justice delivery is not an exception but routine, affordable and timely.

8. **Freedom to move, express, choice in an environment of plurality.** Curbs on civilian voices are exceptional in good governance, and options and choices, too. They are not restrained. There would be no restrictions in availing freedom and rights of the citizens and their role in facilitating implementation of creative plans and proposals.

9. **Facilitative support to avail rights and entitlements.** In a good governance scenario, support is facilitated in availing the rights and entitlement of ordinary citizens and far off communities. This could be done within the civil society and stakeholders.

10. **Free and fair polls for representative governments.** Free and fair elections and free press are equally important for democracy

and good governance. They are two sides of the same coin. No individual or group can or should enjoy special advantage in the poll process. Press or mass media is free but not driven by 'conflict of interest'.

11. **Poll promises and fulfilling them.** In a good governance atmosphere, there would be restraints on luring voters with all kind of promises. Even more, there would be obligatory provisions or precedents for implementation of such promises in a timeframe.

12. **ICT as a level player.** Access and use of ICT has become a key element now, with increase in options for availing newer technology and greater access to software and with every house connected digitally with affordable access to Internet, cable TV and telephone/cell phone. Centralisation and privacy concerns of individuals and communities is not under threat and ignored. Digitalisation would be to the advantage of citizens rather than only of the government and a privileged few.

13. **Level playing opportunity.** How proactive, citizen-centric and concerned for society are the mass media also matter for good governance? Reflecting the woes of the common citizen in mass media should not be an exception. Access to news coverage should add the voices of the society too. Mass media should be no one's monopoly. Access and fair play to mass media is critical for good governance.

14. **Transparency of political parties/system.** Each of the six pillars of the state—legislature, judiciary, executive, media, society and political parties—should function in such a competitive and complimentary way that no one is seen as going overboard in their respective function and responsibility. Sustainability of good governance depends on this balance and equilibrium in the system. Political parties should shift their concern from GDP-led and growth-centric pursuit to human values such as quality of life and capacity building at every sphere.

A consistent holistic view of development is a prerequisite. Good governance is not limited to what government of the day does but depends on how well the pillars of the State perform their role, actively, proactively and inclusively. The desirable and undesirable features of good governance are examples and indicative only. In the ultimate analysis, it is the citizens who have to find the difference in governance from their own lifestyle, perspectives and practices.

Notes and References

1. In writing this book, I have benefited not only from several published works of Dr Subhash Kashyap but also from discussions with him more recently. There are many books and several more articles by Dr Kashyap, e.g., World Bank (http://www.worldbank.org/); Britton Woods (www.brettonwoods. org/); International Monetary Fund (www.imf.org); http://www.imf.org/external/pubs/ft/exrp/govern/govindex.htm; https://www.imf.org/en/About/Factsheets/The-IMF-and-Good-Governance
2. 'What is Good Governance?' United Nations Escap, 10 July 2009, www.unescap.org/resources/what-good-governance
3. Subhash C. Kashyap, *Concept of Good Governance and Kautilya's Arthashastra*, ICSSR Occasional Monograph Series, Issue no. 3 (New Delhi: Indian Council of Social Science Research, 2003).
4. S.K. Chopra (ed.), *Towards Good Governance* (Konark: IIC project, 1997); Pai Panandiker (ed.), *Problems of Governance in South Asia* (Konark: CPR project, 2000); R.S. Chikara (ed.), *Governance* (HOPE, 2009); Ajit Banerjee and Chandrasekaran (eds.), *Renewing Governance*, UNDP project (New Delhi: Tata McGraw Hill, 1996).
5. Subhash C. Kashyap, *Our Constitution* (2001 edition; New Delhi: National Book Trust, 1995); *Idem.*, *Campaign for Good Governance: Mission Statement* (New Delhi: Rashtriya Jagriti Sansthan, 2010).
6. Banerjee and Chandrasekaran, *Renewing Governance*; Chikara, *Governance*.
7. Irshad Daftari, for example, showed that how half of India's GDP comes from 'discrepancies' and how such discrepancies drive the GDP growth (a tweet on June 1, 2016).
8. Isaac Munene Ndereba, 'World Development Report 2017 and Community Led Development', 15 June 2017, https://communityleddev.org/
9. N. Vittal, *Modi's Miracle: India's Tectonic Shift to the Right* (in press).
10. Kashyap, *Concept of Good Governance*; *Idem.*, *Indian Constitution: Conflicts and Controversies* (New Delhi: Vitasta Publishing, 2010).
11. *Andhra Jyoti*, 25 December 2016 (I attended this at IIC).
12. Presentation by Pai Panandikar, Former President, Centre for Policy Research (CPR), New Delhi, at 'State of Nation' symposium, India International Centre, New Delhi, 22 September 2017; from personal communication.
13. Chief Minister's 'Good Governance Fellowship Programme', an advertisement by Government of Madhya Pradesh, reported in *Mint*, 22 September 2017.

14. N. Vittal, 'Some Positive Trends', *Transparency Review* 1, no. 6 (2008); *Idem.*, 'Trust Vote a Turning Point', *Transparency Review* 1, no. 8 (2008); *Idem.*, 'Citizen, Corruption and Public Services—Reversing a Phenomena!', *Transparency Review* 4, no. 5 (2011).
15. Jwala Narasimha Rao, *This is What Good Governance Is*, English translation of original Telugu *Supari Palana* (Hyderabad: EMESCO, 2017).
16. 'Sustainable Development Goals: All You Need to Know', *The Guardian*, 19 January 2015, https://www.theguardian.com/global-development/2015/jan/19/sustainable-development-goals-united-nations
17. Yogi Adityanand, Chief Minister of Uttar Pradesh, speaking at Ayodhya Diwali celebrations on 19 October 2017. Reported in mass media on 20 October 2017.
18. Chandra Babu Naidu, Chief Minister of Andhra Pradesh tended to quote statistics out of nowhere and out of context as do many other leaders in power.
19. https://www.indiatoday.in/magazine/state-of-the-states/story/20171127-india-today-state-of-the-states-survey-bibek-debroy-1087461-2017-11-17; https://www.indiatoday.in/magazine/cover-story/story/20140414-bibek-debroy-suggests-eight-mantras-for-good-governance-801853-1999-11-30
20. Balwant Rai Committee was the first high-level government committee after independence to suggest decentralisation of government.
21. 'What is Good Governance', UNESCAP; cf, note 2.
22. Uppala Gopala Rao is an RTI and anti-corruption crusader in Hyderabad for the last four decades. He has published several leaflets in Telugu on the topic.
23. *Hindustan Times*, *Times of India*, both December 5, 2016.
24. Dewang Mehta was the first Chief Executive of NASSCOM who crusaded for scaling up of ICT initiatives for governance.

CHAPTER 4

Pillars of the Republic

This section first discusses the critical pillars of the State and then argues for six pillars instead of just the three that are traditionally considered as constituting the government. While the media is already viewed as the fourth estate, civil society and political parties too need to be considered as the fifth and sixth pillars of the State as their active participation is critical for governance, and especially for good governance. Should education be also considered a part of civil society? Yes, it should be. In view of its unique role and functions, education should also be treated with special consideration for its long-term implications and mind-setting role. This chapter presents an overview of the dilemma confronting the six pillars of the republic.

Over the past seven decades, the public stature and standing of conventional pillars of the State have declined and, in some cases, have come under increased scrutiny. Since their combined functioning is what constitutes 'governance', how can we expect better governance today without their active role? Even in the case of conventional pillars, it is increasingly being realised that their scope and role depends on political parties and civil society.

Since political parties are the driving force of the government, they need to adapt to newer challenges and avail of newer opportunities to be representative, transparent and accountable. Today's political parties show neither of these qualities. They are not accountable to the

Election Commission of India (ECI). The legislature, the executive and even the judiciary as well as the media are being driven by the electoral system and the way polls are being conducted. Such a situation cannot be moderated without active citizenry and civil society. The education system and ICT are the other differentiators of the functioning of the pillars of the State and the republic.

While legislature, judiciary and executive are State apparatuses and constitutional institutions, political parties are as much established, structured and ongoing forums as mass media. The degree of representation in and transparency of political parties, the electoral system and its practices, and the evolution of the electorate and the motivation to take part in it are just as important, if not more, as legislatures and even the bureaucracy.

In a parliamentary democracy, the political system consisting of parties and the electoral system matter as much as the legislature, the judiciary and the executive. Because of the domination of political parties, it could have an even bigger role than what is perceived. Civil society, comprising individuals as citizens and social beings, organised communities, professions or functionaries, and interest groups who do not pursue power, play a significant role in deciding the course of representative democracy. And yet civil society (the 'WE' in the Constitution) is viewed as the receiver and the government as the provider (giver). Civil society and the political system offer a balance. The conventional three pillars of the State are not enough to explain and take corrective measures in governance. They are required to play an active role without being submissive to or dominating over the others, their eventual goal being the same. These all need to be considered together as correctives to maintain the overall governance and equilibrium between them.

Political Parties

Without political parties becoming more representative, responsible, accountable and transparent, democracy cannot be meaningful. These features are what differentiate democracy from other types of political systems. Going by the functioning of political parties in India over the past 70 years, several questions need to be raised, debated, relooked and repositioned. Some of them are discussed in this chapter. This exercise, however, cannot be inclusive and all-encompassing. Some of these concerns have been gone unaddressed for years, even after recommendations of several parliamentary committees and other commissions, like the Second Administrative Reforms Commission (2010).[1]

The kind of governance that prevails during any given time period depends on the political parties and their efficacy. Notwithstanding political theories, political parties in India are preoccupied with fighting elections to come to power. The notion that political parties are to serve their members, protect their interests and represent them in various bodies formally through an election or otherwise is no longer omnipresent. Parties make claims merely as a formality. And all parties indulge in this practice. Seva Dal in the Congress party, for example, which was at one time the muscle of that party, is a sidelined activity today. The Bharatiya Janata Party (BJP) too has independent units, in fact many more of them. Political parties are expected to have distinct objectivities, ideologies and principles. But one hardly finds any such differentiation between them. They are all viewed as the same in their outlook and operations. And as to priorities, their main concern is to contest elections to win and come to power. Why do all parties need to contest an election if service to people is not a prime motive? Should there be not some criteria for parties to contest an election? It is even important that voters have options and alternatives rather than only one party to choose from, as in some Communist countries like Russia and China.

Should all parties registered with the ECI be allowed to context elections? Although more than 1,500 parties are registered, hardly 50 of them have ever contested an election. Why then did they come into being or what they were otherwise engaged in is a subject for a different study. Instead of a party being eligible for all elections once it is registered, for each round of elections, the ECI should announce the number of parties that are eligible to contest that particular election. It is good that the ECI had notified some parties to explain their existence and account for any revenue collections[2] and that it has sought powers to disqualify some parties from contesting, the same way it does with individual candidates.

Some think that the more the number of parties, the better the democracy. More is not merrier for democracy or for the kind of electoral system we have adopted: that is, the 'first-past-post' system, where votes get divided and fragmented to such an extent that the winner may get to power with hardly one-fourth of the 'polled votes', which can in turn actually result in a party coming to power sometimes with hardly 20 per cent of the 'total electorate'.

As can be observed, there are five characteristics of political parties for ensuring good governance and for sustaining it: (a) How democratic is the party itself?; (b) How representative is the party's outreach and how well do its elected members represent the concerns of the people?; (c) Is the party functioning transparently and proactively?; (d) How responsible is the party and its leaders in their performance?; and (e) What kind of accountability mechanism does the party have for its leaders and for the promises it makes in its election manifesto?

Political parties are registered by the ECI, an independent constitutional body, based on certain particulars provided by a political party. This includes its membership and criteria, constitution of the party regarding its formation, the person/s appointed to run its affairs, the procedures followed in its periodic elections for its office bearers, etc. Political parties are to indicate their adherence to the Indian Constitution in their own party constitution.[3]

The ECI has classified 6 parties as 'national parties', 54 as 'state parties' (against 48 in 2009) and 1,593 as 'registered unrecognised' parties (against 702 in 2004). It is not clear as to why some are described as registered but 'unrecognised'. There is no clarification as to whether they are engaged in any political activity like sensitising voters about their responsibility or doing citizenship sensitivity activities or the reason for which ECI has to register them at all in the first instance, unless it is a first step after which a registered body has to establish its objectives and credentials.

There is hardly any party which is following its own constitution by holding periodic elections to choose its office bearers. That is how some parties have become family outfits, with same person(s) continuing in the same office for years. There is no reliable method to establish or validate the membership of parties. In the last few decades, no party president has been popularly elected by the members in a free and fair contest.

The number of registered national parties has declined from 14 in 1951 to 6 in 2014, and the number of state parties remained 39, the same as in 1951. But the number of 'unrecognised' parties increased from 10 in 1962 to 419.[4] Until recently, the ECI was more often a silent spectator about the functioning of political parties. It never derecognised any party and parties never have to worry on that count. But why cannot ECI strictly enforce its own rules and issue notices for violating the rules of the process instead of its powers being limited to 'after' a due process of issuing notices. It has been asking for legal powers to suspend a poll (for one assembly)—as in Tamil Nadu in 2016—if it was found that money power was at play. ECI also sought the power to disqualify any candidate who has been convicted in any court.

Membership claims of political parties remain as estimates and mere claims as they are never authenticated or validated. Middle men in parties file the names of members paying the membership fees in such a way that not all persons whose names are shown in the roster themselves know that they are members as they have never even interacted with any party functionary or paid the membership fees. There are no 'primaries' for members or any such method for vetting those being considered for membership.

No political party can remain secretive about its operations, particularly about its sources of funding and expenditure. Poll strategies may remain confidential, but not revenue and expenditure; parties are expected to file a poll expenditure statement with the ECI annually and more specifically at the end of a general election every time. But very few parties are filing their annual statements as required with any regularity. It is only more recently (after 2014) that the ECI has been issuing notice for not submitting the statement, but nothing beyond that has been done so far!

Political parties have perpetuated four practices which are detrimental to the very functioning of parliamentary democracy. The first has to do with the way the parties nominate their candidates to contest the elections. The second is the basis on which elections are contested and votes are sought. The third is the whip system in vogue in the legislatures that has been imposed by political parties after getting elected, and which has curbed and curtailed the potential role of members of parliament (MPs) and members of legislative assemblies (MLAs). The fourth is that all this has reduced those elected to power to remain partisan and function more in the interest of the party and their own selves instead of their constituents.

The present practice of selecting party candidates has been criticised for years, and some rightly consider this practice to be the root cause for bad politics and for the poor quality of governance. Party manifesto is yet another document which showcases certain plans, proposals and promises if the party comes to power. But more often, over the years, the manifesto has lost its significance. It has lost relevance with voters and leaders, and even the ECI does not take it seriously. Whip order practiced by parties in legislatures has been a hindrance for representative nature and a threat to the potential of a parliamentary system. As a result of the whip system, we cannot expect the MLAs and MPs to function in the interest of local people. After getting elected, the winner is expected to work for the interests of everyone across party lines, and not merely those who voted for him or her. But, instead, the party that nominated him or her has been the consideration or the party that is likely to be in power.

Decline in Representative Character of Elected Ones

As the country is gearing up to become a more active citizenry as India approaches its 17th general election, we need to ponder about certain broad trends in the electoral process. We should be concerned that over the years, the electoral process has fallen short of the expectations of a parliamentary democratic system on three counts. These are also the undercurrent hindrances for good governance taking off.

First, the fragmentation of polity continues to cause frequent uncertainties (instability) in the functioning of legislative bodies. Second, the representative character of the electoral process has remained static and declining. Third, the party that comes to power continues to operate more or less on party (partisan) lines rather than representing all sections/regions. As a result, inclusiveness of elected governments, credibility of elected leaders and efficiency of their performance for the 'greater good of the greater number' is at stake. (Tables 4.1, 4.2 and 4.3 explain these trends. This analysis and trend hold as of 2018.) How can we expect good governance with the elected leaders remaining partial or partisan?

With an increasing number of candidates getting elected to state assemblies and the Lok Sabha with less than one-third of the total

Table 4.1 *Declining Representative Character: Lok Sabha Winners*

Won with Votes of	1977	1980	1984	1989	1991	1996	1998	1999	2004	2009	2014
Less than 40% of polled	6	84	28	66	115	170	107	100	109	167	112
41% to 50% of polled	62	157	136	160	215	224	257	223	213	255	233
More than 50% of polled	474	288	378	303	204	149	179	220	217	121	198
Total seats	542	529	542	529	534	543	543	543	539	253	253

Source: CMS Analysis of Election Commission Data (article in Indian Politics).

Table 4.2 *How Representative Was the Ruling Party?*

State Assemblies	1990–1991	1993–1995	1996–1998	2002–2004	2007–2008	2012–2013
Rajasthan	12	8	10	11	17	4
Madhya Pradesh	14	10	16	20	27	6
Uttar Pradesh	96	31	19	105	77	117
Delhi	-	1	2	1	3	5
Karnataka	-	21	9	14	7	16

Source: CMS Analysis of Election Commission Data (article in Indian Politics).[5]

Table 4.3 Decline in Representative Character of Party in Power in Key States: Percentage of Votes

State	2000–2004	2005–2008	2009–2013
			(Per cent)
Punjab	35.81 (INC)	37.09 (SAD)	34.73 (SAD)
Uttar Pradesh	25.41 (SP)	30.43 (BSP)	29.13 (SP)
Bihar	28.34 (RJD)	20.46 (JD (U))	22.58 (JDU)
Delhi	48.13 (INC)	40.31 (INC)	29.4 (AAP)
Gujarat	49.9 (BJP)	49.1 (BJP)	47.9 (BJP)

Source: CMS Analysis of Election Commission Data (article in Indian Politics).[6]

polled votes, what kind of accountability could be expected from such representatives? The number of those who got elected with less than 30 per cent of polled votes in Madhya Pradesh, for example, had gone up from 14 in 1991 to 27 in 2008. In the case of the Lok Sabha, the number of those who got elected with less than 40 per cent of polled votes had gone up, instead of declining, from six in 1977 to 167 in 2009.

With parties coming to power (as a single large majority) in states by winning less than 30 per cent of polled votes (which in fact accounts for hardly one-fifth of all its citizens), what kind of governance could be expected? The situation is even more complex in a coalition regime. (BJP ruled in Rajasthan by coming to power in 2004 with 39 per cent of the polled votes. Even in 2008, Congress party came to power in Rajasthan with 36.8 per cent of the polled votes. In Madhya Pradesh too, BJP came to power in 2004 with 42.5 per cent of votes polled, which in the 2008 assembly election had gone down to 37.6 per cent). BJP came to power in Karnataka in 2008 with 34 per cent of polled voted, which went up only marginally to 36.5 per cent in 2013. That was despite the contest in these states being primarily between two parties.

In one of the large states of India—Uttar Pradesh—representative character declined further from 30.4 per cent in 2008 to 29.1 per cent in 2013, but increased to 49.1 per cent in 2017. In Punjab too, it declined from 37 per cent in 2008 to 34.7 per cent in 2013. In Bihar, the representative character of the party had declined from 28.4 per cent in 2004 to 22.5 per cent in 2013 and to 16.8 per cent in 2015.

Despite an increased exposure to news media and increased coverage of poll process by news media in the last 15–20 years, the representative character of elected leaders has not improved. In fact, it has declined. What has been the effect of the number of news channels, which has gone up to more than 500 by 2018? And what was the effect of pre-poll surveys and exit polls which too have proliferated during this period despite contentious credentials? Even voter turnout has improved only marginally despite the all-out efforts by the ECI, media and civil society. The voter turnout declined from 60 per cent in 1977 to 57.5 per cent in the 2004 Lok Sabha poll, and increased to 66.4 in 2014 with all efforts and promotion worth more than ₹2 billion by ECI alone (Figure 4.1). Some increase in voter turnout since 2014 is more on account of an update of the voter list until the last fortnight of the poll.

Even the increased 'note-for-vote' phenomenon across the country and across sections of voters has not enhanced the representative character. The percentage of voters who were paid cash on the eve of polling in 2008 was more than one-fourth of the total voters, according to a first-ever CMS study in 2007. And this percentage had gone up on the eve of the 2014 general election to more than one-third of the total voters, and to more than 60 per cent in five states.

CMS Media Lab, which analyses contents of news channels, has brought out an analysis of how constrained and 'more of the same' phenomena of coverage of news media has been. One-third of the content of news bulletins is about poll campaigns during the election season. I attribute this dilemma of democracy to this phenomena of 'pre-emptive journalism' and 'pre-emptive electoral practices' where voters get demotivated from going to voting. We need to be concerned about these trends of 'dampening democracy' instead of 'deepening democracy' by increasing the representative the character of elected MPs and MLAs.

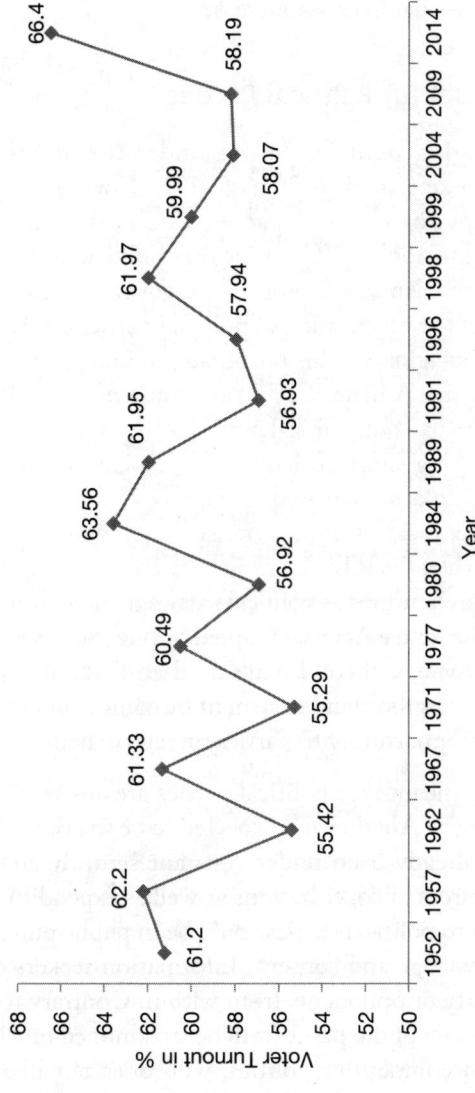

Figure 4.1 *Voter Turnout for Lok Sabha Poll*
Source: CMS analysis of Election Commission data.

Another aspect hindering good governance is the 'conflict of interest' of legislators at the Union and in the states. That is, the number of MLAs and MPs with interests in one or other profit-making advantage enterprises has been on increase.

Is RTI the Best Bet for Political Parties?

Why should bringing political parties under the ambit of RTI Act cause a rage like it had in 2016–2017? How come everyone concerned—except for political parties—described the Central Information Commission's (CIC) order that political parties should come under RTI as a landmark order? The government's argument that RTI will affect the functioning of political parties if CIC's[7] order is implemented is imaginary. This retrograde thinking is the same as the United Progressive Alliance (UPA) government's, which considered an ordinance to bail out political parties from coming under RTI. Such a view is nothing short of depriving democracy of its credible instruments. But thanks to increased activism of civil society, political parties can no longer escape from the transparency wave sweeping the country. In 2005, when the RTI Act came into force, most bureaucrats too had similar apprehensions as political parties do now. But after the Service Delivery Guarantee Act was adopted by one state after another, no such reservations were there. I had said then that, after an initial period, political parties too stand to benefit by coming under RTI. In fact, RTI offers an opportunity to parties to 'revive themselves'.

The CIC order meant that political parties are answerable to the citizens of the country. Are they not expected to be so even otherwise? But parties have already been under constant scrutiny about their funds and their sources of contributions as well as expenditure? Even those contributing to political parties could be in public purview even without their knowledge and consent. Information seekers could be of an opposing party or opponents from within. Contrary to what is feared, the functioning of the parties will be streamlined much sooner than otherwise. In competitive politics, who does not like to gear up better for the future and consolidate. This is what adopting RTI provisions amounts to. This opportunity is not possible for political parties any other way.

As it is, it is already mandatory for political parties to file their income returns (although they are exempted from paying such a tax) and also file the same to the ECI. Their accounts are expected to be audited by a registered chartered accountant. Apart from this, the contesting candidates, irrespective of the poll outcome, have to file affidavits on poll expenditure to the ECI within a specified period. And candidates are obligated to file an affidavit as to their assets and finances, and give details of their criminal background. As such, there is no justification for knee jerk reactions to the Supreme Court's enquiry on non-compliance of CIC's order by political parties. The sooner political parties get to adopt RTI, the more credible they could become. To that extent, our democracy will be robust and responsive.

Has the declaration of finances and criminal background by contesting candidates in the case of state assemblies and the Lok Sabha made any difference? Most states had at least two elections since such a declaration has become obligatory. Voters were expected to choose the candidate based on such information declared at the time of filling of nomination before a district authority. And parties are expected to select those with no or least criminal background. And yet the per cent of those with criminal background in the Lok Sabha, for example, has hardly declined. Assets and finances of many have increased unusually between elections, going by their own declaration. With RTI in force, the scope for 'conflict of interest' in political donations could perhaps be exposed and minimised. Ultimately, it is the voters who could make the difference. With parties under RTI, the much expected change in the functioning of people's representation could come faster. RTI now offers a way out for political parties stuck in a *chakravyuh* (labyrinth)-like situation. They are otherwise not able to get out of a vicious syndrome, however much they wish to get out. RTI provides them an opportunity to do so.

Avail Suo Motu Clause

Initially, there would be all kind of queries for information—almost a deluge. But that is something parties need to gear up for and get used to in an inclusive spirit rather than get panicky about. A provision in the RTI Act is Section 4 with suo motu clause. Under this, parties could put out information on vital decisions and operations on their own for public purview in a pre-emptive way. If parties put out information on their finances and their sources, most of the suspense is over. Lok Satta did that in Andhra Pradesh and Aam Aadmi Party (AAP) too did that initially in Delhi. Some of the recent scams would not have hogged headlines had the concerned leaders bared the facts in a suo motu way.

However, there is one area that could be of concern for political leaders. And that is to do with the poll strategies which parties tend to come up with to score over their adversaries. Leaders do not like their opponents knowing such competitive information. But this is only a short-term problem. Given the kind of competing news media we have, and political parties themselves owning news media, they are already playing the game of snooping for tactical information. In the last couple of national polls, parties have coped with such a reality, including bringing to book 'quid-pro transactions'. So, the apprehensions of the government or/and parties could only be short-lived, but the benefits in the long run would be all round and for all stakeholders. We need to see that political parties stand the test of time by coming under RTI. The RTI should be welcomed and adopted fast by major parties even at this stage, just as CPI and AAP did.

Considering the far-reaching implications of the RTI regime for consolidating the democratic practices, we should not look at the CIC order in legal terms. The issue is not about whether our political parties should be considered as 'public authorities' or not. If a political party does not take any benefits from the government but is active in electoral politics of the country, is it going to be exempted from RTI? The more important issue is, should they come out of a syndrome scenario and function responsively? RTI has immense potential to help everyone in a win–win way, particularly the political parties. In a spirit of 'checks and balances', parties need to gear up, adopt and move into better systems and practices, and come out of the current gloom that political parties generally are in today.

As I suggested, it will be beneficial for political parties to come together and welcome the opportunity to come under RTI and to indicate their anxiety to move on to the next level of a parliamentary democracy. They could also come to an understanding and reflect on their determination to put information on a suo motu basis, particularly wherever the potential for a conflict of interest exists. They could even come up with proposals for consideration of the CIC for certain exemptions. For example, access to files or minutes of party meetings or giving information beyond a five-year time reference as well as giving information pertaining to specifics about regional units of national parties could be exempted. They could even appeal to citizens not to seek information which is already put in the public domain and not to expect individual replies as they are not geared up to respond to every applicant.

Transparency should be seen as part of public culture, a movement for good governance and in an inclusive way. RTI should not be seen merely as a tool against corruption. It could also help foster free and fair elections, the representative functioning of legislatures, and a more responsive administration and political parties. That is why CIC's order needs to be seen beyond its legal scope. The government affidavit before the Supreme Court should not give a cold shoulder to the initiatives of CIC and the Supreme Court.

Polls and Campaigns

Elections are the key instrument of democracy. Democracy is showcased and justified more by periodic elections than by what it accomplishes in meeting constitutional objectives and obligations. The system of elections and its efficacy varies from country to country even among democracies. We have an independent constitutional authority to conduct polls 'freely and fairly' for the Parliament and state assemblies. Local body elections are the responsibility of the state governments.

In India, there is no ceiling on the number of political parties or independent candidates who can contest an election. The more the number of independent candidates, the more the reflection on the representative character of political parties. But no corrective has been initiated as yet.

The system that India had adopted and which has been vogue all these 70 years—spanning over 16 general elections and over as many rounds of elections to state assemblies—is that, the tenure of the Lok Sabha and state assemblies being five years, there is supposed to be an election every five years, unless the incumbent government loses confidence earlier than that. The winner in the electoral system is whoever gets a 'simple majority of polled votes', with no minimum votes required to win. We never seriously considered a 'proportional representation system' that is in vogue in some countries. Under this system of election, the parties in contest nominate candidates by the proportion of votes it has polled. If this system is not feasible, then we must take to preliminaries where parties first shortlist their candidate internally, with members of that party being the electorate in that preliminary inner party selection process of a candidate.

Can an election be on a non-party basis? Why should elections at every level be on party lines? More than five decades ago, the Balwant Rai Mehta Committee recommended that elections to local bodies (Zilla Parishad, Panchayat Samiti and village panchayats) be on non-party basis, and that was how it was until the mid-1970s. Somewhere along the years, it was changed, and elections even at village panchayat level are on party lines ever since. Since then, I can observe with ample first-hand knowledge that not only has corruption multiplied, including by way of note-for-vote, but the elections cannot be called fair and free as they were before when polls were on non-party lines. Way back in 1955, Gora, a sociopolitical reformer of the time, advocated for 'party-less democracy' to which India never gave a fair chance. He even contested for assembly from a (*Bezawada*) *Vijayawada* seat just to demonstrate how a least-cost positive campaign could be conducted.

While political parties have increased their influence on the government, their democratic and representative character has been on the decline. So also has their moral standing. They are being increasingly viewed as the problem, and political leaders are being viewed as being responsible for many of the ills and indisciplines, to the extent of being perceived more often as the villains of the time. Despite leaders who are younger in age and have increased education levels emerging in every party more recently, there is no indication of any change in the functioning of political parties.

Recently, there has been debate in favour of setting minimum education qualification for contesting in local bodies in Rajasthan, Haryana and Madhya Pradesh. Those who oppose such qualification maintain that any such practice in the case of state assemblies and the Lok Sabha deprives illiterate voters and those not having a toilet at home where that has been made as a prerequisite to contest. I have been advocating that, in the case of state assemblies and the Lok Sabha, the candidate should be local, as many contesting elections in some states are from a faraway city with economic interests there. But the Constitution provides that a voter can contest to a state assembly and the Lok Sabha from anywhere in India. Although this provision has been there all along, hardly a couple of voters from a faraway state have contested. In a recent exceptional case—the case of Jaya Prada— it was because the candidate was a popular Hindi cinema actress. Although she hails from Andhra Pradesh, she contested from Uttar Pradesh, and had won once and lost the second time. My suggestion is to ensure that those who get elected from a particular constituency take some interest in the affairs of the people of that constituency. There is ample evidence today to indicate otherwise.

If the ECI could decide and declare parties as national, state, and registered and others based on certain criteria, why can an amend-ment not be made in the People Representative Act to declare that the candidate should be 'local' and also has a vote locally (as in the case of Rajya Sabha)? What are the pros and cons of this corrective?

Free, Fair and Credible Polls

One of the practice that contributes to partisan and divisive politics, even after an election, is the selection process of the leader of the House who becomes the prime minister or chief minister. The party which gets the majority, even by one vote, elects its leader in the party meet, and the governor or the president administers the oath of office. The party which had won more seats could, however, elect its leader within its party meeting. Why cannot all the members of the House, cutting across the party lines, elect the 'leader of the House' the same way as the Speaker of the House is elected? The elected leader would obviously would be from the party with the majority. But the fact that members of all parties join in that process of formally electing the leader would add to the velocity and moral authority of the chosen leader as the chief minister of a state or as the prime minister of the country, as the case may be. In this formal process of election, there should not be a whip system, and the election should be open and not by secret ballot. Such a process facilitates better functioning and productivity of legislatures.

With elections being too frequent, and taking place round the year at one place or for one or level or another, governance in many states is not getting consolidated. The cost of elections has been increasing election after election in such a way that affordability deprives many deserving persons from contesting an election. More importantly, the phenomenon of note-for-vote has been vitiating the very process of elections.

Political parties are supposed to indicate in their manifesto what they would do if they win the election and come to power.[8] This document is expected to indicate the kind of ideology, approach to development, priorities and programmes that the party believes in and proposes to take on if elected. The candidate should also indicate what they would do for the constituency, more specifically if they are elected, in such a way that the poll campaign should be based more on issues than on personalities and prejudices.

Not only should elections should be 'free and fair' but elected leaders representing people should have the least or no conflict of interest. The poll process should ensure a level playing for anyone contesting the election. The poll campaign should be based on a poll manifesto outlining the options offered by each contesting party. The entire process of election should be completed fast instead of being stretched over several weeks. Voter turnout should be much higher than merely two-thirds of the electorate. Poll campaigns should draw out more people to vote, and they should be well aware of their options and choices. The poll process should not divide people or add to animosities between communities that would go beyond the polling period.

Three contentious and critical aspects affect the scope of governments and their governance. First, the transparency of political parties. Second, the electoral lures used by parties and the note-for-vote phenomenon. And third, the implications of simultaneous elections to the Lok Sabha and state assemblies to governance.

Poll campaign is the most significant phase of electoral process and the process of governance. Campaign practices, particularly the expenditure involved in campaigning, is critical for having free and fair elections. The elections should not be restricted to rich and resourceful people because of the advertisement expenditure, particularly in media. The campaign is expected to facilitate voters with enough reliable information to make wise choices.

Parties may start the campaign one year prior to a poll, but the actual campaign picks up once the ECI announces the schedule. The poll codes of the ECI come into effect from the time of the announcement of poll dates. The campaign reaches its peak once the candidates' nomination starts. The time for campaign could be 15 days, starting from the time of nomination withdrawal phase, when only voters know the candidates in the field. This duration has been reduced from over three weeks two decade ago to two weeks at present.

First, all candidates should file an affidavit with their criminal background, assets and revenue sources, and educational qualifications along with their nomination. The national polls in 2019 are going to have a third round since such an affidavit was made compulsory. There is no evidence that the affidavit, while essential and worth continuing, has made a difference to the outcomes. If someone has multiplied his or her assets several times after getting elected the previous time, the conflict of interest becomes obvious, and yet there is nothing that can be done. On the contrary, there is a higher chance of such people getting re-nominated by their respective party.

Not only ECI officials but even political parties should first scrutinize these affidavits before considering them for nomination. In fact, parties should get such affidavits from persons seeking nomination of the party and analyze them beforehand.

The ECI has been increasing limits on poll expenditure by candidates over the years, despite most candidates filing their election expenditure as being much below what they were allowed to spend. What does this mean? Either the ceiling should be brought down or the campaign expenditure statement should be scrutinised and action taken for irregularities. Campaign expenditure is monitored and reviewed, and candidates have to file an expenditure statement multiple during the course of the campaign and, finally, after the poll results within a few weeks. In 2016, the ECI had rejected or disqualified some 200 nominations for not filing an expenditure statement for the previous election—something that had never been done before.[9]

Not all expenditure incurred by parties is scrutinised by the ECI. But a certain portion of the party's expenditure on poll campaign in the constituency is added to the candidate's poll expenditure account. The Bahujan Samaj Party (BSP) has been claiming for years that all its donations were of less than ₹2,000 so that the source need not be disclosed. Even Congress has not disclosed source of 87 per cent of its donations and the BJP for 65 per cent (2017).[10]

Instead of regulating poll expenditure, in 2017–2018, the government exempted parties from disclosing donations received through electoral bonds.[11] It further removed the cap on corporate contributions to political parties. These recent moves are more likely to facilitate the increase in poll campaign spending. The idea of electoral Bonds is good only if it could help minimise black money in polls.

How does the ECI's observation on expenditure or weekly filing of expenditure by candidates themselves not made a difference? It is common knowledge that some candidates spend several times more than what they are entitled. Independent studies, including some by CMS, have extensively documented the expenditures, which is contrary to what was declared. The ECI is obviously not able to control or restrain election expenditure.[12]

The ECI should explore legal possibilities of discouraging TV advertising by disallowing such an extent of expenditure or prescribing certain limits. It is obvious from the experience of US elections that 'TV advertising' intrudes and stifles the free and fair character of polls—the amount spent on TV ads in the US presidential polls is much higher than the national budget of many countries. In the 2016 poll, over one billion dollars were spent on TV advertising alone. This means an increased dependence of parties and candidates on corporates, which in turn translates to conflict of interest. Paid News and Fake News on the eve of the polls is yet another phenomena which is increasing, despite ECI and the Press Council of India's (PCI) concern. PCI had issued notices for the first time to over a dozen newspapers. But that trend is on the rise in the case of TV channels of late. Nobody seemed to have taken this issue seriously so far (2018).

Note-for-Vote

Money being paid to voters for their vote is a known fact to those who are familiar with grassroots politics of India. We now have data for the magnitude of this phenomena. When this data is viewed together with the 2007, 2008 and 2014 pre-general election surveys, it is evident that the trend has become of threatening proportion to the very fundamentals of democracy. *India Corruption Studies*, which CMS had started in 2000 as an annual series, found certain linkages between the bribes citizens pay in availing basic public services and the quid-pro-quo practice of voting.[13]

The first ever-empirical study on the 'note-for-vote' phenomena was in 2007 with 23,000 BPL (below poverty line) families. The second round was in 2008 with a sample of 18,000 voters from 19 states. CMS has also been tracking the trend in individual states where the practice is blatant, in the context of both assembly and Lok Sabha elections.

It is obvious that relatively more voters from economically poor families are lured across all states. In some states, it is more than twice among BPL voters than among all voters. Kerala seems to be an exception. As the CMS study confirms, money for votes is not limited to rural voters but is a national phenomenon spread across rural and urban, among different age groups and irrespective of the educational level of voters.

Prevalence of note-for-vote is more in the three southern states of Karnataka, Andhra Pradesh and Tamil Nadu. Among BPL voters, the percentage was higher—in 2007 it was 37 per cent among BPL voters against 22 per cent among all voters in 2008. In those three southern states of Andhra Pradesh, Karnataka and Tamil Nadu, well over 70 per cent of BPL voters were given money for their vote. Even in Chhattisgarh, Haryana, Rajasthan, Assam and Odisha, much more than 40 per cent of BPL voters were given money in a quid-pro-quo way. A much higher percentage of voters in Karnataka, Tamil Nadu and Andhra Pradesh acknowledged receiving cash as an inducement 'in the last 10 years'.

A sensitivity analysis of responses brings out that money was distributed notwithstanding which party was in power and that all the key contending parties/candidates were involved in this practice. CMS pre-poll surveys on expectations or perceptions of voters about cash lure brings out two things. First, the expectations are much higher than their experience a few years ago, and second, the states in the north (Uttar Pradesh and Madhya Pradesh) are fast catching up with the states in the south on the extent of cash lure.

Relatively more percentage of voters were paid money for their vote in the case of assembly election than in the case of Lok Sabha election. The amount was even higher in the case of municipal and district panchayats as in the case of Andhra Pradesh in 2014.

Mother of All Corruption

The best bet to counter the menace is voters themselves. They need to reject the lure of money and realise the potential of their vote for getting the government they deserve. But political leaders have been suggesting that voters take notes from other parties and vote for him or her, or his or her party. Voters need to understand the linkage between note-for-vote and the 'unofficial money' that they end up paying as bribe to get basic public services that they are entitled to get from the government for free. And, only then will we get more responsive representatives and only then could we except good governance.

Despite the intensity of the phenomena and the way it was covered by news media, the malice did not receive serious or larger attention. Political parties and leaders accused each other and as often, but they not condemned the very practice of note-for-vote. Its implications and linkage to overall corruption in the country was not even referred to by any of the political leaders as if it is all a concern of the ECI.

Over the years, it is so obvious from CMS tracking studies that a major reason for the increasing poll expenditure is this note-for-vote phenomena. But worse is what it meant to the accountability of elected representatives on the one hand and prevalence of corruption on the other. At this rate, how can Indian democracy assures good governance to its citizens?

Media Coverage of Lures

News media not only promotes and increases the incidence of note-for-vote, it compels other candidates too to give or offer money in a competitive way and make the practice an essential part of contest. With one-third or more of news media in the country slipping into the control of corporates and political leaders, can we expect to curb the phenomena of paid news on the eve of elections? 'Quid-pro coverage or reporting' has now acquired threatening proportions in driving the public opinion trends and priorities of the day. This has been my summative observation based on field studies in the last two decades.

Taking money in lieu of vote during poll time amounts to taking a 'bribe' (some voters do not view it as a bribe otherwise). Both taking as well as giving a bribe is illegal and punishable. This needs to be reiterated by the news media as often as possible. In fact, political parties themselves need to take on this malice critically and publicly. Leaders should encourage voters to complain about givers as well as takers of money in lieu of vote instead of encouraging the practice.

Although corruption is much talked about as a national malice, one aspect that has not been seriously pursued is that this corruption by way of 'note-for-vote' is depriving good governance and is threatening the roots of democracy and development. And that, in fact, it is the source and origin of cycle of corruption in the country. That is why I described it as the 'mother of all corruption' in the country. This phenomena has not become a priority concern of either corruption crusaders or political leaders, or of mass media as it should have been by explaining to voters what accepting doles in lure and in lieu of vote would mean to them individually next five years.

By hyping in their coverage that candidates are *crorepaties* (millionaires), contractors of rich families, news media is unwittingly adding to the expectations of voters. Based on its studies, CMS had indicated that voters would in all likely end up paying individually a few times more over five years as bribe for availing basic public services that they are otherwise entitled in the normal course, simply because they succumbed to the freebees and cash on the eve of elections.

The ECI views and approaches these trends more as curbing black money in election campaigning rather than its implications to good governance. There is a limit what the ECI can do in this regard without serious realisation on the part of the voters, political leaders and the news media. We need to ponder over the continued desirability of the first-past-post system of elections itself. 'State funding' of polls is being talked about. Political advertising on television on the eve of polls need to be regulated too before it vitiates the very poll process. Can news media/social networks be promoted specially in such a way that enormous amounts need not be spent on poll campaigns? I feel a search for alternative ways of electing peoples representatives have to be explored for making a difference in the governance model.

The discussion on political parties has been done at length here because no other activity or pillar of the State including the legislature and the executive makes as much a difference to governance as political parties and the processes they follow and practice make. And yet, much needed reforms in this regard have been avoided over the decades as if the linkage aspect to governance is not fully realised or followed up seriously. Can we expect a change in the gears in our development paradigm without taking on political parties? No good governance can be expected without political parties become democratic in their functioning, and transparent and accountable in all their operations, and without delinking elections from the lures of quid-pro-quo.

Do Simultaneous Polls Help Good Governance?

The idea of simultaneous elections for the Lok Sabha and state assemblies has gained ground in 2017–2018. In fact, it has been recommended by a parliamentary standing committee (2015). This could be done by either extending the duration or cutting short the duration of tenure of a legislature by up to six months. Even NITI Aayog echoed the idea (2017), although coming up with such an endorsement is not in its purview.

Simultaneous elections has its pros and cons. On the face of it, the idea is good. Particularly because the ECI's election codes curtail the powers of the incumbent government, which results in the government being barred from exercising some executive powers and being blocked from making any new moves in the name of development. The core argument for simultaneous elections is that conducting elections is a considerable expenditure and the government is unable to moderate this trend. This argument assumes that such efforts give advantage to the incumbent party and that simultaneous elections curb the expenditure of the government as well as of the parties and candidates. It is argued that frequent elections are a hindrance for sustaining development projects.

On the other hand, the arguments against simultaneous elections include that it amounts to adopting a presidential form of government without declaring so, and that it facilitates one-person domination without the country formally opting for such a system. This federal system is diluted in favour of centralisation. This means homogenising the country instead of sustaining plurality, and promoting local and regional leadership. And yet, some ministers advocate 'one nation, one election' ignoring that India is a country of many states and is under a federal structure. How it could be 'one election' unless it means 'one leader' for the country as well! Can anyone say that 'one nation, one election, one leader' is good neither for democracy nor for equitable development course, and even for sustaining a federal system or for free and fair elections?

Simultaneous elections should not deprive states of having a popularly elected government. Neither should it stop a majority government from stepping down when and if the ruling party at the Union loses majority and goes for a mid-term poll. That should not imply that states should dissolve the assembly and hold elections irrespective of their five-year tenure. Then there is the question of imposing President's Rule in a state on a new ground! Simultaneous elections should not offer yet another opportunity for the federal government to impose President's Rule. So far, since the formation of the republic, popularly elected governments in states have been removed more than a hundred time to impose President's Rule. Only a few times it has been because the House could not elect a leader in the normal course. Most of the time, President's Rule was imposed at the discretion of the leaders of the federal government or its agent in the state, the governor. There is no transparency in the process, and suo motu announcements have become a practice. Instead of curbing such a practice, this idea of simultaneous elections amounts to denting the very democratic process and going against the political plurality that is necessary for tackling social diversities. Also, it addresses symptoms rather than a root cause.

Instead, the need of the hour is to find alternate ways of conducting free and fair elections at all levels with the least cost. For this, poll time codes could be looked into again. Second, we could find ways of curbing or making it difficult for the incumbent party to misuse the government machinery to its poll advantage. We also need to discuss whether we should go for one agenda and one leader driving the poll process, which would mean that local concerns, issues and interests would become secondary. The distinction between elections at different levels get blurred when voting is done simultaneously. The question has to be looked into from aspects of both feasibilities under Constitution and desirability with regard to democracy, development and plurality. From these criteria, simulations election could be reasonably pursued, if and when we formally adopt a presidential system.

PM Modi is in a comfortable situation (because of the absolute majority) to take on the real issues of political reforms and thus make a difference. This debate for simultaneous elections should not overshadow the more important and long-pending poll reforms. First, it is time to replace the first-past-post system that we have experimented with over seven decades with a proportional representation system. Some parties have already been arguing for this change. This could also reduce poll expenditure considerably. A debate on this is more pertinent. Second, political parties should be brought under a regulatory framework and into a regime of transparency by bringing them under RTI. Third, the prime minister and chief ministers should be elected in the same way as the Speakers of the Parliament and assemblies. Fourth, the whip system should be curbed and limited to exceptional situations. Fifth, even more urgent, curb poll expenditure at all three levels—by the government, by political parties and by candidates themselves—and come up with compliance mechanisms to cap expenditure including by curtailing the duration of poll process. Several parliamentary committees have looked into these aspects over the decades, but no follow-up or firm decision has been made.

Simultaneous elections in India, the notion of 'one nation, one election', is antithesis to good governance, to deepening democracy and for consolidation of development on ground. The idea of one election is against regional parties, local leadership and regional agenda. It promotes the idea of one leader and one party, and increases the chances of misdirection by stoking passions and populism. The charisma of such emotions has threatening implications for the spirit of federalism and strategies of development. Certain key persuasive instruments that are available today for country-wise 'consensus manufacturing' were not there during 1952–1967 when we had held simultaneous polls. Instead, India would be better off if it pursues more critical political reforms. It is easy to adopt the idea of simultaneous elections but it has threatening implications and doubtful complexities in its implementation. The basic poll reforms, on the other hand, are difficult to push through but have durable positive implications to the parliamentary democracy and federal system that we have adopted.

The argument that the country is spending too much for frequent elections does not hold because the value of democracy is such. And if there are concerns for the costs, governments do not spend as much or more on avoidable publicising and advertising their 'achievement in media' without sensitises people.

Declining Legislatures

Legislative bodies (parliament and assemblies) are the key institutions of governance in India. They make laws, oversee the functioning of the government, prioritise and monitor government spending, and reflect the expectations of people in all such functions.

Parliament and assemblies as the highest forums of democracy is on the decline. Anyone who has been following the functioning of Parliament and many of the state assemblies in session in recent years wonders whether these floors of legislatures have been reduced to wrestling rings of tit for tat. More than a quarter of the time spent in parliament sessions in last three years (2015–2018) had been wasted. On the other hand, the number of days of the House being in session in a year is declining from over 120 days a few decades ago to less than 75 days in the last few years (2016–2018). Also, the number of ordinances being brought is increasing. The number of bills being passed has declined over the years, and in most cases without any debate on the bills. Even budget demands for grants were being passed without much discussion. And most of the bills were passed by voice-vote. Hardly 10 per cent of the bills were passed on record as to who voted for what. Even half of Question Hour was being lost to disruptions. The 2018 budget session was a 'washout session'. There were also bills which became acts without any debate in the House, including the RTI Act in 2005. Even parliamentary committees and standing committees operate behind closed doors. The Rajya Sabha, which is supposed to be the House of Elders, is no exception for witnessing unruly acts of members across party lines. The leader of the House, both in the case of state assemblies and the Lok Sabha, should be elected in the House by all elected members, irrespective of their political party, even if notionally. If this one change could be made in the present practice, it will have an overall impact on many other ills hindering the floor debates in legislatures. If the ECI could add NOTA (none of the above) to ballot paper option after 60 years, why can Parliament not make this change in the larger interest of parliamentary democracy?

Members of legislatures, both in the states and the Union, should consider their position as honorary without any 'fixed salary'. Do they really need such a salary? Most members not only come from relatively better financial backgrounds but also have additional sources of income. They, however, are provided free accommodation and travel, and their actual expenditure in serving the constituency is reimbursed. They are provided paid staff for research and secretarial services. A parliamentary committee recommended (February 2016)[14] the formation of a permanent body to periodically revise the salary and other emoluments given to the MPs. What a pity this is! For 'many MPs think their salaries are lower than even senior bureaucrats even as parliamentarians enjoy a higher status in the warrant of precedence'. Ironically, in 2018, the parliament passed a government proposal to increase 'salaries' substantially, despite the lack of order and the din prevailing in the House at the time.

That our laws are not effective is obvious from the fact the Anti-Defection Act made no difference to the trend of crossing the floor from one party to another in the legislatures. In fact, such incidents have increased since the amendment to this act. The loopholes and ambiguities in this regard need to be removed even with the amendment. Anyone who changes their allegiance from the party through which they got elected should be considered as having crossed the floor, and the Act should apply to them. The only exception could be if one-third of the members of a party decide to do so, proving this in person to the Speaker of the House.

Most such MLAs who cross the floor to the party in power argue that they are doing this so that their respective constituency could be developed, and that they would not develop otherwise. By saying so, they are reminding the people that the governments are partisan and do not work for or serve all sections of people. In 2003, an amendment had provided for the defection of one-third of the members of a party. On the floor of the House, the Speaker has the final word. Implementation of defection comes under their judiciary. The lure of money or position through quid-pro-quo is so obvious in most floor crossings. This is a threat to parliamentary democracy and is happening across the states. The anti-defecation law takes away the decision-making power from MPs and MLAs, and yet parties do not seem anxious to take corrective initiatives. The recent (2017) case of defections into the party in power in Telangana and Andhra Pradesh assemblies are extreme examples of this.

The role of the governor has been clarified by a five-judge constitution bench of the Supreme Court.[15] The governor should not intervene in the Speaker's prerogative as to party-wise numbers in the House. Supreme Court Judge J.S. Khehar voiced concern in February 2016 over frequent removal of governors under every government. 'It is a serious issue', he noted. A new precedent was made in the Pondicherry assembly in 2017 when the governor on her own nominated three members who belonged to the opposition party in the state, but the ruling party at the Union. But the Speaker refused to allow them to even enter the House (2018).

Legislatures are expected to transact an agenda by having the elected representatives of people in the interest of immediate and long-term interests of people go through an orderly debate. Once certain motions are passed by the House, all the members are expected to work for its implementation in a non-partisan way. But this is not what is actually happening.

The whip system vitiates or constrains the function of legislatures as representatives of the people. Legislative power resides with parties instead of with individual legislators. Individual members reflect the party interests more than the interests of the people who elected them. As Manish Tiwari pointed out in his recent book, legislators have become 'virtual hostages of whip-driven tyranny'. He called for liberating legislators who are bound in the name of party discipline.[16]

Certain conventional precedents and practices are not allowing legislatures at the Union and in the states to set an atmosphere for good governance. Since the goings-on of these legislative bodies is visible for the larger public, the current trend of decline in debates need to be reversed. Only then will laws have a better compliance record. The legislators are not salaried employees. They are elected to serve the people. As volunteers to represent and serve the public, legislators should not succumb to the grip of party whips. The leader of the House should truly reflect and carry all the members of the House across political party affiliations. No good governance can be consolidated without bringing legislatures who are representative, more responsible, transparent and concerned with grassroots realities.

The Executive/Civil Services/Bureaucracy

There has always been the need to reform, reorient and reposition the executive or civil services, and several efforts have been made to discuss how to go about this matter. Several committees, commissions and studies from within government as well as from outside have given their perspectives over the decade. As of 2018, there is hardly any evidence of any visible change in the functioning of bureaucracy. This remains as a bigger challenge as in the case of poll reforms. The executive includes the civil services and all other services engaged by the government at the time.

In the ultimate analysis, it is the bureaucracy which is engaged in the functioning of a government and in the delivery of its services to the people. The face and the fate of a government depend to a great extent on how efficiently the bureaucracy functions. The scope of governance depends on the functioning of the civil service as much as it does on how gracefully political leadership takes its responsibility and how independently free and fair polls are conducted. And together they have to work in tandem to differentiate the standing of a government.

Enthusiasm to reorient bureaucracy is eternal. Increasing challenges of multiplying programmes, schemes of Government and compulsions of democratic system call for renewed initiatives. What could be the interventions that could be taken to give a facelift to the government's functioning?

The executive is supposed to function independent of the political system while following the policies of the party in power. Because of the services and cadre system that India has continued from the British, the executive can retain their stature irrespective of the party in power, despite the government controlling the appointment and promotion of the executives. We are expected to continue to have professional functionaries to run the government in a dispassionate way, and to follow the framework of checks and balances. While we continue to rely on this model, a certain *jugalbandhi* phenomenon is sweeping the country where political bosses and cadre functionaries work with an understanding not always in public interest but sometimes in a quid-pro-quo way. The Indian Administrative Services (IAS) has done well to ensure that the country is held together and the development course is being pursued. The same could be said about most other services (Indian Police Service, Indian Cost and Accounts, Economic, Forest, etc.).

The IAS deserves to be strengthened and made attractive for a new generation of talent. The pride in the service and in the stature of the position needs to be restored so that it functions confidently and independent of political parties, and does not succumb to the pressures of the party or the ministers in power. They should function through push and pull forces, and work for the concerns of the country. Those who are found to be a misfit should be retired through a transparent and uniform system of performance review and appraisal. Individual bureaucrats should be allowed to have strong and direct impacts on development endeavours. Such officers should be publicly acknowledged. There is no uniform legislation to ensure the accountability of the executive.

Often, it is difficult to determine responsibilities, as the appointment letter does not specify the functions that the functionary is responsible for. Every time a government employee is appointed or transferred, the letter should indicate his or her functions and responsibilities. A more recent classic example is of the Supreme Court proceedings on the PIL on *Chikungunya* fever in Delhi. Even the minister could not name the specific officer responsible for frogging in Delhi. Then how anyone could be accountable? Of course, in this case, the minister himself was fined by the Supreme Court. The government should first identify and describe the responsibilities of each executive functionary at the time of their posting.

The RTI Act should help restore the unique independence of the bureaucracy. In a short-term view, RTI is considered by the executives as an inconvenient law as it adds to their work load and can even put them in vulnerable situations as they have to record the compulsions for certain discretionary decisions. But in the long run or over time, RTI helps them disassociate from discretionary favours of political bosses and also reduces the work pressure. Once Section 4 of RTI Act is put out in a suo motu way, people's respect for executives/officers will increase. If sincerely implemented, the Citizen Charter too compels government officers to comply with deadlines and serve the public better. The payoff from its sincere implementation by the executive is critical for good governance. The Service Delivery Guarantee Act in many states, in fact, is another opportunity for the executive to catch up with aspirations of the people.

IAS and other cadre officers should declare their assets annually in a suo motu way and should also declare any 'conflict of interests'. They could take certain bold decision like sending their children to local public schools. This will not only enhance their credibility and respect but add to their grip on the administration and even the respect of colleagues. (As of mid-2018, only one senior IAS officer, Mrs Radha in Chennai, has admitted their child in a corporation public school.)[17]

Professional associations of executives should take on certain social services outside the government voluntarily and of their own interest, even if just symbolically. The sensitivity of government officers towards conflicts of interest could change the very face of the government and force the political masters to take on such suo motu disclosures. Senior officers could have 'open house sessions' with the public, general or specific, at different locations every two or three years on locally relevant concerns that are bothering many families or communities.

The two mechanisms of complaint redressal and allegations against executives and of internal disputes should be settled faster and in such a way that they become an example for good practice. Corruption allegations against senior officers should be dealt by the Anti Corruption Bureau (ACB) on priority so that the case is not prolonged at the cost of the public image of the cadre. A more recent trend was to use the anti-corruption drive as a symbol by showcasing the expose of senior functionaries in the government in isolation of (political) associates.

Officer postings and promotions should be far more transparent than they are at present. The criteria for such decisions should be posted on the website instead of needing an RTI to access the information. They need to be protected against arbitrary and politically motivated transfers and postings instead of being excluded from enquiry forums or commissions. Government's permission for enquiry against senior functionaries by enquiry agencies should be exceptional.

A parliamentary panel has backed a move to bar anti-graft agencies from probing into bribery allegations against public servants without government approval. This was despite opposition from the Central Bureau of Investigation (CBI). Even otherwise, bureaucrats are protected by a procedural requirement after completion of the probe. They cannot be tried without the government's sanction. Why does this retrograde step, this provision, still exist and is at the root level of governance?

Indian Institutes of Management have been training thousands of people every year, and several thousand institutes have been offering MBA degrees for over two decades. What difference have they made in professionalising the Indian bureaucracy? And in streamlining, many of the government's public services are delivered more efficiently. The scope of governance has been changing with frequent elections and promises of political parties. This obviously means that the executive is gearing up for new challenges. Training in management skills is expected to make a difference. Responsiveness and accountability methodologies could be more appropriate to different services and be better in catering to different groups of people through further training.

A quick analysis of my own dealing with half a dozen ministries and a dozen departments over four decades, mostly from the outside, convinces me that the executives/bureaucrats are not sensitive to the provisions that are already in place and are not proactively enthusiastic to avail the various methodologies available in their functioning. This is one reason why the credibility of executive has eroded and why they are often blamed for delays and for prevalence of corruption. There are of course exceptions.

Why should employment with the government be viewed as 'permanent'? Why it cannot be based on tenure or on a contact or linked to an outcome? If Medical Council of India members are restricted to two terms of five years each, why can that practice not be adopted in many other functions? If NITI Aayog is concerned with a 15-year development plan as an agenda for the country, the executive could be geared for such a tenure.

The expenditure for salaries of employees in some levels of government and services is more than half of what it collects as revenue. In fact, many municipalities could pay salaries only by taking overdrafts from banks or loans from financial institutes. The government is unable to cope with increasing aspirations and deliver public services, and yet more departments are being created.

There are no initiatives and outcomes in the course of bureaucratic functioning to recognize the merits of the bureaucrats or to keep up their morale. Nor is there much ongoing independent appraisal of their functioning. Year after year, we have been sending officers for short-term courses to US and UK academic centres. But what difference that has made in bettering government functioning, and whether it has made any difference at all, is a different story.

Is the government understaffed or overstaffed? This question is raised often, particularly against the background of public–private partnership, the privatisation of certain services and enterprises and the increase in taking to newer technologies. The government, however, continues to be seen as an employer and a source for employment. With the advent of computerisation, the government may have to curtail the number of staff by reassigning tasks with newer network technologies. With the use of better technology, officers should find it convenient to perform and even respond proactively to RTIs, the Citizen Charter, independent social audits, etc.

Too many schemes are there for a District Collector to be engaged with. As many as 2,500 schemes or project programmes are on file at a time, although hardly two dozen of those are of immediate concern at any point of time. New files are always being added; closing schemes has been rare. As a result, the role of district officials is devoid of any focus on outcomes and benefits or on implementation at the ground level. With frequent change of ministers and governments, priorities change or files get relabelled each time, with the brunt being taken by the executives.

A former chief secretary of the Uttar Pradesh government was convicted in a two-decade old plot allocation scam. Any action on the verdict was pending for a few years even after the Allahabad High Court upheld the 2012 verdict. The Central Vigilance Commission expressed its concern that momentum in the case of nearly 600 cases involving government executives had been pending and that the progress was slow.

As N. Vittal, former Central Vigilance Commissioner, has written, 'The Culture of bureaucracy will realize that larger the organization and larger the score, slower it is bound to be in operation.' Vittal has rightly pointed out, 'If honest public servants become fifth columnists in favour of bringing about good governance and checking corruption, they will be able to bring about much better check on corruption than what can be achieved by outside agencies.' [18] That was why I suggested to the minister much earlier that B.G. Deshmukh, a former cabinet secretary who had just retired then and was known for his upright reputation, should be a member of India's first social audit panel, which I coordinated for four years (2002–2006) at the Ministry of Communications.

There could be no good governance without a proactive executive. But realising the new compulsions of the times is essential to avail newer and more challenging opportunities. Independent, dispassionate and specifically appointed bureaucracy could contribute far more to governance than a committed one.

Justice System and the Judiciary

In January 2018, the standing of the judiciary of India had a jolt like it never had before from within. The Chief Justice of the Supreme Court of India was questioned by four sitting senior judges of the Supreme Court itself. They had cautioned that the independence of the judiciary was under threat. By their unprecedented public outrage, they raised the basic issues of independence, accountability and transparency in the judiciary, the same way as the other pillars of the republic (the executive and legislation, and media) keep facing from time to time. This crisis was described as a 'wake-up call'. The letter written by one of these four to the Chief Justice in April 2018 and the subsequent remarks bring out the friction between the judiciary and the government, and within the higher judiciary.[19]

Since the year 2016, India has been experiencing certain unease in the relations between the judiciary and the legislature. The desperation in judiciary was obvious when the Chief Justice became so emotional in the presence of the prime minister and many chief ministers that he had to wipe tears of helplessness because of mounting pending cases and vacancies in the judiciary. On the question of appointment of judges, the differences between the judiciary and the legislature have led to open provocation of each other and each exceeding its own domain yet again. While the Chief Justice of India had expressed his concern about the government's intrusion in to judiciary, the Minister of Law and Justice in the Modi government had pointed to the long delays in the courts and noted that 'legislation must remain the preserve of legislators'.[20] The former Chief Justice of India, talking at two different programmes on the same day, made some relevant statements. At the meet of All India Administrative Tribunal, former Chief Justice Thakur reminded the people about the 500 vacancies of judges in high courts for which clearance had been sought from the government. Speaking at a Constitution Day function on 26 November, Justice Thakur said, 'Judiciary has responsibility to intervene any legislation which is against Constitution provision and that judiciary has responsibility to see that pillars of the State function within the purview of constitutional provisions.' In July 2017, the government wrote to the Supreme Court reminding it about the ongoing controversy on the appointment of judges and collegium system which the Parliament had brought in October 2015, and which the Chief Justice of India had questioned in December 2015.

Is the judiciary encroaching into the legislature and the executive? Yes, that was what a senior cabinet minister, Minister of Finance Arun

Jaitley, himself an eminent lawyer, had said on record in the Rajya Sabha, 'Step by step, brick by brick the edifice of India's legislature is being destroyed.'[21]

People Are Craving Justice

Justice Gopal Goud, a Supreme Court judge, had said in a 2016 Kurnool meet of judges that ordinary people are not getting the very basic rights created or provided for that purpose, as if 'rights are in cold storage', and they need to be brought out.[22] Around the same time, speaking in a legal cell meet in Jammu, former Chief Justice of the Supreme Court, Justice T.S. Thakur, said that while 'jails are getting filled and overcrowded, people are craving for justice'. In another occasion, the Chief Justice observed that 'judiciary is facing crisis' and that 'credibility of judiciary is at stake' and that judges need to be more accountable.[23] A week earlier, former Chief Justice Thakur had called for 'raise in bench mark of the profession'. One would find more than a couple such reports in the Indian news media in one week, as if intensity of concern about functioning of judiciary is on the rise. The Chief Justice had earlier announced that the Supreme Court had decided to set up a constitution bench to 'to evolve a fitting mechanism to once and for all clean up legal profession.'[24] Nothing much has been heard about it since.

Nearly 15 per cent of the total households in the country have sought one or other type of service from the judiciary at one level or other (between 2007 and 2018). It is much higher in Bihar, Gujarat and Punjab. A finding of the CMS national study done some years ago (2007) and also more recently (2018) was that less than 5 per cent of those who deal with the judiciary pay bribes, and twice as many think that corruption is there in the judiciary as well. But more than half of them think that it is the lawyers who are involved in this corruption, against 30 per cent who think it is court officials and 15 per cent who think it is through a middleman that corruption in judiciary takes place. That report noted that lawyers who are supposed to uphold law have become a conduit for corruption in the delivery of justice. There have been more than a couple of instances in the last couple of years of retired senior judges talking about corruption in the judiciary.

Big Reforms Needed

So many panels at different levels had come up with suggestions for much needed reforms in judiciary, but no comprehensive correctives had been taken up. That the judiciary system is dilatory, expensive and beyond the reach of common man was indicated by many analysts over the years. The misuse of powers by those in judicial positions at various levels was also brought out by many reports.

There are too many lawyers and too many vacancies in the judiciary. There are over two million lawyers, as if more than the number of lawyers the country needs are getting into this profession or that there have been no efforts by agencies like the Bar Associations to uphold the standards. Field studies have indicated that corruption in the judiciary is more via lawyers.

An increase in the number of vacancies and delays in the appointment of judges have hampered the judicial process, and the number of pending cases is increasing. Former Chief Justice T.S. Thakur accused the government of dragging its feet in filling judicial vacancies. There is no change in the position the judiciary was in 2018: there were 40 per cent vacancies in high courts, more than 25 per cent vacancies in district courts and 19 per cent vacancies in the Supreme Court. Of the over 70 names sent to the government by the collegian, only about half were approved as of November 2016, after several months of delay.[25] In 2018, the seniormost judge of the Supreme Court reiterated this issue and alleged that it was the government which was responsible for the delays.

There is considerable debate on the appointment of judges and about the very process of shortlisting a panel. Judges are appointed after a panel is shown to chief minister, the Governor and the minister of Law and Justice, and it then goes to the Supreme Court Collegium. In between, the Minister for Information and Broadcasting also learns the names under consideration.

Outdated Laws

One of the first thing that Narendra Modi did on assuming the office of prime minister was to form a group to come up with list of outdated laws. By the end of 2015, 300 laws were already declared as being irrelevant. Another 1,400 were awaiting to be declared even after they had been identifying outdated. About 1,200 laws were cleared by early 2016.[26] Some thousand laws on book were estimated as being outdated and need to be off loaded. Thereafter, there is no evidence in 2018 that this process is being pursued seriously.

Transparency in the judicial process, although in a relative context with other pillars of the State, is viewed as being better, it is not yet that transparent as incidents of corruption in the system are increasing. The alternative methods of adjudication, arbitration and conflict resolution have not gained ground. The application of newer communication technologies with their immense potential has hardly made a difference in the system so far. The judicial system is overburdened with prolonged pending cases of government. With over 6,000 vacancies of judges at various levels, there were 2.8 million cases pending as on April 2016, and more than half were criminal cases. Of these, 58 per cent had been pending for more than two years. The cases filed by the governments at the Union account for over half of all pending cases!

The judiciary has been increasingly accused of 'judicial activism' and interfering in the legislative and the executive. Certain distrust between the judiciary, executive and legislative is frequently reported more recently as if reminding that the judiciary is required to uphold and safeguard the Constitution. After the prime minister's observation on the Good Friday in 2015 at the conference of chief justices and chief ministers about 'seven star activism' driving judicial process, a wrong impression had gone around in the country that 'activism' is bad or unwarranted.[27] There cannot be any disagreement that robustness of the pillars of democracy comes as much from the activism of citizens. Any number of studies have indicated that passivism is at the root of many of our problems. Realising that our Constitution has provided for checks and balance in a very unique way, Justice P.N. Bhagwati, as Chief Justice of India, had come up with the landmark initiative of 'PIL'. That was more than 40 years ago. This was not first time that a prime minister had expressed his concern about 'PIL activism'. Even some judges, including some of the Supreme Court, had expressed their concern earlier. In fact, some judges are known in the Bars across the country for their pro- or anti-PIL views.

The concept of PIL recognizes that the poor and the voiceless should be defended, and it provided for a pre-emptive opportunity to intervene in favour or for the cause of larger public. PIL allows proactive initiatives for justice on the part of citizens, irrespective of their legal standing and the affordability of a normal legal route. We need mechanisms for self-assessment and introspection of such interventions. Even if one-third of PILs are on account of lobbies or of 'five star' nature, it is of great significance, as rightly envisioned by Justice P.N. Bhagwati at the outset. The kind of revelations that PILs have helped to unfold and expose, including corruption scandals in the country in recent years, do not justify any limits on PILs. By the time judges reach such a level in their legal career, they should be capable of differentiating grain from chaff.

Prime Minister Modi was apparently reminding to the people of such activism, as against judicial activism, so that confidence in the judiciary is not dented. The empowerment that citizens derive from this opportunity of PIL is significant in consolidating the roots of democracy. In fact, the best of each pillar or estate of State would be obvious when each one of them has some extent of activism and are proactive to respond to the aspirations and anxieties of people and also facilitate a level playing field in citizenry.

Introspection by each of the pillars of democracy of its own role as well as in the context of other is a desirable aspect of good governance and should be appreciated and welcomed. The fact that we are in a transparency era should come handy for such a process of introspection. Also, taking to 'too many' PILs should not necessarily mean hindrance to independent judicial functioning.

The number of PILs should have gone up after rights regime in the country, particularly the RTI Act in the last 13 years. With Service Delivery Guarantee Act too taking off in many States, the quality of PILs in terms of substance and sustainability should have gone up. But there is no evidence of that is a different aspect. News media's coverage of PILs more often is because of public interest angle many

PILs reflect by way of a lapse on the part of one or other institutes of democracy.

Best bet for good governance and deepening of democracy being citizen activism and sustaining checks and balance between pillars of State, PIL, RTI, Citizen Charter, etc., are available as legally provided mechanisms. Both UPA and NDA governments tried to scuttle RTI movement by describing applications under the act as 'frivolous'. Odd abrasions should not curb or curtail mechanisms available for citizens. Nothing should be done to tamper or hamper RTI, PIL and the like. Introspection helps avoid shortsighted view otherwise. In July 2017, the Supreme Court reversed its own view on RTI jurisdiction about constitutional functionaries. Infect, in July 2017 it recommended that the Constitutional Functionaries, including the Governors and the office of Chief Justice of India should be made amenable to the RTI.[28]

Good governance expects law of the land is accessible, available and affordable and effective across socio-economic–political backgrounds. It is not merely shortage, delays in appointments and vacancies of judges but gearing up with alternate methods of justice and scale up to newer technologies is what likely to make governance standout. In the 2015–2016 Rule of Law Index of the world justice project, covering more than 100 countries, ranked India as 59 against 46 of Brazil and 19 of USA. This was based on perceptions in the public about constraints on government powers, absence of corruption, law and order and security and other issues related to fairness in society.[29]

Basic Dilemma of the Fourth Estate

Why is mass media viewed as the fourth estate of the republic? Of course, there is no reference to media anywhere in the Indian Constitution, unlike the other three estates (legislature, judiciary and executive) and unlike the First Amendment in the US Constitution. And yet certain privileges of State are bestowed on the media by the governments, not only by way of subsidies and concessions but also by way of certain entitlements, including access to powers and privileged information. All that without mass media coming under any specific provisions of accountability or responsibility. This is because the media is considered as a purveyor of information, essential for communities, societies, governance and businesses to function and 'serve' for the good of most people, as are the other pillars of the republic.

The media is expected to crystalize and mobilise opinions of people, at the level of individuals, groups and large public, and provide, in the process, a level playing field. It was in acknowledgment of that kind of relevance and role that public opinion plays for the functioning of modern state—that its fourth estate status relies on—that purveyors of news were described as the fourth estate for the vital role it was expected to play. Of course, democratic States claim and allow 'free media' and 'independent media' outside the government and parallel to the other branches of the republic.

At the outset it was called press, then with news media—radio and television—acquiring mass, it has come to be known as mass media, and with the increase in newer media, social media as being different from mass media has become a phenomenon. Initially, the process was more of a crusading mission and a watchdog of people, With technology becoming a key driver for scaling up, media has also become 'business propositions'. First 'viability' and then 'profitability', and now deriving advantage in a competitive scenario is what determines the scope of contents of media with 'quid pro quo' culture creeping into news media. 'Fake news' have come to stay, going beyond 'news plants' and 'paid news' and 'PR', which were known earlier. It is no surprise that Gartner Research predicted that by 2024, most of the news around in all media would be fake news, which could also be said as being irresponsible contents. Despite press expanded with media going for entertainment, and things other than news and information, they continue to enjoy a special status.

Shift in Paradigm

Media today in the 21st century is not the same as press was 200 years ago. Not only have its structure and composition changed but, even more, its control and contents have also changed. It is no longer 'freedom of press' (meant for newspapers); it is 'media' comprising a range of media (radio, television, websites, etc.) that are mostly technology driven. They are no longer 'trusts', but are profit-driven and profit-motivated; they are now corporate media with conflicts of interest involving other business interests. The more the role and significance of public opinion, the more manipulated media tends to be as to their contents and priorities. They are no longer independent and objective as they were expected; they are now part of a *jugalbandi* phenomenon when they are not part of one or other (motivated) political campaign.

They are no longer run in a mission mode nor are they trusteeship oriented. They are more in pursuit of propaganda, profit maximisation, and corporate interests (not the community concerns with which they started). They are no longer society oriented as much as market concerned. Promoting consumerism (not consumer interests) is their hidden agenda. Where is the win–win concern hallmark of the fourth estate?

And yet media continues to enjoy the status of fourth estate. It continues to set the agenda, drive opinions of people and political regimes, tilt the balance of political power, and empower some citizens but influence more citizens as consumers and voters. In many countries, the government has some control or regulates media formally. Despite all these trends, democratic countries claim 'free press' or an 'independent media' as something desirable. Some describe it as a deceptive syndrome!

The idea of fourth estate is somewhat outdated on the face and structure of media today. No wonder some analysts described it as being ironic to call press as the fourth estate. But then the power of public opinion, dependence on media for information and trust in them for reliability in a relative context makes media a viable instrument.[30]

The numbers today are mind boggling. Most of the numbers are estimates. Officially the number of mobile phones is over 1,110 million mark against 100 million landlines. But the number of TV viewers has already crossed 500 million against less than 200 million TV sets. The number of PCs has crossed 50 million against the well over 260 million internet users. Twitter alone claims over 200 million users of its service. Over all, one could say that today there are 500 million 'active users' of new and old media put together, and it could be a billion well before 2025.

Nevertheless, news media plays a critical role in ensuring that good governance is well acknowledged. But in what respect or to what extent that role is being played is known in a disjointed way, and not in a long-term context. Perhaps because such a role is neither consistent nor continuous, and is in one direction. In any case, there is no concern for dimensions of effects and implications of media contents even over time.

In the last few years, since 2010, the role of news media role has been a little better in reflecting civil society concerns and in pursuing the issues bothering the people, locally and nationally. More specifically, this is to do with corruption in government and decline in public services, transparency at micro and macro levels of policy decisions, and in exposing ills and contradictions in different sectors.

I have been a critic of news media over the past decades for their concerns, priorities and even impact. Its role as an agenda setter and as a moulder of public opinion was never in doubt. All that, however, has been changing more recently with the rise of civil society activism and social media. Increasingly, there have been an increasing number of examples of mass media triggering or prompting a change in the very outlook and preferences in the implementation of public schemes and operations of public systems. Coverage of larger public concerns by the mass media has been better than in the case of political parties. The question is, how much coverage of grassroots reality and concerns of certain sections of people is covered, as in the case of rural, poor and underserved by the government.

There has been a recent rethink among media operators for a relook into their concerns and priorities. But compulsions for their very survival are such that they are not able to come out of a 'conflict of interest riddled media'. These concerns are also at variance more often with those of 'fourth estate' notion. 'Consumerism' being a driving force of mass media, the scope and limits of media including news media are set by such ultimate and ulterior interests.

In my book[31] *Unleashing Power of News Channels* (2012), I contended that news channels are not able to come out of the clutches of certain fallacies in order to reposition themselves and showcase their potential. This is a dilemma today for all media. News channels should find a way out, individually and together, to remind themselves of their role as the fourth estate. News channels of late have been catalysts for sensitising larger sections of otherwise passive citizenry. Second, there should be certain turns or twists in the way the controversies involving large masses are covered (instead of individual-centric controversies as before). Third, the focus should be on basic public issues instead of going by events (of short-lived nature) where they can fill telecast time with concerns and aspirations of people.

News media is giving an opportunity to civil society, which had never been such coverage and reflection before. Using the RTI Act, news media is able to expose failures in the implementation of much-hyped public schemes, and in the very performance of the government and its functionaries, including the ministers. However, negative portrayal in their coverage is more evident than positive endeavours in public domain. As a result, the contribution of news media has been echoing more negatives. And one of the fallacies in media operators is that such negative coverage attracts more viewership or readership!

Ombudsman for Media ... in a Nutshell!

Never before has the need for an Ombudsman system for media been as great as it is today. But, also, the chances of a conventional ombudsman coming to play have never been so bleak, as none of the players who matter are enthusiastic. There was never a serious movement to go for ombudsmanship at any level, the exceptions being hardly two or three short-lived examples.

With the increasing phenomena of self-righteous claims of individual media, the very idea of ombudsman needs to be repositioned. Without distinguishing right from wrong in a given situation, and motives from ends and a transparent mechanism for doing so, there cannot be any appreciation for the idea of an ombudsman. This requires an atmosphere where there is a concern in the media for the society, for long-term implications and for upholding eternal human values.

Today, given the kind of complexities, an ombudsman exercise is needed at multiple levels, but it is critical at the individual media and association levels. The system works if parallel efforts are there at six levels, independently, transparently and with different methodologies at each level. The six levels include the most critical level of individual media; 'industry' association or operators; civil society groups; associations of journalists/editors; and academic and independent professional groups. The role of government agencies in this regard should be the last level, and only in exceptional instances. They all need to work together and deliberate on guidelines and compliance mechanisms for ensuring a creditable media scene in the country.

For more than two decades, there has been a realisation for repositioning the PCI, but there has not been any initiative for doing so. The News Broadcasters Association (NBA) and News Broadcasting Standards Authority (NBSA), outside the government, have demonstrated better initiatives, although they represent hardly a quarter of all TV channels. The journalists' associations had never seized the opportunities arising out of the vacuum as did not the academics. Exercises such as the Hoot or CMS remained exceptions. The Telecom Regulatory Authority of India (TRAI) is a more recent active player.

Multiple ministers have observed that self-regulation by industry is not working. Even the Supreme Court questioned the provision of self-regulation as being a good enough argument (2012), having observed that regulation 'should come from within'.[32]

A CMS experiment carried out along with Shyam Benegal for three years independently 'naming and shaming' of Telugu news channels (18), although made no difference, offers insights into a comprehensive, transparent and participatory system. This model sensitizes viewers towards a more active role and offers a win–win model. This approach could yield better results if it is tried for at least five years with no 'sponsorships'. Three measures are required for an ombudsman idea to take root. First, the media should welcome RTI and come under its regime. Second, an ombudsman system will not work without some such mechanism in place at five other levels, independently. Third, the journalist–editor system with a responsibility for content of media should not be in doubt as it is today.

Civil Society—Is It Not the Fifth Pillar?

Civil society is an essential element of good governance, and it directly contributes to expanding the scope of governance. It not only performs watchdog functions but also offers a more reliably pulse of people, sensitises citizens and mobilises public opinion for and against public policies. It also advocates the interests of sections that otherwise do not get space and voice, and individuals who otherwise cannot take on powerful political and bureaucratic establishments. The scope of governance depends on how well civil society is organised and keeps up in an ongoing way.

Civil society activism was evident in the earlier decades (more in rural communities) as a result of the exploitation of one section by another. Some were accused of joining extreme groups like the Naxals and taking to violence. This was mostly to do with agrarian exploitation and inequalities. With the rise of the middle class and an increase in corruption involving citizens availing basic public services, civil society activism has witnessed a steady rise in recent years. With the fast growth in urban poor, and access and decline in the representativeness of the elected, citizens seeking ways other than electoral politics of activism (such as agitations, protests, processions, petitions and boycotts) have gained prominence in news media.

This has been happening more often since anti-corruption has become a rallying point. With Anna Hazare's India Against Corruption movement gaining ground, it led to birth of a political party taking to the electoral route. We now have different kinds of activism. First, aggrieved citizens taking to political, judicial or bureaucratic methods solo or as local groups. Second, dissenting people formally organising themselves into common interest groups. With access to social media, these groups have received a boost, becoming wide spread networks. They are mostly confined to the urban middle class. Third, taking the electoral route by either trying to contest the polls or becoming a political activist expecting a voice sooner or later, either from within existing political parties or by forming a new one. Fourth, seminar groups or think-tank forums and libraries with newspaper readings have increased their prominence in the urban landscape. And last, activists (and whistle blowers) at grassroots level taking to the mechanisms provided for legal remedies. As a result of all such activism, India witnesses a million or more 'hotspot' activities of civil society every week (as per my estimate).

Good governance requires conflicts to be resolved peacefully and through existing outlets and channels. But with increased electoral alienation of the poor and middle classes, the trust in existing institutions to resolve or redress is declining. Disproportionate coverage in mass media is yet another factor for civil society activism. It is also motivated by dissatisfaction with the prevailing political processes. That helps governance become responsive and participatory.[33]

Until the mid-1960s, postcards were used by individual citizens to reach out and convey their support or dissent, or to make suggestions to the leadership at different levels. Now this is done by individuals and networks of citizens through social media. We have large mobilisation of the public to express solidarity or demonstrate against one or other public policy. Then there are small groups in one city enlisting the parallel support of civil society activists in other cities using social media and smartphones. Many cities in India have well-known locations, hotspots, where civil society activists congregate, formally or informally, such as on morning walks or meeting in public parks. Earlier it used to be the Parliament or assembly premises, or the secretariat or some such symbols of establishment. But now most cities have one or more prominent location where activists come together. Ramlila Maidan (for large groups) and Jantar Mantar in Delhi, Marina Beach in Chennai, Peoples Plaza and Dharna Chowk in Hyderabad, Subhas Bose Town Hall in Cuttack, Shaheed Minar and Brigade Parade Ground in Kolkata, Matwari Maidan in Ranchi, Hazari Bagh in Lucknow, and Lal Bagh or Cubbon Park in Bengaluru are some example of these 'hotspots of citizen activism.'[34] At the height of the India Against Corruption (2012) movement, civil society activists held simultaneous and parallel demonstrations in over 40 cities of the country. It was these civil society leaders during this period who came up with innovations in reaching out and networking which the government could not do until then. For example, the idea of giving a 'missed call' on a mobile phone to express interest and endorse a proposal by a concerned person was an innovation of civil society. 'Not in My Name' meets in 16 cities simultaneously in a matter of a couple of days in July 2017 was another example of citizen activism. Of course, even the government started using IVRC and such other new technologies, but most of them were used for one-way transmissions. The discipline with which a massive rally of 40,000 over 185 kilometres was undertaken in April 2018 has become an example to trigger more such mobilisations of people.

More recently, signatures of a large number of concerned citizens, from a few hundred thousand to a few million, were collected to convince the authorities of certain interventions. Civil society has recently taken to conduct ballot paper voting against one or other decisions of the government. This often helps break an impasse in public policy-making. Civil society and active citizenry have been more organised, transparent, innovative and inclusive of late. In this process, it has also convincingly signalled that civil society could rise up to become a parallel forum to the elected one. The example of Lok Satta becoming a political party had not made a mark the same way as its role as an oversight civil society organisation and as a body of surveillance on the functioning of the government has made. Social audit is yet another instrument that active citizens or expert citizens could use for better implementation of public policies for the common good such as Aruna Roy in Rajasthan or Janaagraha in Bangalore have been using.

A few bad elements in civil society, the same as in political parties or the legislature or even in the government, should not amount to condemning or belittling the kind of role that civil society plays in upholding the Constitution. Writing in *The Wire*, Suvojit Chattopadhyay[35] noted that there has been an abuse of law to curb free speech, NGOs are being harassed and there is a tendency to put restrictions on and curb free press; all these indicate the decline of civil society and an increase in signs of authoritarianism. Such trends should not gain ground if governance has to gain in scope.

The recent efforts of the government to involve civil society groups in support of programmes like Swachh Bharat remind us that the days when government could do anything and everything alone or on its own, particularly positive things, are long gone. Governments can no longer fully implement massive schemes on their own. Also, the days of imposing decisions are over, even by the governments with a mandate. It is essential that citizens should feel and find onus, and should participate in the process of implementation, including in protests. As Divya Ravindranath maintained in 'Making Ahmedabad Mine' in *The Wire,* 'ownership of a city only when one could protest'. She rightly contends that protests espouse rights.[36]

More than 50 years ago, when the power of public opinion was found to be critical, the 'press' was given the stature of the fourth pillar (the other three being the legislature, the executive and the judiciary). To this, I had suggested that civil society and political parties be viewed as the fifth and sixth estates of the republic respectively.

Governance no longer means the government comprising the three pillars, as was viewed until recently. Today the participation of civil society is just as important and sometimes, and on some issues, even more important—as in the case of Swachh Bharat or the RTI. Together the power is more than each of the five pillars individually. The combined outcome could be much more than the sum total, and that is when governance is unleashed.

In governance, what matters more than control and command is the inclusiveness and efficacy of networks of communities, citizens and self-motivated or voluntary forums, not in pursuit of electoral party politics. A certain equilibrium between the pillars of the republic and in a checks and balance way is required and expected for governance to become good governance.

Governance is encompassing more than what the government at the time does. We need to end a certain misnomer in this regard. Governance includes what citizens and communities do on their own. The rights regime means nothing outside of legislations as in the case of RTI, Right to Education (RTE), Service Delivery Guarantee Act, etc.

Today civil society, such as mass media, matters even more. In fact, for good governance, the proof of the pudding is in the eating. That is why I have been advocating that civil society should be viewed as the fifth pillar. Together the five pillars matter even more than any one does individually. Civil society is the fifth pillar of the republic with a critical role in governance along with the government, the media and the political parties. Only when civil society is actively involved and counted on is good governance possible and could be claimed.

Organisations like those of residents associations or senior citizens, etc. are all self-motivated and self-driven voluntary organisations. They set their own priorities and agenda. They are not remotely guided. As such, they should not be considered as being an 'NGO', which tend to act at someone else's tune or priorities. Of course the government of the time tries to use 'control and command' methods to set the course, direction and priorities of the time.

Some recent events have seen civil society espousing the status of fifth estate. Civil society deserves that for the stellar role of individual citizens, as a community, and as a network for common cause and with community concerns. It is not the first time that civil society has stood up to see that the government works for the common people, upholds participatory democracy and crystallises public opinions. The extent of civil society's involvement being what it is, Swachh Bharat is a good example for the government recognising the significance of civil society (2016–2017).

The role played by Mohandas Karamchand Gandhi, never holding any formal post, remains the best example for civil society's contribution in policy-making. I am also reminded of some earlier instances like Professor N.G. Ranga's anti-cooperative, farming movement in the late 1950s using a postcard in the wake of the Avadi session of the Congress (1956–1957). It resulted in Prime Minister Nehru changing the course of that proposed amendment. Anna Hazare's movement changed the course of the government as well. Based on years of research on public participation, public opinion and government responsiveness, I suggested to Mrs Indira Gandhi the implementation of a social audit model by independent professionals to ensure that concerns of local public are headed (1981–1982). She encouraged the idea but could not take it up. Even Rajiv Gandhi could not follow-up on the idea. But with same note as mine on the social audit approach, Rajesh Pilot constituted the first social audit panel in India (1992–1996) along with me, Justice P.N. Bhagwati, Kushwant Singh, B.G. Deshmukh and a couple of activists. One idea was to involve citizens in coming up with correctives in the system and take this voice into account. We used 'public hearings' across the country to elicit and enthuse stakeholders. But that did not become a mass movement as it could not be taken beyond an experimental stage. There are several such isolated experiments in different sectors by independent civil society activists. Aruna Roy, as a pioneer with several such initiatives starting from Rajasthan, could effectively change the scope and course of public policies. Sharad Joshi, V. Kurian, Rajendra Singh, Subhash Kashyap, Dr Jai Prakash Narayan and Bindeswar Dubey are the other such activists. They changed the thinking and the very future course of leaders. Some of these leaders succeeded in sensitising the powers to become transparent, give up a proposal or even to include one, as in the case of RTI, Right to Food, Right to Employment, etc.

The role of civil society is much more and beyond having an 'oversight' function. It could also be the agenda-setter along with news media, and as much as the legislative bodies and political parties. That is what citizen activists, residents societies, senior citizens associations and the like are engaged in of late. With a regime transparency being around (RTI Act 2005), there is yet another opportunity for the pillars of the State to gear up, clear through and be more transparent as well as be responsive to large clientele and be community centric. That is what former President Pranab Mukherjee called for in his inaugural speech at the 77th Indian History Congress in Trivandrum on 29 December 2016.[37] He said that 'freedom to doubt, disagree and dispute intellectually must be protected as an essential pillar of democracy.... Nothing should lie outside realm of discussion and argument and such freedom is vital for the progress.... Civil Society is the source for ensuring democracy'. He was so convinced of this that he reminded the nation a year later on 27 May 2017 at the Ramnath Goenka lecture that 'the need to ask questions of those in power is fundamental for the preservation of our nation and of a truly democratic society'.[38]

The role of civil society remains important in ensuring that the work of legislators remain people-centric. Residents' welfare societies, senior citizen groups, consumer protection acts and RTI acts are a good example of that paradigm. Certain polarisation in adversarial positions between the government and some responsible members of civil society needs to be understood in that larger context. There is an accumulated anguish and anger over politicians in particular and those in powers in general, prompting a polarised view of civil society leaders. A root cause for this situation is the declining representative character of those getting to legislatures, many of whom, being elected by hardly one-third of the people, barely devote any time for the concerns and aspirations of the local people who elected them.

Civil society should sustain its role and broaden its scope, and not get blurred with party politics. Of course, corruption has to be a continued concern and sustained pursuit of everyone. In that endeavour, political functionaries, higher judiciary and bureaucracy and also the media should be concerned. They need to work in a spirit of checks and balance, transparency and responsiveness. The formal and informal role of civil society as the fifth pillar should remain a unique feature of Indian democracy. Governments should recognize, respect and avail this strength. Civil society in turn should work so that the elected ones become more representative and accountable, and development becomes more inclusive.

No Good Governance Without Citizen Activism

In the ultimate analysis, what distinguishes one government from another? More particularly, what should differentiate a government from an *aam aadmi* perspective? What would qualify a government to be described as being a good government? One of the common denominators is when ordinary people get basic public services delivered promptly without having to pay anything extra or without requiring a contact or an approach to get at it. There are between 10 and 20 basic public services that a citizen seeks from one or other government departments, either occasionally or frequently. A good government is the one which is concerned with and enables the delivery of these services transparently and responsively. But 'good governance' requires not only what the government does as a minimum responsibility but also the role that civil society plays in that process.

While the responsibility for delivering a service is that of the government, it should also be the concern of the civil society to ensure that citizens in fact avail those basic services and that their concerns are reflected. To facilitate this process, governments have recently created certain administrative mechanisms. These work better and more reliably with the intervention and initiatives of civil society. A series of India Corruption Surveys of CMS[39] in the last decade have indicated that between 2 and 12 per cent of those citizens seeking one or other of these basic public services did not avail the service as they could not afford to pay the extra amount needed for the service, or had no approach or contact to get at it. This is the challenge. No governance could be considered as being good if the percentage of such deprived people is more than 1 per cent at any one point, in any one public service and in any community.

A better way for ensuring that good governance is not merely more and more reforms or proliferating government, but that existing instruments or mechanisms are taken seriously and are implemented both by the government agencies and the civil society groups. In my opinion, this approach works faster and more reliably. This is what I call a citizen-centric approach. In this approach, these enabling instruments work better in combination rather than expecting any one approach to yield the desired outcomes. RTI activists should also take to the Citizen Character and the Right to Delivery of Public Services Act (which has already been adopted by more than a dozen states) together to make their interventions far more effective, notwithstanding provisions in the whistle blower legislation. I have put this proposition in the form of a formula to reiterate an integrated approach for getting better outcomes from these various mechanisms. I have explained the modalities in my book *Good Governance: Delivering Corruption-free Public Service* (2013) with specific reference to 10 basic public services.[40]

Education: A Differentiator

As a public opinion analyst for over four decades with continuous field research, I was never before so perturbed as I am today. This is because concern about primary education is not gaining movement as it should have been, even among those who talk of a knowledge society and about the future of the country. We do not seem to realise that primary education is just as important for the success of reform initiatives and the very future standing of the country. I have seen neither a political party nor any of the news media being concerned about primary education and pursuing the cause. The problem has become even more complex since the enactment of the RTE Act of 2012.

For sustainment and success of governance, the educational status of people is critical. Even more so because of the decline in the grip of parents in shaping the future citizens of the country. The role of school and teacher has increased in regard to guiding the destinies of children, moulding their mindset and breeding futuristic concerns. The ease with which citizens avail public services and actively participate in a democratic system depends on the kind of foundation that children get in early childhood, particularly from the school system.

Foundation for a knowledge society has to be the schools and school education. Knowledge society is an important contributor for the kind of governance that takes root. It comprises the public media, access to communication channels and how they are availed by citizens. For active citizenry, a skills and knowledge base is critical. And its origin for most part of that process is early schooling.

The present scenario in the country, however, does not convincingly vindicate education as a differentiator when it comes to governance as in the case of some indicators of social development. Nevertheless, the chances of transparency in public affairs and citizen activism are key features of good governance. They become differentiators when education is widely spread and becomes a leveller. The World Inequality Report 2018, which observed that 'India's record on inequality is the worst', advocated higher public spending in education to reduce income in equality.[41]

Most academics have faculties of economics, social work, sociology, political science, anthropology, psychology, etc. Each of these faculties could indulge in linking up the policies and schemes with surrounding communities, and addressing societal issues, with independent and objective feedback and evaluation support, which could make all the difference in the scope of governance, both at macro and micro levels. But unfortunately, there are hardly a dozen faculties in the country which are taking active interest in public policies and making a difference in their efficiencies. For sustaining governance, active involvement of academics is critical. Special initiatives in this regard are compulsory for sustaining governance beyond a change in governments or the party in power.[42]

Primary Education

The number of public primary schools being closed down is on the rise. In the two Telugu-speaking states, for example, some 40,000 schools would have closed by 2019–2020. The only reason for this is that enrolment in these schools had gone below the minimum cut off number (20). This, however, does not mean that there are no children who don't yet go to school in those locations. In fact, in many of these locations, enrolment in private schools had gone up. Then why are schools being closed without making an effort to enrol local children?

'Civics' as a subject should become a part of the curriculum from the mid-primary level. As political science is more about political power, civics should not be removed as a subject from the curriculum as it is about citizenship and responsibilities. Education, starting with the primary level, should create sensitivities about fundamental duties and basic human values, and with futuristic perspective in such a way that understanding remains a foundation for living, behaviours and for pursuing a career. The tendency to depend on the government and to expecting the government to do everything can be tackled at the school-education level. This view has to be corrected and reversed. It cannot happen without imparting sensitivities from an early school education itself.

Without citizen contribution and community involvement, many of the welfare and development schemes cannot be explored fully and yield the desired outcomes. The Planning Commission recognised this fact at the very outset (1957–1970) and made most local infrastructure projects subject to at least 25 per cent local participation by *shram-dan,* or local participation or contribution. Unfortunately, such a condition has been diluted or removed a couple of decades ago and a 'dole-out culture' has been promoted since then. Citizen as voters have been lured and pampered with freebees in such a way that the citizen is made to think of the immediate benefits and not the long-term adverse implications. In recent years, this has become a threat to the very democratic process, and that is telling for the very scope of governance. No good governance can be expected without citizens being sensitive to such threatening trends. Threats to governance could be coped with and countered only with education system taking them up. Only school education could be reliable enough to prevent such malice. Instead of doing that, children are made to view dependence on government as a desirable feature. For example, the Rajasthan government blatantly[43] deleted a chapter on the RTI movement from the Class Eight social science textbook as if RTI was objectionable to warrant such blocking. This is lamentable even more because the RTI movement started from Rajasthan and that it is viewed as a classic case for good governance movement in the country.

A key feature of our Constitution is the 'checks and balances' provision between the pillars of the republic. If the significance of this provision is not fully understood, can we ever expect to ensure good governance? None of the schoolbooks refer to or explain what checks and balance is all about. The idea of checks and balance is a way of life, a time-tested way of finding a better option in a conflict situation, towards an equilibrium between public institutes and to get the best out of existing systems of governance. Some such understanding is possible only when the concept is included in the high school curriculum.

Not just in some parts of India, but even in primary and secondary schools in the USA, these days one hears about incidents of children forgetting the difference between ballot and bullet, and pen and pistol. Perhaps one sees the effect of a pistol or bullet immediately; not so with pen or ballot. Capturing power at any cost, or showing off power, has become a criteria for success. Such a trend cannot be reversed without imparting knowledge and awareness from an early upbringing and through the school curriculum.

But school education across the states of India is languishing as if it is being allowed to decline! The national education policy is being ignored or bypassed. The trend for privatising school education, without any concern for basic quality and standards, has a threatening significance.

A 2017 meet of the National Education Advisory Council of Ministry of Human Resource Development (HRD) had brought out several alarming trends that have to do with primary education which were never covered in any of the news media. One of the reasons for closing public schools is the student–teacher ratio. There were over 900,000 vacancies for the post of primary-level teacher. In many states, more than 40 per cent of the teacher posts were vacant. And another 10 per cent of the teachers were untrained.

The shortage of teachers at the elementary and secondary school level has reached alarming levels in several states. This has come out of data released in the Lok Sabha by the HRD minister. In Uttar Pradesh, half of the secondary-level teacher posts were vacant in 2016–2017 against 71 per cent in Jharkhand. At primary level, over 17 per cent of teacher posts are vacant at elementary schools against 34 per cent in Bihar and 24 per cent in Delhi.[44] According to a statement given by the HRD minister in the Lok Sabha on 21 November 2016, in Andhra Pradesh alone, 19,000 posts of teachers in public schools were vacant as of March 2016. And in Telangana, 13,000 posts of teachers were vacant. The situation in private schools is no better. In fact, even with regard to drinking water facilities, playgrounds, boundary walls, libraries and science labs, private schools are worse than public schools. And yet, the impression is that education in private schools is better. Of course, the school fees and other recurring expenses per child in a private school is significant. The same week, the Supreme Court had admonished Telangana government for not appointing teachers since 2012, and asked both the Government of

Telangana and the Government of Andhra Pradesh for an explanation in this regard. And yet, as of mid-2018, no specific initiatives have been taken to fill the vacancies.

On 22 November 2016, the Supreme Court expressed its anger on the neglect of basic facilities in public schools. It lamented the lack of teachers and, surprisingly, adversely commented on the neglect and slow progress about toilet in schools. In the meanwhile, the chief minister of Andhra Pradesh was talking of broadband connectivity to schools when other basic amenities could not be provided for and teacher vacancies could not be filled (2018). The syllabus at primary and secondary school levels requires serious consideration, taking the dilemma of development, democracy and governance into consideration.

ICT: The Double Edger

For the idea of beyond good governance, ICT is a major factor as it enables a turnaround in the functions of the pillars of the state. Indians have emerged as major players for the paradigm shifts taking place globally in governance, commerce, leisure, education and relationships. Successive governments in India have realised this potential and have come up with ambitious plans and initiatives. It was years ago that successive governments announced big ideas and plans to leverage the potential of ICT for reforms in administration, efficiency in education, health services, land records, and so on.

But it is interesting to recall that there have been apprehensions about ICT among certain sections. Initially the impression was that ICT promotes centralisation, polarizes political control and even curbs individual freedom. That was how certain political parties argued even in the Parliament. Online transfer of money from the Union government to districts, and online tracking and monitoring, for example, continues to be a contentious issue politically and in the union–state relationships. The Big Brother view of governments will continue to be a live issue. The next hurdle we had to overcome was the impression that ICT takes away jobs and adds to unemployment in the country. That was why, for example, trade and employee unions openly resisted computerisation. The impressions then in many quarters was that ICT causes and leads to divides between rural–urban, rich–poor and educated–uneducated.

In 2016, both perceptions and experiences were the opposite of what they were a decade ago on the same counts. ICT is credited with helping decentralisation and empowering individuals. Today ICT is viewed as major source of employment, irrespective of government support and policies, and with hardly much investment in infrastructure. It is considered as a hope for knitting the country and bridging the divides. Government departments in the states and at the Union are competing to champion ICT. But even today, private initiatives and individual proactivity continue to determine the pace and scope of digitalisation, speed of broadband connectivity and the range of their applications.

The realisation that large public services could benefit from ICT was seen as early as the mid-1970s when N. Seshagiri, a pioneer in computerisation, took initiatives that eventually lead to the start of NICNET which became a catalyst for many computer networks in India. The first in this series was the application of computers for passenger reservation in Indian Airlines, Indian Railways and the State Bank of India by the Operations Research Group (ORG). At that time, the Internet was not known. It has been two decades since the Internet took off in India. Its penetration picked up only in the last few years, after 2010.

It was Rajiv Gandhi's emphasis on 'computerising' government offices and operations which had internalised and triggered the process. But this phase ended more in showcasing computers, with many remaining unused or remaining idle for different reasons, and wherever they were being used, it was more for basic data entry purposes. Citizen and service delivery were not the core concerns. With Sam Pitroda coming on the scene the idea of communication networks and linkages took off. All these initial efforts have become essential infrastructure to avail and scale up the use of information technologies. Shortage and criticality of training and software skills, and application specific packages got a boost. Dewang Mehata's call (1998) when he launched NASSCOM, for '*Roti, Kapada, Makan*, and broadband', had brought to the fore the need for a more durable infrastructure foundation for ICT in India.

Nadella Satya, chief of the global giant Microsoft, in his recent book (25 September 2017) reminded people that ICT should not be at the cost of human values. And that ICT should empower people and also make them unique in a soul searching way.[45]

Digital Divide

Digital divide is a decade-old apprehension of social critics. Even in 2018, it remains a contentious issue. With the launch of digital India campaign as a government programme (2015–2018), even politicians have become critics of this issue. The percentage of people or households in the country that have reliable access to any of the tools of information technologies, including social media, is unclear. In early 2017, this number could be anywhere between 30 and 60 per cent depending on what is considered as cut off for access. Access does not mean much by itself unless one is able to avail of these tools and also benefit from their usage, and affordability is an intervening variable for that. For real-time governance, it is important that the tools offer two-way communication in an interactive and reliable way. Only then will information technology facilitate good governance.

The affordability and capability of information technology tools is changing fast to create a level playing field for all people. The mobile phone has now become an integral part of lifestyle and is a basic requirement for enhancing one's skills and availing opportunities. Although over a million phones are in use, only 700 to 750 million people have access to them (2018). This number is expected to rise to a billion by 2024. Most of these devices will have access to the Internet and even to Internet of Things (IOT). But then, this access by itself is not a contributing factor for good governance. On the other hand, anything that betters the living conditions and the standards and productivity of people could be encouraged or taken up. Also, a national percentage in this regard does not always mean much. Because the percentage of those with more than one mobile and more than one device may be high. That is how the percentage of those who do not have access to any of these technologies or information sources is more than 20 per cent. In fact, one estimate put that as high 60 per cent (not including simple mobile phones).

Recent initiatives to use and increase the number of applications are helping to bridge the digital divide. Rail, air, cinema and bus reservations through net and mobile phone, and locally relevant functional applications are helping scale up the use of one or other device. And even the range of communication devices is increasing. With many of the apps being available in local languages, the scenario is bound to change further and faster. The schemes under digital India such as Andhra Pradesh's broadband scheme to every household and school for ₹149 per month, with internet, telephone connectivity and access to multi channels of television, could be expected to change the face of communication when the government could be expected to be on finger tips for citizen and citizen for the service providers. Once these ambitious plans materialise in the next couple of years, the governance scenario could be expected to go through a paradigm shift, even more so if the devices have the capability for two-way communication and also are interoperable.

The Andhra Pradesh government has planned to induct (2017–2018) 5,000 high schools for digitalisation and the Telangana government plans for 2,000 schools where children will be exposed to all kinds of devices and teaching will be through an interactive stream.[46] This initiative could be expected to speed up the process. Computers in schools should help induct more young people. This scheme, however, deserves some serious repositioning. Hardly half of computers in schools are in working condition, and even when they are in working order, instructors are not available. No panchayat or city could become smart without the local schools becoming smart first.

An electronics service delivery bill empowering citizens to electronically and digitally communicate was allowed to lapse and is yet to be reintroduced even after the government changing in 2014. This bill makes all public services obligated to respond to any RTI questions and to complete the redressal process. Once such a bill gets through, it is bound to give a boost to the scope of good governance and its consolidation.

Digital activism has changed the process of governance. Smartphones and the Internet have changed the way political events, protests and feedback are organised. The existing ways of reaching out to people and campaigning are changing. An ICT-based alternative of organising society, governance, markets and economy is in the offing.

E-voting, preventing farmer suicides and real-time governance are discussed here to indicate their potential in expediting the digitalisation process and pursuing broadband with internet connectivity to access reliable and affordable applications for availing a wide range of government services. Any benefits from such infrastructure are possible only when the citizens are sensitive and skilled enough to avail of e-governance.

The national e-governance programme started more than five years ago is yet to make its mark. There is no evidence that the national e-governance grid is fully operational and linked with state-wide area networks (SWAN), district- and block-level data centres and common service centres. Despite budgetary allocations, for this process, the progress is slow and not commensurate as is being talked by the government leaders. Unless non-governmental players take interest, e-governance will not become a way of governance.

Preventing Farmer Suicides

Farmer suicides have been on the rise in state after state for nearly a decade now, as if it is nature's curse! And as if a series of relief packages have not worked. If technology cannot come to the rescue in this context, how could it better deliver public services? I think farmer suicides could be prevented using e-governance the grid launched in 2011. Under this programme, it should be possible to know the season-cycle-wise likely farm yield beforehand and simultaneously also to know about loans borrowed by individual farmers or a group of farmers from different sources of lending, even if not included in an insurance scheme. Every other record of the farmer and his family, including health, could come from the ID database and the record of past crop yield and past credit history from sources such as banks, local cooperatives and local moneylenders. Property records come from the land registry. Simultaneous efforts could be deployed to guard against any unforeseen vulnerability. The concerned agency should be able to identify and reach out to such farmers on a real-time basis, and to take pre-emptive or proactive initiatives. This of course assumes that information on vital parameters is put in place reliably, is accessible for an app, and that the data is updated often. Equally important, the responsibility to keep track of such data should be assigned specifically to a concerned functionary. Under such an integrated application package, it should be possible to make projections two or three times during and before harvest season and to identify 'hot-spot farm-clusters'. Even specific farmer households that are prone to financial difficulties could be reached out to well before the farmer comes under distress of one kind or other. Why has this approach and app not already been a priority? However, such efforts were made in the in order to reach and persuade voters in the context of elections.

Farmer's agitation in Madhya Pradesh in June 2017 that resulted in the death of seven farmers in police firing is yet another example of the failure to use state-of-the-art information technology to track and forecast cropping area, crop yield forecast, market arrivals and prices, which could have prevented such a scene.[47] This case signalled new compulsions on the agriculture front. For, Madhya Pradesh, it was a case of ineffective crop pricing in the wake of improved farm produce causing a crash in the prices of produce and upsetting the farming community.

Real-time Governance, Not Necessarily a Good Governance

Real-time governance is a recent concept in India. Its implications are something that most countries aspire for. It is even viewed as a desirable ultimate in governance. In simple terms, in real-time governance, one need not seek out or wait for a service or solution. Rather the system works proactively and attends to or resolves the situations amicably in a pre-designed course without going through a process or a chain of decisions, and without discretionary interface. Real-time governance is much beyond online services. But an infrastructure of online facility is a prerequisite for real-time governance. Online is somewhat like providing access to facilitate quick attention, and may involve human interface. Not so in real-time. Unlike in a conventional model, real-time combines the stages of awareness, attention, access and availing a service almost parallel. The idea of 'good governance' encompasses features of real-time governance.

Real-time governance is derived from the manoeuvrability of constantly evolving information technologies for different field situations and governance issues, and from auto-course correctives and availing predictive methodologies. In this approach, for example, farmer suicides could be prevented. Crop insurance could be target-specific and dynamically adjusted to risk. Analytics-backed methodologies facilitate real-time processing. Real time is not merely for simple demand–supply type situations, but is meant to meet complex and peculiar instances and emergency situations going by auto feedback and loops.

At the moment, real-time governance in India (2018) is only an idea. It has not been deliberated at any level until recently (August 2017) when the chief minister of Andhra Pradesh claimed real-time governance based on his management of the 12-day Krishna River Pushkaralu festival. When could one claim real-time governance? Does the government use of IOT for control and command purposes entitle it to claim 'real-time governance'? What are the minimum prerequisites?

First, reliable availability of state of the art and affordable infrastructure, particularly of information technology. Andhra Pradesh could be a state to experiment with even partially by 2020 if the planned broadband connectivity with IOT facility materialises. Access to smart television sets (at ₹150 per month in Andhra Pradesh) and to smart mobile phone with video or audio conferencing capability would double by then. Second, completion of the digitalisation process, at least in some services and functions, by then. Third, availability and accessibility of cloud computing source technologies as the future is all cloud computing. That wave has just began, and it has a long way to go. Fourth, availability of huge databases amenable for analytic operations. Fifth, availability of specific skilled support at different levels with visionary leadership. Sixth, reliability of hardware and constant upgrading of application software. Seventh, linkage and coordinated functioning of various services and departments, including public–private partnership operations. Eighth, massive adoption by people in such a way that at least one person in a family could access and avail information devices and get connected. Ninth, unambiguous criteria for eligibility of various state and Union schemes and social justice programmes. Tenth, ease in availing information technologies, apps and software in regional languages. And eleventh, how well federal, state and district level linkages have been recognised and reliably. How soon mobile devices get upgraded also determines the efficacy of this process. What is needed are apps and not merely hardware.

To move on into a real-time scenario, the education stream in the country should get linked to real-time technologies. The real-time model should take into account citizen and civic society groups as much and as often as possible, and invariably as a matter of course. The academics should get into certain foundation courses such as artificial intelligence, cognitive skills, scenario-building technologies, outlook for envisioning futures, socio-economic demographic, anthropological dynamic typologies, simulation models in real-time situations, data analytics, visioneering, network technologies, etc. for parallel and continuing efforts. The capacity for critical thinking should not get lost in the anxiety to go for IOT and such for other new devices.

All this depends on the kind of democratic traditions pursued. For example, in the times of transition in power from one political party or alliance to another post a general election resulting in shifts in policies, priorities and criteria, if the definitions and criteria, for example, about eligibility, remain ambiguous, one cannot expect the real-time system to works smoothly. In a parliamentary democracy, based on a federal system with checks and balance, real-time governance should not tilt the balance or undermine any of the features of the country's Constitution and the fundamentals in it.

External or independent audit of real-time strategies should be an essential component of real-time governance. Also, issues such as privacy, centralisation and equity concerns should not be ignored. Implications of real-time governance on employment opportunities need to be addressed. For example, India is estimated to lose more than 100,000 jobs because of IOT.[48] This will remain a politically contentious issue. Care should be taken to ensure that this issue will not become a stumbling block for real-time governance.

Hacking (like fake news or data misuse) is another threat that lurks around the corner, ready to disrupt the governance itself. What alternative or standby arrangements could be provided for? What kind of insurance coverage is possible? Confidentiality remains an issue particularly because of access to codes of devices and hardware infrastructure, and at critical times. What management controls do countries like India have on IOT, if at all, to rely on it for governance? Preventive security measures need to be adopted to tackle this problem.

Impediments in going for real-time governance include partisan politics. Some states under different political party rule may cause uncertainty for the government. Real-time governance cannot happen without taking the idea seriously and following it up proactively. If the judiciary is not geared up, for example, it could jeopardise the very process (as we see in the context of Aadhaar). But real-time governance becomes realistic more when it is in a bottom up mode from a village or district. Or it could be specific to certain services, or functions or occasions as in the case of Krishna River Pushkaralu (a once in 12 years' festival). Real time could be operational in the functioning of the textile sector, health service delivery or MGNREGS operations where time series documentation is there for some years and digitalisation process is on. Analytics methodologies are not yet being availed to move in the direction of real-time governance.

In a real-time governance, there is no need for a huge physical structure for a state capital as it is viewed now. In fact, I advocated a few years ago a 'digital capital'[49] idea for Andhra Pradesh instead of a number of high raise buildings in Amaravati. In real-time governance, if the government of the time does not heed and respect the views of bottom quarter of people with correctives that advantage of real-time technologies is not of much consequence to consolidate good governance. Not a top-down, but a bottom-up approach and linkage is a prerequisite.

With all that is being claimed in Andhra Pradesh, why is the state going for huge high-rise building complexes concentrated at one location, Amaravati? Why has the state not thought of 'digital capital' or some such innovative government functioning? Where a citizen can reach out the government any time on video conference mode and similarly any government officer or agency could reach out any citizen any remote corner without physically going out. I had discussed this idea of digital capital in my book, *Chronicles of a Village Boy in New Delhi* (2015).[50]

The IOT is viewed in many quarters as the technology to usher in a beyond-good governance regime with the help of real-time operations. While IOT is credited with multiple advantages, the associated concerns of people cannot be ignored. Over emphasis on tools at the cost of human touch and democratic principles in country of plurality and sensitivities may end up as a mere quantitative exercise. It cannot be an auto-pilot route. Nor is reaching and tracking large numbers in one go good enough for a real-time regime! Nor will discretionary powers to individual functionaries help. Good governance includes happiness, and satisfactory levels and privacy of individuals as well as belongingness to a community. Individual identities continue to matter and make a difference. How well real-time could be sensitive to this?

Around the time chief minister of Andhra Pradesh was claiming launch of real-time governance, there were instances of 'out of the way' even in a strict online system![51] Tirumala Tirupati Devasthanams, managed by the government, is a good example of better online systems for most of its services. There is no discretionary quota for the *darshan* in the temple. Yet one could get into an out-of-the-way measure even in the formal online route! How? Thanks to a public–private participation arrangement. Real-time governance requires addressing such limitations or ways in short circuiting by interest groups. Another example is the digitalisation of land records. Despite availability of special software, *Bhoomi*, it remained incomplete for more than a decade. Why? The issue of repeated leak of competitive examinations question papers should be also analysed. Yet another example is the increasing frequency of fatal road accidents at a time when claims of introduction of information technology in all these functions are being made as if they are a solution.

Real time governance could happen only in a step-by-step way. It cannot be a one-shot affair or tenure-specific to be accomplished in one tenure of a government. Neither can a Microsoft (even its Klijala or Dash Board) trigger real-time governance. Only in a mission mode and with the support of political leadership can the process achieve a threshold level. Real-time infrastructures is an opportunity for good governance. But it need not be a guarantee for good governance. That is possible only if a holistic view and a sustainable plan is pursued, where political concerns and responsibilities are matched to real-time discipline, and where pillars of the state, including the media and civil society, gear up and adapt to the discipline of real-time methodologies.

Tabs and biometric tools need to be widely available and used by functionaries at various levels of government agencies. The interoperability of devices should be a reality as well. These functionaries need to be sensitive to avail and adopt. They are expected to collect information, review and assess the scope of information together with the database, and help take simultaneous actions as desired. And the cycle includes wide-range feedback on interventions. Klijala, Dash Board and many such tools are now available for real-time governance. These 'readymade apps' need to be pre-tested to local conditions and adopted. A better option is to develop apps locally, (the e-office, me-seva, Teem friends to support, Eravake innovations, Health for life care etc. apps of Andhra Pradesh are some example in this regard).

Will Digital India Deepen Democracy?
The Case of Our Electoral Process

If digitalisation empowers citizen with better access to governance and makes citizens the centre of governance, it would mean the deepening of democracy. Digitalisation has this potential, as and when every citizen of the country becomes familiar with and begins to use inter-operable digital devices. In the meanwhile, once broadband connectivity spreads to every nook and corner of the country, and communities become more reliably connected to internet and mobile services, Wi-Fi and cloud technologies, the governing process becomes more efficient and transparent. Even more so, the cost of our elections, for example, would come down significantly.

These days, everything is being talked about in terms of becoming 'smart'. How soon would citizens too become smart, and what percentage of citizens of the country would be considered to be so. More importantly, will citizens become active rather than remain passive? The future and quality of governance and democracy depends on this process. The electoral process could be benefited, and if the electoral process could be made least cost based, it amounts a paradigm shift in governance. If digitalisation helps people to distinguish between good and bad, and need and greed, only then can we say for sure that it will take democracy and governance to newer heights. Both are equally important and reinforce each other.

The Aadhaar Way

If in a year or two, Aadhaar gets universal broadband coverage in India, and if gets linked to a mobile or a PC, it could add to the potential of digital for online voting. That is because the Aadhaar number ensures one's identity with their finger prints (of all five fingers) and iris. (Assuming the possibility of impersonation with rubber gloves will be ruled out). However, the scope of unauthorised tracking and tapping of Internet and cloud services needs to be addressed. Even when Aadhaar covers every citizen of the country (not just every resident), not all of them are expected to have access to a mobile or any other device at home and to use at will. A billion phones do not mean billion citizens. Perhaps only half the citizens would own a phone, and there is no guarantee that every devices would be in operation on a given day and time, say on the day of voting, and are also inter-operable. Also, there is no guarantee that the person using the mobile device is its eligible or registered owner or that when a message is sent from a device, it is done so voluntarily, independently and confidentially, just as the voting right implies and requires.

What Difference Should It Make?

From my four decades of insights into elections, I look for certain desirable outcomes in the coming years which would amount to consolidating governance. First, the duration of poll schedule should be much shorter if it cannot be completed in one or, in the case of assembly polls, two phases. Second, the process of selecting candidates and candidates being selected by parties should have a better representative potential. Third, the expenditure being incurred by the state, by the parties and the candidates should be drastically decreased. Fourth, the election campaigns should become more rational, issue-based and more positively driven than what it is at present. Fifth, the entire process should be truly 'free and fair'. Sixth, winning or losing should not be on account of 'lures and doles' but should be on the merits of candidate and be based on the propositions put forward to the voters. Seventh, voter lists should become more accurate and polling percentage should increase. Eighth, reporting of polls and campaign in news media should become more analytical and sensitive, with a voter-centric concern. Ninth, there should be transparency in the 'conflict of interest' of the contestants and of those who are elected. There could be more such criteria flowing from our experience of last couple of years with e-money and digitalisation of economy. And, of course, the electoral process should be free from controversies like the ones concerning the reliability of EVMs (electronic voting machines).

Online Voting?

The idea of electronic voting or online voting in the wake of digitalisation is a good one and sounds fashionable as well. The Indian electoral system gets a face lift, albeit a psychological one. Although technically possible, online voting cannot be made compulsory in the next two or three national polls. A cashless and digitised economy should expedite the process of e-voting. It cannot be viewed as a substitute or an alternative. It cannot be an option either. In any case, it cannot be put in practice in the near future. Also, there is no guarantee that online voting would be free and fair or any better than what it is at present. However, we need to strive towards such a possibility as it requires considerable and prolonged promotional efforts at the grassroots of the country. Voting becomes credible only when doubts and apprehensions about potential to manipulate and misuse of digital devices are removed.

Digitalisation could make a difference in the process of the ECI tracking the election process. Political parties could better network with their field functionaries and even candidates could reach out and interact with voters. Digitalisation could help reduce the overall election expenditure and even help reduce poll eve corruption, particularly campaign costs, help increase transparency. Digital tools can make voter lists be far more reliable and up-to-date. Counting of votes can be made far more precise, faster and transparent. A recent study of Bristol University in UK[52] (of Professor Stephan Heblich) on voting before the Internet era in 2000 and after the spread of broadband in municipal elections of some countries had indicated a decline in voting percentage because of lack of clarity or confusion of campaign information on the Internet. To prevent such a thing from happening in India, precautions are required.

Digital India is being considered being done in a big way with big budgets, specific time schedules and responsibilities. Once the envisioned infrastructure becomes operational, perhaps in the next couple of years, we need to explore digitalising the electoral process, including online voting. But a debate towards that should start now so that extensive promotion and elaborate preparations can get underway, including the sensitising of citizens, political leaders and other stakeholders.

In the next couple of decades, ICT is expected to cause revolutionary changes in the functioning of the governments at different levels, and redraw the contours of governance and the scope of democracy itself. Hence, the discussion here is beyond what is sufficient in the immediate context. If ICT could change the electoral practices or the way the officers function and the representative character of elected ones, the very relevance of governance, especially good governance, is bound to standout.

Notes and References

1. See *Second Administrative Reforms Commission*, 2010, https://darpg.gov.in/arc-reports (Accessed 24 July 2018). The second commission was chaired by Veerappa Moily, a senior minister who was later in the UPA government.
2. *Times of India* and *Hindustan Times*, 24 December 2016. https://timesofindia.indiatimes.com/ https://www.hindustantimes.com/
3. There was a rare incident of Telugu Desam Party not including this clause when it filed first its constitution with ECI for registration. It was later, after someone approached them, that this particular clause was added.
4. As per the ECI, the number of registered parties was 420, number of regional parties that could contest was 39, and national parties 6 (having a minimum percentage of votes in more than three states).
5. Compiled from results of assembly elections from the ECI. See http://eci.nic.in/eci/eci.html
6. N. Bhaskara Rao, 'On Good Governance', *South Asia Politics* 14, no. 5 (September 2015); N. Bhaskara Rao, 'Good Governance Not Without Citizen Activism and Civil Society Concerns', *Transparency Review* 8, no. 3 (September 2015).
7. CIC ordered that the top six political parties should come under RTI Act. But this order has been withheld at a higher court with the connivance of the government despite appeals and PILs so far (January 2018;). See http://cic.gov.in/
8. C. Narasimha Rao, *Prajala Manifesto* [*People's Manifesto*] (Hyderabad, 2012, 2016), and discussions with this author twice in 2016–2017. This publication identified what a manifesto of parties should include. An English version of the book is expected in 2018–2019.
9. See http://eci.nic.in/eci/eci.html
10. 'Analysis of Donations Received Above ₹20,000 by National Political Parties —FY 2016–17', https://adrindia.org/content/analysis-donations-received-above-rs-20000-national-political-parties-%E2%80%93-fy-2016-17 (Accessed 24 July 2018).
11. *Indian Express*, 1 June 2017.
12. The ECI is not able to restrain election expenditure despite taking measures in the field and analysing of expenditure submitted by the candidates. According to such an analysis, more candidates in the Lok Sabha poll showed that they spend much less than what they were allowed to spend. And, yet, the ECI endorsed increasing the ceiling.
13. CMS reports on corruption and 'note-for-vote' survey of 2007 and 2008 and the subsequent surveys on poll expenditure.

14. *Hindustan Times*, 11 February 2016.

15. 'Governors Are Political Animals,' *Live Mint*, 12 August 2014, https://www.livemint.com/Opinion/n09gaoRLVrBh1GqTA2wTeN/Governors-are-political-animals.html (Accessed 24 July 2018).

16. Manish Tiwari, 'Decoding a Decade: The Politics of Policymaking', *Business Standard*, 14 November 2016.

17. This is what a recent judgement of Allahabad High Court suggested.

18. N. Vittal, 'Citizen, Corruption and Public Services—Reversing a Phenomena!', *Transparency Review* 4, no. 5 (December 2011).

19. *Hindustan Times*, 8 April 2018.

20. *Times of India*, 26 November 2016.

21. Sagnik Chowdhury, 'Judiciary Is Destroying Legislature Brick by Brick: Arun Jaitley,' *Indian Express*, 12 May 2016.

22. *Eenadu*, 28 February 2016.

23. *Indian Express*, 13 March 2016.

24. *The Hindu*, 5 March 2016.

25. *Times of India*, 12 November 2016.

26. Professor Bibek Debroy, member of NITI Aayog, speaking on 'Walk the Talk' of NDTV with Sekhar Gupta on 9 May 2016.

27. *Times of India*, 4 April 2015.

28. Gandhian Seva and Satyagraha Brigade, 'Effort to Improve Judicial Governance', *Newsletter of Gandhian Seva and Satyagraha Brigade* 7, no. 8 (August 2017, New Delhi).

29. *Times of India*, 26 April 2016.

30. Kathy Gill, 'Stop Calling the Press the Fourth Estate Unless You Are Being Ironic', ThoughtCo, 26 March 2017, https://www.thoughtco.com/what-is-the-fourth-estate-3368058 (Accessed 24 July 2018).

31. N. Bhaskara Rao, *Unleashing Power of News Channels* (Vijayvada: EMESCO, 2012).

32. N. Bhaskara Rao, *Hotspots of Citizen Activism* (forthcoming).

33. Poulomi Chakrabarti, 'Urban Middle Class "Tryst With Politics"', *Business Line*, 28 September 2016.

34. N. Bhaskara Rao, *Hotspot of Citizen Activism in India* (forthcoming).

35. Suvojit Chattopadhyay, 'Non-Authoritarian States Can Practise Everyday Authoritarianism Too', *The Wire*, 11 January 2017.

36. Divya Ravindranath, 'Making Ahmedabad Mine', *The Wire*, 9 July 2017.

37. History Congress in Trivandrum on 29 December 2016. See http://www.uniindia.com/prez-inaugurates-77th-indian-history-congress/states/news/733464.html (Accessed 27 August 2018).

38. 'Ramnath Goenka of Indian Express Has Become a Symbol of Freedom of Expression for His Role During the National Emergency: This Annual Lecture Has Become an Event', *Indian Express*, 25 May 2017, https://indianexpress.com/article/india/president-pranab-mukherjee-ramnath-goenka-lecture-live-updates-4673167/ (Accessed 27 August 2018).

39. India Corruption Surveys of CMS; N. Bhaskara Rao, *Good Governance* (New Delhi: SAGE Publications, 2013).
40. Rao, *Good Governance.*
41. Gireesh Chandra Prasad, 'Income Inequality in India Worsens, But Slower Than Russia and China: Report', *Live Mint*, 15 December 2017, https://www.livemint.com/Politics/0W83vrWtlQBpJ4qR5zZYyI/Income-inequality-in-India-worsens-but-slower-than-Russia-a.html (Accessed 27 August 2018).
42. *Live Mint*, 18 September 2016, New Delhi.
43. 'After Nehru, Rajasthan erases RTI Act from textbooks', *The Hindu*, 17 May 2016, https://www.thehindu.com/news/national/other-states/after-nehru-rajasthan-erases-rti-act-from-textbooks/article8608438.ece
44. *Economic Times*, 6 December 2016, New Delhi.
45. Satya Nadella, *Hit Refresh* (London: Harper Collins, 2017).
46. *Telangana Times*, 24 December 2016, Hyderabad.
47. *Indian Express*, June 2017, New Delhi.
48. *Eenadu*, 25 August 2016, Hyderabad.
49. Digital Capital idea was suggested for newly formed state of Andhra Pradesh, instead of going for huge high raise buildings. See N. Bhaskara Rao, *Chronicles of a Village Boy in New Delhi* (e-book, Authors Upfront, Amazon Kindle, iBook, Kobo, Nook and Google play, 2015).
50. Rao, *Chronicles of a Village Boy.*
51. *Eenadu*, 24 November 2016. Hyderabad.
52. 'Bristol University in UK Study', *Saakshi*, 18 September 2016.

CHAPTER 5

Facilitators and Destabilisers

Certain minimum facilities or factors are essential to accomplish good governance and for it to gain ground. What are the practices that distinguish a government-driven system from a citizen-centric approach? These should be practices that help build reliable delivery of public services, going beyond what the government network does. For this, the way executives are positioned and professional bodies are available, the kind of primary data, databases and analytical support that is available become essential. A few examples are briefly indicated.

Change in the party in power or even of individuals at the helm of affairs over the seven decades has not made much of a difference in the quality of governance, in development outcomes and in reducing socioeconomic disparities. We are nowhere near fulfilling even obligatory provisions in the Constitution, electoral promises repeatedly made and the basic needs of the people. And, yet we clung to a polarised model of federal government, where states are reduced to mere satellites of the Union. Even when the signals are otherwise from the electoral results, as if popular verdicts make no difference. What have we learned from the trends in the verdicts of 16 general elections? Clearly it is time to explore options and alternatives or find correctives to make a difference beyond marginal.

Negating Trends of Governance

While governance is as old as modern state, good governance is a phenomenon evolving out of dynamic political processes and deepening of democracy in 20th century. In that course and process, the role of the 'negating trends' is critical. Such trends reflect dynamics particularly from their linkage with the potential to hamper the path to good governance. Some simple and common examples are indicated here briefly.

In an election-centric parliamentary democracy, political parties have their compulsions to focus on winning rather than on the process of following or observing certain discipline and setting good precedents. Which aspects matter and are important for sustaining governance? Some negative trends are outlined here as they are more often noticed. This account of course is not inclusive. It is important to be sensitive to nagging and 'negating trends' which neither allow the process of governance gain momentum nor allow cumulative growth. This section reminds the eternal dilemma between promise and performance, what is advocated and what the extent it is actually pursued is.

Way Forward

The current paradigm of governance, development and democracy is top down. Centralisation implied in this model has made development and the state–union relations complex. And the pursuit for equity and social justice was neither consistent nor sustaining. 'Centre' is a myth, N.T. Rama Rao said that more than 35 years ago. What we have is a 'Union' and a Federal system. States are not subordinates, as they are viewed and treated more and more, as if there is a 'big brother' in New Delhi. For, the Union ministers tend to dictate their ideas and wishes in so many different ways. The basic public services required by citizens are the responsibility of a state. And yet in the present order, Union has been proactive and prescriptive more often than not.

Union should confine itself to its core responsibilities and its mediating role, leaving out the basic development responsibilities to the states. The Union ministries and departments which replicate those of the states could be confined to infrastructure and coordination functions. Powers of the state and responsibilities in such cases need to be restored. Power from the bottom up should result in bottom up administration as well. Too many hyped schemes of the Union government are deployed in states with norms and guidelines developed in Delhi expecting uniformity even when it is well known that India is a country of continental proportions with various distinct climate zones, cultural traits and resources.

In January 2018, three states Kerala, West Bengal and Odisha opposed the proposal of the Union government to appoint its officers 'to oversee development work' in 115 backward districts. These states maintained that such a tactic and mindset of union was 'an impediment to development'.[1] Even before roping in the state governments, the prime minister had already spoken to the respective District Magistrates and named nodal officers for the districts.

B.R. Ambedkar's last address to the constituent assembly answered the critics of the federal system. He clarified as early in 1949 while finalising the draft constitution,

> States under our constitution are in no way dependent upon the centre for their legislative and executive authority.... It is wrong to say that the states have been placed under the Centre.... Centre and States are co-equal in this matter ... over ruling powers to the centre are for emergency only.

Today, the balance in decision making and priorities is heavily tilted in favour of the Union. Even consultation forums have become mere formality and endorsement occasions. This scenario needs to be corrected. Relationships between Union and the states need to be repositioned. For sure, we need to think beyond a short-term perspective. Digitalisation, e-governance, cashless economy, Aadhaar, direct transfer and similar schemes should not lead to further centralisation and polarisation. If initiatives are not taken deliberately now to that end, further centralisation is likely to happen, threatening the very harmony of the Union.

Why the chief ministers of West Bengal and Tamil Nadu had to ask for 'adequate powers to states'? Both the chief ministers talked about their sovereign rights and the imposition of policies from New Delhi. Mamata Banerjee went a step further and questioned why the Union government should have so many ministries. She even suggested that Union should confine to only four ministries. Praveen Chakravarthy and Vivek Dehejloo, senior fellows at IDFC Institute, found in their study that India is the only large federal country that is experiencing an economic divergence among its states and economic disparities among states and these are only widening and not narrowing. If such a trend continues, what would be the implications to states and union relations?[2]

A retired senior IAS officer once narrated an incident involving Rajaji on his assuming the office of the chief minister of (then known as) Madras, after serving as the first Governor-General of India. After reading a front page news in a local newspaper about a 'Central team's visit' to Madras on a fact-finding mission, Rajaji phoned Prime Minister Nehru and is supposed to have told him: 'Jawahar, what business do you have to send your observers' and abruptly put down the phone. The prime minister immediately cancelled any visit of such a 'central team' to Madras. This perhaps explains how the growth of Madras State was far more impressive in the first 15 years of Independence.

Is the Government a Continuing One?

A government is expected to be a continuing institution no matter which party or which leader is heading it. Keeping continuity is an essential feature for good governance. What has been our experience in this regard?

If every leader tried to rewrite about or redo the past afar coming to power, it will go down more as 'his-story'. If it cannot appreciate whatever was good in the past, any government preoccupies itself with only new initiatives, and indulges in criticising the deeds of the previous governments and leaders. Claims of good governance by such government are more likely to be a political rhetoric, which then becomes a precedent for the next government. Although 16 general elections have taken place in the country, a different party came to power at least four times at the Union. That has been the case in many states also. We have seen different modes of transition in power from one party to another. How smooth and graceful the transitions kept up with the process of development? For, development of a people too is a process, not an overnight affair as change in the party in government is. If each time a party in power wishes to start all over again or claim as if only it could come up with initiatives, how can the government be in continuity and insights be accumulated? The issue is not about the prerogative of the incumbent government to change the course or rechristen titles of the schemes in vogue, it is about sanctity and precedence that such an approach in transition imply. Justification for good governance comes from some continuity that the institution of government implies. Of course, policies, priorities and practices of the party in power have to be as declared in the manifesto or otherwise advocated for getting the support of the people.

In a parliamentary democracy no party will be in power for ever. It is there for running the government for a tenure or as long as it has a majority on the floor of the legislature, or people elect it. The party in power is expected to be a custodian, a caretaker, a trustee, an administrator or all of them in one proportion or other, depending on its priorities. Common people of the country should not suffer or be affected when the party in power changes, even if they do not benefit somehow. Such a change or transition should not divide people, if it cannot unite them. Has that happened over the years every time there was a change in the party in power?

The system, that is the government, continues with different labels, focuses and even goals. The state as described in the Constitution of the country includes elected or nominated government. Change in party in power should not intervene or unduly influence or destabilise none of the other pillars of the state; rather all of them should function within their limits. The party which has won the mandate should function within the limits of the Constitution of the country. The idea of amendment to Constitution on the floor of the legislature with absolute majority is to enable the party in power to help itself in fulfilling the promises it had set for itself and promised to people to get the mandate.

Of the 16 general elections since 1952, four elections showed a different party in government. Congress was in power for six terms without break (1947–1977) and three terms later at different points for almost 20 years. BJP or its alley Janata Dal although had won the election six times, it came in power for a full term only once in 1998. Janata Dal with the support of BJS and other parties although won the historical election in 1977, that coalition government lasted only for two years (1977–1979). During all these years, except for the five years BJP was in government, transition of party in power did not cause much of a hindrance to process of governance in the country. Being an elder, liberal hearted humanist himself, the Atal Bihari Vajpayee government offered an amicable governance and yet with policies and programmes with developmental impact that were worthy of precedence.

However, Janata Dal government could not complete the full term because of internal squabbles and its negative outlook and approach, notwithstanding the towering and upright personality of Morarji Desai at the helm. It wasted time with an enquiry commission to expose a Constitutional aberration which was so obvious that it required no preoccupation of the government of the day. The transition in the government left bad precedence of seeking vengeance than maintain continuity in governance. With a regional leader, away from New Delhi, winning an impressive majority in 2014, primarily on his oratory skills and positioning as an underdog, has indeed led to the transition from a two-term unpopular previous government, despite its landmark initiatives on several fronts which it could never effectively put across to people. The transition in governance in the last four years (2014–2018) has been such, as if to disown the very idea that government has been a continuous one. Although the Narendra Modi government has nearly a year to complete its term, its mark on governance is unprecedented, as if the government is blatantly determined to disconnect from the previous regimes of 70 years and rewrite the history of independent India. Its modus operandi though deserves to be taken note of. With creating new definitions and benchmarks, closing or reframing the past, the government being relabelled and restructured in terms of its scope, and taking to centralisation in the name of decentralisation—it looks like as if whatever the government was offering has been a way towards good governance. The government continues to be centralised around one man but the leader's frequent interactions with public makes it an open government, although civil society groups are often being snubbed under the regime. The situation in different states is no different. Nilanjan Mukhopadhyay, who analysed Modi's public performance and wrote his political biography, observes that union–state relations have never been as hostile as they have been since 2014. He questioned the unfair branding as antinational of those who question official policies.[3] Modi government had set a good precedent for how and what could be accomplished by consultations cutting across party line and regimes. Goods and Services Tax (GST), initiated by the UPA government, was taken forward and it was demonstrated that government as an institution is continuing. Implementation of the Aadhaar identity system introduced by the UPA government and the way MGNREGS is being continued are only a few other examples.

Coming to state governments, let us look into three different models in vogue in the country. Kerala and Tamil Nadu have been witnessing change in governments between two parties. While in West Bengal, it had been one party government until recently and the change in 2014 was after more than 30 years. In Uttar Pradesh, on the other hand, five different political parties changed in the government since 1952, spanning over 16 elections of the state assembly.

What has been the experience? Did we see continuity in the system of governance? How smooth have been the transitions? Were there any initiatives for transition to consolidate the state governments towards facilitating good governance? In West Bengal, clashes between the winner and loser in the elections have been unprecedented during 2014–2017. If a changeover in government is not widely accepted as a basic routine principle of parliamentary democracy, how could we claim good governance? The leaders of the contending parties have been questioning the party in power, especially its leader, and demanding his resignation from the very first year of the regime itself.

One practice that has not changed, with the change in party in power is that government programmes are not organised inclusively yet. That is, when the government organises a public programme, those who attend it belong to only one party—the party in power, though it is a non-partisan affair. Even local representatives elected from other parties are not involved most of the times. This is a glaring example of hindrance to governance taking roots and development becoming inclusive. When invited to such public programmes, leaders of other parties tend to either avoid or boycott such programmes under one excuse or another. This trend is not recent though. Even when a development programme's success depends on a non-partisan engage-ment, one doesn't see that happening. For example, Prime Minister Narendra Modi inaugurated five different projects on 7 August 2016 in Telangana when the participants with him were from the party in power in the state, TRS, and the party in power at the Union, BJP. He could have taken care to see that the leaders of the Congress too accompanied him and be seen involved with the 'official programmes'. For, the programmes are for the development of the state. The practice is even alarming in many other states, Take the case of TDP in Andhra Pradesh, for example. Chief Minister Chandrababu Naidu seldom invites the leaders or representatives of the opposition in official government programmes. In fact, the other parties are kept out as if it is a routine. He was not even willing to call for an all-party meet or delegation on critical issues before the state. And there has been not even one such meet in four years. The TDP government organises a formal official programme as if it is a party affair. This is the case in many states. Quite often, one cannot differentiate a party programme with an all people affair for inclusive development. This practice of parties in power prevents the government being viewed as a continu-ing system. In such a scenario, how governance could be expected to be good? How the leaders of the party in power could claim good governance or even inclusive government?

I suggested a corrective, which may not be a solution, but could be tried out. Leaders in the legislature, that is prime minister and chief ministers get elected the same way as the Speaker of the House—that is, by all elected members present in the House (of course, without the whip system). Effectively, this means that the leader of the party with majority gets elected, which is the same thing as is currently practiced. Only the process is different. It could be perceived as if the prime minister represents all parties in the House. A more lasting solution, however, has to come from the leaders of political parties themselves.

Midway of the Modi term, an affiliate of the ruling party worked on an idea of putting (placing) its active members (trained) as officer on special duty (OSD) to Union ministers with the specific goal for coordinated work in the ministries between the government and the party, and see that the agenda of Hindutva and aspects are kept in picture. Such OSDs meet once a month and review functioning of key government departments and ministries.[4] During the Emergency years, Mrs Indira Gandhi had such a system of OSD to Union ministers in place and through them her office (PMO) coordinated and kept track of affairs of the ministers and ministries. Those OSDs there were mostly of the IAS or a similar cadre. But after realising the futility of that arrangement, the system disappeared once the Emergency was lifted. In the process, though, 'Office of the Minister' (in addition to Prime Minister's Office) has come to stay as another tier in government decision-making.

Adding to partisan official programmes of successive governments, if the prime minister and ministers continue to talk, even halfway after coming to power, about the ills of the previous government or hold it responsible for the continued basic problems of people, how the current government could be viewed as a continuing one and how to differentiate one regime from the other. This is what successive party leaders in power have been doing as if they have forgotten the lessons from the 1977–1979 Janata Dal government. How and when such governments can ever become inclusive? How the development process can become participative?

Whether governments are in continuity or not, electoral politics is being pursued endlessly with ministers holding party meetings, making political speeches and statements as if they undermined the fact that they were on official field visit. Ministers are more often poll centric, wooing voters rather than motivating them, and are often engaged in 'quid-pro manners'. They talk more of what has not been accomplished by previous governments than what need to be achieved now and in future, and how and what exactly should be the role of various stakeholders. In such an atmosphere, which more often is vitiated, vindictive and/or in search of an alibi, how could one expect the government of the day to be inclusive and facilitating good governance?

Change is bound to be there in policies and even in programmes as per the promises of the party being elected. But should that be by reversing past decisions non-transparently or without following a procedure, destabilising the institutions and systems in the process, instead of going back and forth, for the betterment of people? One undercurrent contributing to such a scenario is leader-centric elections and polarised decision making in the party that comes to power. Despite 15 to 16 elections of the state assembly in West Bengal and Kerala, the transition was between two parties. While in the case of Kerala it was between two ideologically different parties, the transition problems were fewer, in Tamil Nadu, the transition was as if it was more between two individuals than between ideologically different parties with distinctly different agenda. Politics are more quid pro-based in Tamil Nadu. Kerala has been under President's Rule six times up to two years. Good governance should have taken root in Kerala far more than in Tamil Nadu or even in Uttar Pradesh, where too the transition has been more centred on personality. There have been 16 assembly elections since 1952 in Uttar Pradesh with President's Rule nine times. Six different parties have come to power during these years. Government should have been more consolidated there. But what is the scene in Uttar Pradesh with successive governments?

Multiplicity of political parties have cold shouldered governance as most of the parties when in power become even more individual-centric, taking to sectional politics and electoral priorities. Rhetoric and vengeance between individuals dominate the governments. That has not helped consolidation of governance in these states. Neither accountability of government functionaries is different or better in these states nor have grievance redressal mechanisms taken roots there nor has been a serious positioning desirable for good governance. The corruption in the delivery of basic public services is not any different. An undercurrent or a driving factor for this phenomenon is electoral practices based on luring the voters. The competition between parties is not so much for better governance as for wooing the voters to come to power at any cost, unconcerned of the means for winning. How such phenomena and precedents could contribute to a smooth, harmonious and graceful continuity of governance?

There were significant changes, to the proportion of a change in regime with a change in the ruling party, at the Centre, at least three times since Independence, each ending up with different models of transition. Each of these marked reversal in policies and priorities glaringly. Even more was certain vindictiveness about the predecessor as if it was normal and could not be avoided. Or, as a cover for its own underperformance against what was promised in the election manifesto. This is to the extent that benchmarks of performance are modified or redefined as if the previous government had violated government yardsticks or did nothing for the people during its tenure. Ever since the first major change over in the regime at the Union in 1977, such an outlook and approach has become on 'expected lines'. Such a syndrome has been prevalent since then both at the Union and in the states.

In 1977, a coalition government was headed by one of the most respected senior leader, Morarji Desai, of the country. It was the 'system' of the executives that kept the government running and continued with the routine as the party in power got preoccupied with the riddle of punishing the previous prime minister with a (Shaw) Commission of Enquiry. Because of internal squabbles in the political alliance, this regime could not complete its tenure. The two subsequent prime ministers from same alliance hardly got time to come up with serious initiatives except few reversals or renaming of programmes of the previous government, apart from a huge reshuffling of officers with preferred ones in key positions. The government nevertheless continued despite its preoccupation elsewhere.

Indira Gandhi, however, came back with a bang. But soon the prime minister was killed with in her own house by her own security personnel. Rajiv Gandhi came to power and continued by and large with the same policies. His initiatives included Constitution Amendments 75 and 76 in 1986 for decentralisation and reducing voting age to 18 from 21 respectively. But his plan to send funds directly from New Delhi to District Collectors had to be given up. The government continued all through of course with changes in functionaries in various positions.

If a former prime minister stands up in the Parliament and states that as a prime minister he had given some assurances approved by the Cabinet three years earlier and whether that mean anything to the current government and whether those assurances are binding or not on the present government, what is the message he is sending and what is the question that arises? Is the government a continuing one? Or each time a party gets a majority, is it unconcerned with the previous government's decisions and policies and does not bother that some other party could be the one in the government next time?

The transition in power as a result of the 2014 elections, however, was unprecedented. The incumbent party got absolute majority to form the government on its own and the leader who lead it to victory was the one involved in controversies of one kind or another earlier as a chief minister. That being the backdrop, the effect of transition is bound to be visible everywhere beyond posting of officers, in the role of institutions and in terms of concentration of decision making in one person. In that process, there were doubts, even after four years, whether the government would be a continuing one!

Planning Commission, which was there, playing an active role in the previous 60 years, was discontinued first and revived a year later in a new avatar as NITI Aayog with a different set of people and new semantics. Then there was the uncertainty whether massive programmes like MGNREGS, which was implemented during the previous ten years as a flagship programme of the previous government, will continue or not for almost a year and which then was allowed to continue in a subdued way (it was after the Supreme Court's admonition in May 2015 that funds were released for it).[5] The RTI Act was another game changer initiative of the previous government, which the successor government was not enthusiastic about initially but soon thereafter endorsed it, albeit in a subdued way. What is the message?

More widely debated inside and outside the Parliament was the Bifurcation Act of Andhra Pradesh with six promises on the floor made by the previous prime minister on his last day in the Parliament in that capacity. Seeing the reluctance of the new government even after four years to implement it might lead one to think whether each government is on its own? If one government declares a project as a 'national project' for implementation and the successor government scuttles it around, it obviously makes one wonder whether the government is in continuity?

A key element that defines good governance is that the new government makes least changes or shifts in the scope of programmes and minimal reshuffling of the executives. A good governance is where bureaucracy remains in the same positions and continues to function as before. Whereas today not only officers are removed and shifted out or brought in out of turn but even the position and role of the institutions is changed or replaced. BJP-led state government in Maharashtra tried to scrap 95 irrigation projects initiated by the previous Congress and NCP governments saying that they were 'scam' ridden. Changing or removing officers is different from scrapping irrigation projects taken up during the tenure of the previous government.[6] It may be to pressurise or provoke certain political leaders to yield and accuse some other leader.

It is amply evident from the analysis that neither 16 elections have changed the course for bringing out the better in governance nor the transition in power by way of change in the party in government has brought the kind of continuity required for good governance, nor was there any indication that good governance practices were ushered in unless as an exception. This is both in the case of the Union and the states. Such a process of transition of party in power should not be at the cost of a section of people or another. If policies cannot be inclusive, the transition should not cause exclusion of some sections of people, and should not be against the very spirit of a smooth transition. What precedents a government sets for the next and subsequent governments should determine the criteria for good governance.

Relationships between politicians and executives is yet another indication for governance going beyond shifts in power and transfers.

While a minister is there to pursue the policies of the party in power, a civil servant is expected to ensure continuity in governance within the constitutional bounds. How well does this happen, particularly at the time of transfer of power, is another indication of good governance.

Why ministers ask for shifting or posting of particular officers? Of course, officers too seek change or shift in some instances. News media prominently reports about 'sacking' or 'shifting' of certain key functionaries (although appointed in the name of President of India) before completing their tenure in that position as a political removal and make the event a controversy. For example, the removal of 111 Standing Counsel by the Central Board of Excise and Customs (CBEC) was reported as politically motivated 'sacking' since it was soon after a renewal of their tenure. Obviously, such instances send out signals of postings dictated by political interest but which are expected as being above party politics. Similarly, for the changes in the terms of appointments. For example, what message goes out when the government decides 'non performing staffers won't get pay hike'. 'Performance' of officers should not be viewed in the light of whether they have support of ministers or not.[7]

King Yudhishthira in *Mahabharata* called 'death' the 'biggest surprise' and it is true in the case of our political masters. Though obvious that there is a successor around, they do not bother to set good precedents as traditions of governance. Is it not a wonder in a parliamentary democracy?

Corruption—Public Face of Good Governance!

Despite much talk by political leaders, initiatives by the government and extensive and repeat coverage of news media, most people think corruption is on increase and standing in the way of success of governments. And yet, chief ministers and prime ministers continue to claim good governance. How come?

There is no magic formula to curb corruption. It cannot be cured overnight, nor is it a one shot affair. And the task cannot be only of the government; it has to be the concern of all stakeholders. There is no one route or methodology to go to; it has to be a multipronged endeavour. More importantly, it has to be an ongoing concern. It cannot be rooted out without change in the lifestyle of people and elected representatives. Government policies alone will not do; individual behaviour, societal vigil and determination of political leaders, all have to work in tandem. Checks and balance mechanisms and proactive initiatives are essential. However, the extent of success is eventually determined by (a) restrains on greedy behaviour at individual level, (b) criteria of competitiveness at macro level, (c) scope of consumerism nationally and globally and (d) limits on profit maximisation by corporates. In all this, the role of mass media, particularly of the news media, has special significance as they set the national agenda and priorities in the system.

A holistic view of corruption takes into consideration those who suffer more as a consequence of corruption. This approach is driven by systemic improvements in the delivery of public services. Our concern should not be trapped in establishing 'how much corruption' or in making corruption an 'indicator for development'. The pursuit, instead, should be to understand how and why such a phenomenon continues and what can be done to ensure that the citizens can access and avail public services. The functioning of a government and effectiveness of its policies is affected by corruption at the level of citizen–service interface. Corruption at higher levels, based mostly on greed, is more because of loopholes in the laws and decline in political ethics. Corruption in terms of needs of citizens has more to do with governance and grassroots level activism of civil society.

Perceptions about corruption is a phenomenon in the context of the causes, consequences and control of corruption, and it has become a determining factor. Corruption tends to get exaggerated and often addressed in isolation, ignoring the perception about corruption. Perceptions change the sensitivity about corruption. Most corruption surveys tend to be hearsay, rather than an actual 'experience'. Such studies enable only a 'firefighting' view of corruption, based on only signs of corruption but not actual facts. The concern of the government is limited to bring down the extent of perceptions, rather than actually ridding the system of the 'compulsions of corruption'. It has been found that surveys, particularly involving rankings, come up with temporal curbs rather than cures.

The experience and the perception of corruption are different phenomena but both are interlinked and happen in parallel. Perception is based on the accumulated impressions and experiences of oneself and neighbours; experience is based on the encounter one had while seeking or availing a public service some time or another. The two are correlated. One intervening variable that influences or determines this correlation is the way the mass media covers and presents corruption. For example, if television channels broadcast specific corruption cases frequently and accentuate them, the viewers are likely to believe that corruption is all over and everywhere, although that particular audience does not have any first-hand experience of the same. Coverage of corruption in news media over a long period—the way police, public distribution system, land registration, etc. are covered and portrayed—and the perceptions formed out of such coverage and discourse cannot be reversed easily and in a short period. Corruption itself cannot be curbed without dissolving its perceptions. For an objective understanding of the problem and to address it reliably, one needs to desegregate the two.

One of the fallacy is that corruption is an independent phenomenon, and that it can be curbed by preventing 'incidences' of corruption. A perspective missed more often is that corruption has become a part of a system interlinked with the society. Unless this linkage is understood, can we control the incidents? Efforts to eliminate incidences of corruption in isolation while involving the citizen in availing public services remains a temporary cure, rather than eliminating the root cause. This understanding assumes of course that if people do elect those who are concerned about and also determined to curb corruption, they can make a difference. And only then the cause can be addressed and compulsions for corruption can be marginalised. This phenomenon is negative for good governance.

More Is Not Merrier: The Cabinet of Ministers

Prime Minister Modi has reshuffled his cabinet twice in three years. After that the size of the cabinet has gone up to 76 against 66 when he first formed it. He might add four to six ministers more in a few months when the new allies from Bihar and Tamil Nadu need to be 'represented'. In neither restructuring of the cabinet, there was any effort to 'reduce the size of government' as Modi's popular 'less government, more governance' slogan implies. In fact, the number of ministries and departments were increased by splitting the old ones in both reshuffling.

ICT sector now has three ministers instead of the two of old. One for the Ministry of Communication and two for Ministry of Electronics and Information Technology. And all three ministers were assigned additionally one or another unrelated portfolio. Then there was no effort to integrate the ministries with somewhat interrelated responsibilities and portfolio. For example, Broadcasting from the Ministry of I&B could as well have been added with Communication Ministry.

Efficiency could come from an integrated view of the portfolio rather than clubbing of unrelated departments. For example, Yoga, Ayurveda and Naturopathy were separated from the Ministry of Health and Family Welfare. The Ministry of Water Resources comprises River Development, Ganga rejuvenation and drinking water departments. But at the same time, unrelated departments were put under one minister. For example, Textiles and Information and Broadcasting were brought under one minister. Petroleum and Skill Development were under one minister; Finance, Shipping and Chemicals were brought under one minister (even if it was a temporary).

I was hoping that Prime Minister Modi would more 'reshuffle' than 'expand' his cabinet when he rejigged his Cabinet in 2016 and in 2017. It was of course good that he inducted some young blood in his Cabinet. Dropping some ministers and promoting some performers in the Cabinet sends good signals too. By inducting 19 new ministers, Modi has filled the Cabinet with the maximum numbers of ministers he could have. By so doing, as he himself put a day earlier to some journalists, he sent out the message of expansion than that of a rejigging for performance of the ministries.

An appealing campaign theme of Narendra Modi in 2014 was 'more governance and less government'. He reiterated the idea more than once even after as the prime minister of the country as if he was going to follow it beyond sloganeering. The prime minister promptly asked some senior bureaucrats to suggest measures. One important follow-up initiative was to declare over a thousand laws as obsolete. Apart from this, no other initiative was heard of even symbolically to reduce the government in the first four years of Modi government. On governance, a few measures such as using social media to reach out and interact with the public are of course impressive.

Union government as well as some state governments claim theirs as 'good governance'. A basic premise of good governance is 'limited government'. I have been advocating for some years winding up of some ministries and regrouping of some others. Expecting initiatives in this regard, I had even sent to the prime minister why and how the Ministry of I&B, for example, could be wound up both for credible communication of government's performance as well as to symbolically send out the signal for 'less government'.

Prime Minister Modi should be complimented for reiterating that there are too many legislations which have outlived. His government has even identified such legislations and even weeded out more than a thousand laws, and as many more are expected to be repealed soon. There are more than five thousand files of schemes that a District Collector is expected to handle though actually active schemes or projects at any point of time are less than hundred. I consider that if the administration at the district level has to be focused, it is even more urgent that defunct schemes that are of no relevance and no longer in operation, be weeded out too.

The number of levels that an issue passes through before a decision is taken in the government has to be reduced to within three levels (instead of the more than six current) and a time limit be set for disposing the file.[8] Citizen charters are expected to indicate a timeframe for a citizen to get his or her problem resolved. To what extent citizen charters are doing that? That should have attracted the attention of Prime Minister Modi and that would have gone a long way in demonstrating 'less government'.

Good governance involves and implies that it is less government and more governance. This slogan also helped Narendra Modi in the 2014 elections. But, is closer the elections a good time to see whether the country is moving in the direction of good governance? Of course, Prime Minister Modi and his ministers have been claiming their administration as better or different. I advocated more than two decades ago to more than one prime minister the idea of merging ministries and departments for a coherent and credible functioning. But what is often seen is to add on ministries and departments so that more ministers could be accommodated and more officers could be claimed. With developments on ICT and impressive contribution of Indian software experts globally, those developments should have made a difference to our own model of 'more the merrier' approach in government formation and functioning. It would have meant rationalising departments and that would have meant further reducing the time to dispose of matters that come before the government in a responsive as well as a proactive way.

Do we see any such reduction in the time cycle recently with initiatives on ICT? PRAGATI (proactive government and timely implementation) platform is created more to keep the bureaucracy on its toes. A similar software platform in the implementation of citizen charter and the suo motu provision of RTI Act could make government more sensitive, proactive and far more responsive.

A trend that has contributed to expanding the cabinet recently is the increase in centralisation although decentralisation has been the rhetoric of political leaders. When the prime minister expects the chief secretaries of states to report to him and review with him periodically about certain schemes or projects even though they were initiated by him, what is it—decentralisation or centralisation? When NITI Aayog takes to advising district collectors directly, is that centralisation or decentralisation? Ignoring the federal character of union government tends to inroad into standing of states even when it meant going against pro-states provision of the Constitution! This in fact is a contributing factor for ineffective implementation of many developmental schemes and their not reaching the needy people in time or fully or at all. What difference various research reports have made in this regard, including those of Controller and Auditor General of India? On the contrary, there are efforts to impinge on the powers of the states. Maximising governance cannot be expected without a decentralised view and practice as to rules and procedures. Maximising governance is not possible without decentralised functioning of the union government in a participative and inclusive way of going about deciding and delivery of services. Only then good governance could be unleashed.

Was there any effort to rationalise the size of the government as to the number of ministries, departments and functionaries. As regards the ministries, portfolios and departments, there is no evidence that there was any serious effort to rationalise, even after 2014. On the contrary, instances of happening otherwise were more. The size of the Cabinet was 53 in 1969. The cabinet with 76 members in July 2016 was bigger than any cabinet during any tenure of the UPA regime. There is so much scope and even the necessity to regroup ministries for more effective functioning and coherent policies. Such exercise was expected every time there was a Cabinet reshuffle.

Cabinet reshuffles have been more to fill in vacancies on account of deals or resignations or dropping on political reasons and as often to accommodate political compulsions including to win over or prompt defections. Cabinets in Andhra Pradesh and Telangana in 2016 and 2017 were expanded more to induct six or seven 'lured legislators' from one or other opposition party.

As creation of jobs has been a poll promise every time, there is a reluctance to reduce the number of jobs by every government during the tenure.

To show reduction in establishment costs, governments in recent years have taken to freezing recruitment, and resorted to outsourcing of certain functions. This by itself does not mean much for bettering efficiencies or reducing government as to its size. A better option is to inculcate sensitivity in public as to what establishment cost means and why costs of establishment could be reduced and where the payoff for the citizen comes from. Good governance sustains from public institutions and plat-forums of civic groups taking to. Self-administered procedures and more transparent and simplified rules are what make minimum government a durable proposition and practice.

When Prime Minister Modi announced winding up of Planning Commission, I expected that move to be a part of his idea of minimum government. But not so. The country would not have been at loss after winding up of the Planning Commission altogether. If Modi was looking for a think tank in support of government, an alternative could have been to go for a private–public participative model on the lines of Tata Institute of Fundamental Science or Indian Institute of Science or many other successful models whose output and impact has been far more creative, positive and lasting.

In the ultimate analysis, minimum government and maximum governance is not feasible without good politics. And that is not possible without inclusive parties. Good political parties could not be expected without their having good political leaders. No leader could be good without concern for common people, grassroots realities and being responsive to their basic needs and aspirations. No government could claim good governance without common people becoming the focus in implementation of policies and in its outlook for the future. When a higher percentage of people claim or readily agree that the government is their own, then only can a government say that it is offering good governance.

Minimising government requires a conscious determination of political parties and leaders for reforms, both financial and administrative and may even need legislative backup by way of amendments to existing laws and/or new laws. There is ample scope to minimize government much beyond identifying outdated legislations. The best way for a prime minister to show his determination is start with rationalising ministries and departments, which add to bureaucratic delays, and the government funded institutes with no evidence of bringing in efficiencies in government services and agencies.

The RTI Act is a terrific legislation, although, on the face of it, it appears adding to 'layers of government'. But it should be seen differently. For it has an immense potential to bring in efficiency, responsiveness and proactive initiative. Contrary to the general impression, it makes bureaucrats more respected, and even reduces pressure if only the provision of suo motu disclosure in the RTI Act is seriously taken up even for a couple of years.

Minimising government by itself does not ensure maximising governance. But that helps create an atmosphere and optimize efficiency levels in providing services of government departments and institutes. There are good examples to what is often said that 'least the government, the better the performance'. The assumption is that a ministry intervenes, creates stumbling blocks and adds to delays with its policies, orders and layers in decision making. The way software and computer technology has put Indian talent on the top of the world and has become highest earner for the country is a good example of least or no government, which means the least the government, the better the sector flourishes, entrepreneurship enriches and global standing of the country becomes distinct, as in the case of IT.

The size of selected ministries could be curtailed to limit their role to that of facilitator or enabler of creativity, productivity, entrepreneurship, and even for bettering self-employment opportunities within and outside the country, if not wound up altogether.

It is high time to reduce massive ministries and rationalise their structure in such a way that their efficiency and service delivery is visibly improved. One example is passport service, which has seen impressive transformation in the last couple of years. But by continuing with police verification same way as before, the benefit of the transformation of the process is not being fully realised.

The rationalisation of departments/ministries could be in three different ways. First, by merging or bringing together those catering to similar or linked services, as in the case of travel and transportation. Second, by winding up ministries, departments and other establishments as they are based on outdated notions and today's need is less confidentiality and more credibility. For that, a good example is the

Ministry of I&B. Third, reduction in redundant services by outsourcing, with more accountability built into. Some institutes set up by different ministries some decades ago are either redundant or no longer relevant today in the changed socioeconomic scenario and policies in the country. Why are they being continued?

Two examples given here are only indicative. The two Ministry of Culture and Ministry of I&B could be wound up. Winding them up would make no difference and, in fact, would help bring the much needed paradigm shift in the country and enhance the very scope of the services. There are many outlived Directorates of the previous era which have no relevance today. They could be closed down too. There must be more than a dozen such departments, directorates, etc. for such immediate consideration.

There is an ample scope to reduce or rationalise the size of the government. First, the duplication or multiplication within certain ministries needs to be sorted out. Second, adding new sections or departments should be stopped. Third, assessment of what is the best mode and strategy to deliver certain services or functions of the government should be made. This will yield good outcomes from the point of view of the citizen and the stakeholder, particularly in the case of departments which have to do with taxation, registration, information, science, technology, and so on.

Why a Ministry for Culture & Tourism?

Department of Culture was a part of Education Ministry for several years. Later on, it was shifted to the Ministry of I&B. Likewise, Film Censor Board was a part of the Department of Culture for some years although all policies relating to 'film' or 'cinema' were dealt by the Ministry of I&B. The two ministries could be integrated into one. The hardware or technology aspects of I&B could have been integrated with the Ministry of Telecom and Communication. Earlier the departments of Telecom and Electronics (IT) were two different ministries but sometime ago, they were merged. Indian Council of Cultural Relations (ICCR) could be repositioned now to its original status. If necessary, another body outside government with experts could be formed for promotional activities. The government could at best facilitate or support such promotional activities. The institutes that were already there under the Ministry of Culture but were operating as independent entities could be rejuvenated and repositioned to take over functions of the ministry. The same logic applies to some other ministries.

Institutes Under Ministries

Even after 25 years or more of their establishment as 'societies', many institutes of ministries continue to be controlled and funded by a ministry irrespective of their role and contribution. Today, many of some 115 institutes are redundant and adds to bureaucracy but helps in sidelining unwanted officers of the main ministry from time to time. Alternative sources for providing such services need to be explored in each case. May be the ministry could continue to hold the ownership of real estate (land, building, etc.) of some of those institutes. Many of these institutes could be closed down without making any difference to the functioning of the government as they do not add to or serve any public cause. In some instances, on the contrary, they add delays or defer a decision. Many of these bodies could be wound up or merged.

For example, Indian Institute of Mass Communication (IIMC) completed 50 years under the Ministry of I&B. When the institute was recommended by Prof. Wilbur Schram, there was hardly any faculty to train various functionaries of the field units of the Ministry of I&B. However, in no time, in the next two decades, many training centres proliferated all over the country, both in the universities and outside. Some of them have done better than IIMC and made a difference in the standing of the sector. There is no justification whatsoever for this institute to continue to be a part of the government unless its focus is changed and different. In fact, as I observed three decades ago, IIMC sometime misleads the ministry with its delayed or unreliable inputs. When a course on 'public relations' was introduced more than 30 years ago, I argued that this meant more 'managing media' and 'catching eyeballs' than actual performance on ground by the government. A corporation manufacturing consumer products could afford such a priority of taking to public relations, not a government department concerned with larger public, and it could take to public relations as it is practiced now at its own peril.

A couple of years ago, the Ministry of Corporate Affairs built Indian Institute of Corporate Affairs (IICA) with a huge campus in the outskirts of Delhi. Hardly a part of the campus IICA is using even after 5 years of its functioning. With Finance Ministry expecting IICA to start earning (as it is also catering to the private corporates), it is facing difficulty and looking for revenue, but from rentals! I know about many such institutes under union government which should have been wound up or taken out of government years ago. In 1991–1992, I did a review of half a dozen such institutes and came to this conclusion. Today, with Prime Minister Modi's concern being with outcomes, closing many of these institutes could mean 'less government'.

Has the Ministry of I&B Out Lived?

In 1985–1986, I suggested to the then Prime Minister Rajiv Gandhi that it made sense to wind up the Ministry of I&B. I repeated this suggestion with more convincing logic again to Prime Minister P.V. Narasimha Rao. More recently, I pointed out how Ministry of I&B's campaigns tend to put leaders into being deceptive. One PM did refer the idea further to the concerned ministers. With the minister for I&B vehemently opposing the idea for obvious reasons, it could never be taken forward seriously. When Prasar Bharati was formed, about 30 years ago, that should have been the appropriate time for winding up of this ministry. Sushma Swaraj did not consider the idea even when she was holding both the portfolio of I&B and Communication, although only for a short period in 1998.

This idea, however, does not mean that the government does not need help and dedicated support to put across its policies and programmes to a larger public. Yes, it does. But that should be in such a way that in the process the citizens are enlightened, participate in and actively engage with and benefit from governance. It should not be just for more awareness or image-building purpose of a couple of leaders in power. An analysis of the work of various units of Ministry of I&B during the three or four months prior to the notification of elections by the Election Commission will tellingly bring out the kind of wearied perspective that those in power carry, not out of innocence but with greed. Then there were a large number of cases of politically motivated misuse of these units over the years, irrespective of which party was in power.

Why did I pursue the idea and considered it was high time to wind up Ministry of I&B? What was the logic that did not convince the PMs for so long? The suggestion was made based on three different insights. First, my association with the Ministry of I&B as a senior advisor evaluating performance of its media units and later, after a gap of a decade, with the Ministry of Communication as national convenor of Social Audit Panel of that ministry, appraising its benefits for a couple of years along with a former Chief Justice of India and a just then retired Cabinet Secretary of India. One conclusion I reached after studying more than a couple of national campaigns of the government of the time, conducted by the media units of the Ministry of I&B was that those units were not professionally equipped to creatively strategize the campaigns efficiently and credibly. Furthermore, after discussions and appraisal, I concluded that a better option for the government was to rely on professionals operating independently or in an environment having either a Board or a Bureau.

A second source for the idea of dissolving the Ministry of I&B was a study that I did then on Kingsway transmitters (two-thirds of them in Delhi and of neighbouring states were located in Kingsway) and the ones in Himachal Pradesh. They also accounted then for most of the primary broadcasts of All India Radio. And yet, hardly half of the time of broadcast hardware, including transmitters, were being used and the rest of the time, the transmitters including those in states like Himachal Pradesh remained unused when they could have been used to expand the reach and network of telecom services. I tried in vain to make the two ministers discuss the potential. Many in both the ministries have forgotten that initially in 1950, there was only one service of broadcasting in the country. When telecom was carved out, many from broadcasting had opted for telecom service and later to develop it as a ministry. A similar dilemma arose more recently regarding internet and social media.

The third reason for the idea of rejigging I&B was the emerging of the era of convergence, where the synergy of broadcasting, telecom and information technologies was expected to go through rapid change for scaling up and to be able to offer many more value-added services. I was among the earliest ones to advocate convergence of communication technologies first from Social Audit Panel[9] (1992–1999) and later as two times elected President of Pacific Telecom Council of India (PTC India Foundation, 1999–2003). Even a Bill for expediting convergence of technologies was debated countrywide but was allowed to lapse in the Lok Sabha for the same inherent reason of 'losing an empire' of one or other ministry.

Then there is the fallacy that has been across political leadership. They think that control over media or presence in media will give them an edge and offer certain advantage over rivals in the elections. By being in news, a minister gets an ego boost. Basing on field studies, I had debunked that notion several years ago. That is how the Ministry of I&B continues its importance as one of the prized ministry in the cabinet. Even in the case of state cabinets, information portfolio is viewed as more important than what it is in fact. That is why winding up that ministry will send a significant message for New Politics of 2018–2019; even earn appreciation from many in the 'media industry'; go well with transparency era; and even help Prime Minister Modi to distinguish his regime markedly and creatively.

Initially, some 50 years ago, when Press Information Bureau (PIB) was formed, journalists from leading newspapers were inducted to credibly offer media support to various government departments. After that, PIB recruited mostly freshers for the Central Information Service (now IIS) on the launch of the service. Over all, the idea of winding up the information wing of that ministry is a better option for more than one reason. In its place, a functionally independent Board or Bureau is a better proposition to ensure more credible media support to various government policies, schemes and ongoing programmes. When such an Information Board is formed, a more appropriate ministry to place 'broadcasting', both radio and television and related functions, would be the Ministry of Communication and Information Technology. It is a logical initiative. Prasar Bharati, on the other, should be allowed to function on its own with a repositioned role and a more independent standing that it is mandated to.

For better efficiency, credible operations and to cope more promptly with emerging communication technologies, the idea of winding up the Ministry of I&B is appropriate even more now when the concern is for 'minimum government, maximum governance'. That could also save the ruling party from getting into 'fallacy traps'. This explanation should be good enough for the 'new government' in New Delhi to go about with the initiatives that this suggestion implies. Retrospectively, there is no evidence to conclude that Ministry of I&B or its units or institutes have ever positively helped the party in power to retain power. In any case, the latest trend by the ministers is to 'engage' senior journalists on board (not one but several) at a much higher remuneration and demoralise those already on the staff for years. If the chief minister of Andhra Pradesh engages more than a dozen journalists from outside, can the functionaries in the Department of Information be expected to perform to their capacity? This is the case with many other chief ministers and Cabinet ministers in New Delhi. Many ministers have engaged more than a couple of journalists as a consultant or OSD to help the minister (not the ministry or its programmes).

NITI Aayog: The New Planning Commission?

In 1985, I edited a book *India 2021*, which was released by the then Planning Minister Madhav Singh Solanki in New Delhi's IENS HQ. Former Union Minister Dr V.K.R.V. Rao wrote the forward. I contended in the preface and the introductory chapter that five-year planning approach to India's development had outlived and that we needed a long term perspective, given the kind of complexity of our problems like poverty, inequalities and process of behavioural change and societal support needed for the success of many schemes. I further noted that despite 50 years of planning and annual reviews of budgets of ministries of the states and the Union, neither our planners nor officers had acquired sensitivity for outcomes and the processes with budgets and revisions. Even more, neither the Planning Commission itself nor did anyone else at any other level, including academics, acquire interest in 'futures studies'. This is despite that Planning Forums were formed in the early years (1960s) in many colleges and universities to debate the very idea of Five-Year Plans. I benefited as a member of one such Planning Forum in SRR & CVR College in Vijayawada (1958–1960).

Planning Commission had become yet another bureaucratic agency with no constitutional standing and yet imposing its writ on states and ministries. In the process, it lost its significance further with winding up of two of its most important divisions meant to engage public for their cooperation and evaluation of public policies and schemes. The Public Cooperation Division was closed in the late 1980s as if the government no longer sought public participation. The Programme Evaluation Organisation (PEO) was expected to independently monitor and/or evaluate schemes, particularly the ones funded by the Union government and offer mid-course modifications. It was also expected to provide inputs proactively for proposed or potential schemes. With subject specialists in Planning Commission losing out to career bureaucrats, role of Planning Commission had become redundant. Against such a background, the NDA government renamed it NITI Aayog with a different set of priorities. But the Aayog is not yet fully equipped with 'experts with concerns' that a think tank of its kind is expected to have been. More significantly, the government decided to go for 15-year planning in place of five-year plans.

Planning without a perspective into futures, concern for the disadvantaged sections of people and understanding of the linkage between sectors is useless to make a difference. This was what has happened in many sectors, particularly in social development sectors. Hopefully, NITI Aayog will at least not be a pretentious body as its predecessor was. But even to be a think tank, which it is described as and is expected to be, a futures perspective and concern to basics on ground is essential to further the cause of governance. No government can claim good governance or maximisation of governance without having such essential support available reliably and proactively.

The government asked NITI Aayog to come up with a 15-year plan as 'National Development Agenda' on the completion of the 12th five-year plan (ended in March 2017). It expects a review of that agenda every three years. Can a plan or agenda for 15 years be 'larger and more focused' as was claimed, than the one for five years? It needs to be seen how a political party in government for five years takes up a plan as an agenda for the country for 15 years and expects the successor government if it is of a different party, to go along with the same priorities!? Also, how the promises in the manifesto of the same party as well of other parties in some states will be absorbed into an ongoing 15-year plan, particularly in the case of contradictory and contentious proposals of political parties (as in the case of subsidies or privatisation of basic public services, for example)? The perspectives of loan write-offs, future and poll-to-poll priories are more often likely to differ between the party in power and the one in the opposition. What mechanism the NDA government expects to come up with for sorting out such a dilemma? One precondition for such a mechanism to work is the kind of independence NITI Aayog enjoys. The representative character of the members of the Aayog, which has to function in a vitiated political atmosphere, has to be professional and non-political. A situation of good governance is not affected with contradictions as it is expected to have a resilience to sort out the differences.

One other critical factor both for the efficacy of NITI Aayog and its plans and good governance is relations of the Union government with the states and vice versa, also described as 'Centre-state relations'. NITI Aayog should not be dragged into political controversies played out among the parties as a scapegoat (as for delaying or deferring the demands of the states). The National Development Council, which endorses or approves development plans, need to be repositioned with an active role (rather than once a year meet as a mere formality) and its link with NITI Aayog should be stronger than has been so far.

NITI Aayog should reposition itself with a different agenda instead of going into 'more or less' the same agenda as that of the Planning Commission. It should engage more in 'guiding' the states including their priorities and supporting the implementing agencies instead of dictating and prescribing formulas in so many different ways. It should be equally concerned with the qualitative dimensions of 'development'.

Dampening Trends

All governments and the party in power, irrespective of the duration, claim exaggerated achievements and do so by spending huge public money on advertising. The definition of 'achievement' in most of these cases is mere an announcement of a proposal or just an inauguration of a scheme. It seldom means accomplishments from the perspective of delivery of actual reach and outcomes. Despite resented by the Supreme Court the spending of huge amounts of public money for such claims, huge amounts are allocated year after year both at the Union and in the States for the same. Union government has spent to advertise a couple of flagship programmes like Swachh Bharat upwards of ₹400 crores a year. Even the Delhi government has spent so much or more for advertising its various schemes and all claims of its accomplishments. The information on how much was being spent for publicising schemes or achievements has seen the light more from the answers to RTI questions by citizen activists. A quick analysis of what is being spent by the Union ministers and state governments indicates that as much is spent annually for 'publicity' or for image building and awareness building as the expenditure involved for general elections once in five years. What contribute to or dampen the quality of governance? A few other examples are indicated here. These are simple examples that one could observe around easily but which matter a lot.

Claiming Credit for Every Achievement

In a good governance, credit for outcomes in public sphere should not be claimed by a single leader or by one party or a ministry, particularly when it involved more players and the situation called for taking along every party and acknowledgment as a team. Often, the trend in an ideal situation is to give credit to other players for the achievements. That is in a sharing spirit. Taking credit often causes or leads to divisive and partisan politics, whereas acknowledging others' contribution implies inclusive politics and inclusive government. Acknowledging other political party or players for their accomplishments in the sphere of governance is a civilised behaviour and promotes harmony and betters the atmosphere of governance. At the individual level, this is an 'I' vs 'We' syndrome. This occurs many a time involving one or another pillar of the State or any combination of two or more players. Prospects of good governance to some extent depends on it. Taking credit as if by habit for everything going good, and attribute the ills and lapses to a past or a previous regime is indicative of a problem and amounts to going against the very spirit of good governance.

Grabbing credits each time a different party comes to power is a wrong signal for governance. When Congress came to power in Andhra Pradesh, the Hyderabad airport, named earlier after N.T. Rama Rao, was changed as Rajiv Gandhi airport. And when TDP returned to power in 2012, it tried to change it back. But after considerable protests, and as a compromise, it was decided to use both names for different terminals of the same airport. There are other instances of such change in names and/or focus with change in the party in government.

Politicising a hospital fire causing death of patients by accusing the party in government, or praising the party in government for accomplishing a task which any government is bound to take on as an obligation, does not promote governance. Claiming credit for every positive outcome and accusing the opponents on every lapse for whatever reason do not pave the road for good governance. Stable pillars of the State and their foresighted functionaries do not be influenced by momentary political equations, advantages and weightages. The approach should be to find occasions to support, sympathise or appreciate others who too matter for governance. The notion of 'country first' is not evident as often in the rhetoric, reactions and public utterances of political parties and leaders.

'First Time' Mania

A tendency of an incumbent government is to claim as if this or that happened for the 'first time' in their regime, as if it was accomplished when the previous government failed or could not perform. However, whatever has happened now is because of the continuity from the past governments. Governments anywhere try to score brownie points, but doing it by humiliating the opposition and/or its leaders and/or the predecessors is to polarise the public. The public relations experts working for the government anywhere try to present that everything the government claims has been for the first time. It is just like news channels claiming a number one position in viewership. In the process, the government try to redraw benchmarks or reference points in such a way as to give an impression that a lot more has been accomplished by the party in power. The definitions or criteria are changed to suit such a claim. For example, a government can show that it has increased jobs as never before by rigging the previous counts or by defining differently or setting a different baseline. Similarly, inflation rate or even the way growth rate of economy is so claimed too. In the process, the government tend to lose its focus from where it should be focussing, instead of engaging in this 'one-upmanship' or in manipulating desired outcomes for such claims.

Is Everything Done by Previous Government Irresponsible?

Taking excuses by attributing failures to the previous regime has been the approach and pastime as if it is a privilege of successive leaders. Political functionaries in power tend to attribute failures, even much after the elections, to the previous regime forgetting that they will face the same music from the successor is a matter of time. This is no way of enriching democracy or democratic traditions. Setting precedents on which the successor can improve upon should be the outlook. Problems can be faced better together and 'for better future' should be the outlook. Such a spirit paves way and creates an atmosphere for good governance. 'Modi may have repackaged 23 UPA schemes, but most are working better now',[10] speaks well how a succeeding government could bring in improvements over the previous government. This adds to the credentials of Modi government even more if the government itself puts out and upholds that trend.

Missing Mutual Respect

Graceful transition of power from one party to another party and leader reflects respect to each other and confidence in the system. But how often does this happen? The loser accusing and alleging the winner with malpractices and rigging the poll. The inherent problems in the electoral process cannot be addressed unless both the winner and the loser come to terms. The ongoing mudslinging between parties and leaders and winners and losers, including in the Parliament or Assembly, has to be stopped first for claiming good governance and inclusive development.

Not acknowledging the different viewpoints of political opponents, as it often happens, adds to the lack of cooperative spirit and to the discontent between political parties and leaders. Cooperative spirit between opponents could be improved by openly acknowledging each other's stands (not necessarily arguing). Once the contentious issues involved in this process are identified, the chances of a 'cooperative politics' improves. This was one of the theme I discussed in my book in 1977. This, however, doesn't imply that the losing party gives up its stand and crusade on critical issues bothering people.[11]

Government Is, of and for Everyone

When partisan politics takes roots, leaders in power tend to forget that once an election is over, the party in power is expected to represent and work for all without discrimination. But what is seen today is otherwise. The government gets accused of favouring the people of the party out of the way or preferring those who voted for it. The vocabulary of leaders often is in those lines rather than ensuring an inclusive way of working and making appeal to all sections and taking every section along. This is one factor for development plans remaining unfulfilled. Once the election is over, the 'healing approach' of the incumbent should distinguish the new government and the party that has come to power as a 'better one'.

Why Politicise Everything Every Time?

Politicising in the Indian context implies viewing things in a partisan way of advantage–disadvantage to the political parties, unconcerned with its implications for the future. Politicisation also implies ignoring of facts and real issues and diverting public attention to the trivial. Whereas once the process of an election is complete, the political parties and candidates are expected to cooperate to reap more benefits out of the system for their people and region. Parties and leaders may disagree on principles, ideologies and the paths to cherished goals, but on development projects and issues to do with security and welfare of the people, they are expected to cooperate and work for the benefit of the people irrespective of the divides on party lines. This is exactly wherefrom good governance derives its spirit and base. Instead of such a win–win outlook, claiming credit for oneself and playing the blame game is a block for good governance. Where accusations between political parties is open and continuous, chances of good governance are less. Worse is situations where political parties are not even willing to listen and acknowledge each other's point of view. This is when parties and leaders tend to take extreme positions on an issue and conflict and controversy follow and polarise the scene in different ways at the expense of the people. The 2018 budget session of Parliament witnessed over 20 days of such ugly scenes among the parties. Why they were there?

Politicking or politicising a public issue is an outcome of trying to own up achievements. A development project or a programme never achieves its intended outcomes without the support of all. In such events, news media prompts or even provokes political parties or leader's claim of achievements and polarised views with bytes and hypes. Spirit of competition may be better than trying to own up credits in an exclusive way. In the context of contemporary politics, the party in power naming projects, programmes, public institutes or establishments after active political leaders reflects a limited outlook. Such naming of public services and establishments profusely after politicians is more likely to send negative vibes both when a party is in power and even more when it is out of power. That so many public places were named after Pandit Nehru, Indira Gandhi and Rajiv Gandhi when Congress was in power, was ridiculed and continues to be a soar issue even after decades. Even in the case of performance and achievement of the governments, the 'India Shining' campaign by Vajpayee government in the 2004 elections boomeranged and was widely talked about. Likewise, *Gareebi Hatao* was supposed to have helped Indira Gandhi with a sweeping victory nearly 40 years ago. Earlier (in 1975), the 'Decade of Achievement' claim by Indira Gandhi boomeranged. The Andhra Pradesh government named an insurance scheme 'Chandranna Bhima', thereby in a way, putting the longevity of the scheme in doubt. For, if another party comes to power in the next election, that government may not continue the insurance scheme. Also it sends out the message that the scheme is available only to the voters of that party. There are too many such examples contributing to public apprehensions, civic passivity, and voter apathy.

Too Personalised Politics at the Cost of Basic Issues

In an atmosphere of personalised politics, good governance could only be a temporary concern. It is institutions, systems and setting precedents what paves way for the consolidation of governance. Political parties are individual-centric; elections and campaigns are fought with an individual in focus; issues, manifesto, and ideology becoming secondary or no concern at all. This approach is concerned more with images and ratings rather than the outcomes and effects or benefits.

More Propaganda, Less Information

Most governments and political parties have taken the publicity and advertising route more to maintain the grip than to inform and involve people at large. This obviously implies image building more than implementation of what is promised and advocated. The model is somewhat like that of sales pitch of corporate giants manufacturing a branded consumer product, with marketing hype. The way information and publicity establishments and budgets have expanded in many countries recently is more than what is for the very development and prosperity and happiness of people at large and for the welfare of disadvantaged, in particular. So, the Ministry of I&B is viewed as far more important than the Ministry of Social Welfare!

I am reminded of why Hemvati Nandan Bahuguna, chief minister of Uttar Pradesh (1974–1978), wanted to expand information and publicity activities not only in Uttar Pradesh but also outside the state including Delhi, when Mrs Indira Gandhi as the prime minister and Chief of the party snubbed such efforts. I know how the two leaders reacted in this context because I was the nominated expert member of a high level committee (1975–1977) of Uttar Pradesh government to reorganise information services of that state. Bahuguna knowing that I was not anxious to endorse his plans, invited me to his house for breakfast to convince me. Of course, I refused to sign the report of the committee because I was hinted of its implications by Jamal Kidwai, then the Secretary of the Union Ministry of I&B. Upendra Vajpai, chairman of that committee and Sarla Sahani, the director of Uttar Pradesh Information Department, both being friends of Bahuguna, went all out to multiply image making apparatus for Bahuguna, eventually making him responsible for his own decline.

Rating Trap

In recent years, most government and public service departments have been the victim of this rating trap where the concern is more to rank higher in the ratings than recognize the ground level realities. Rank in the ratings has become a measurement instead of the difference that has been made in the life of people, living standards and development or improvement in the implementation practices. Temporary improvement or positive perceptions of some people to that effect has become the priority, which means juggling with quantitative scores and focus on the rating methodology rather than service delivery on a qualitative yardstick. The origins of the rating agencies in most such cases is not fully known. If there is a 'conflict of interest' with the rating agencies, it is seldom revealed. The methodology is not fully transparent and it is revised every time such that a comparison with previous years, or previous government, will not reveal the true picture. This rating mania has become a preoccupation of those who are in positions to manage the ranks!

Opinion Surveys

Public opinion is critical for governance, but it cannot be a daily routine or selective or motivated as per the requirements of the public relation experts of the State. Certain sanctity of public opinion should be evident and the process should be transparent. Public opinion on contentious issues should be used as an independent and objective feedback and help take initiatives and correctives in public policies. In an atmosphere where efforts are to 'manufacture' public opinion, surveys often become a means. News media, which often create hype on these surveys and also generate heat between political leaders and parties is more often misleading. Online surveys by old and new media have become more of a menace as they are motivated or the context is not always revealed. 'Pre-emptive capability' of news media is yet another aspect that is availed by inducing opinionated surveys into public media.[12]

Citizen Dependence on Governments

Luring voters is no way to offer a good governance. Citizen activism is critical. But a consistent trend has been to make them depend on the government instead of liberating them from the clutches of governmental agencies and regulative methods. The political parties lure voters with dole outs of all kind, formally as a part of party manifesto and informally even when that is against the electoral codes of the election commission. These lures make the people depend on the government during as well as after elections. There are consistent efforts by successive governments to make citizens and communities depend on the government for everything every time. Governments even block the opportunities for the citizens to get together and express their anguish.

Celebrate Diversities in Cultures, Do Not Homogenise

In a parliamentary democracy, all individuals being equal, civility is in respecting each other. That is the only way of ensuring a united and a stronger country. How good governance can be claimed otherwise? This is a fundamental feature of good governance. Any measures threatening diversity, or efforts in that direction, are no way of claiming good governance. They can only be divisive features. Equality can never be in sight otherwise, so also good governance.

Can those who crave to take credit for everything, claiming first time accomplishment and politicising every opportunity with a propaganda, be expected to be inclusive in their initiatives? These are distractions. These are traps and diversions from the core concerns and criteria. If the government of the day relies more on such tactics and technics, governance can never be expected to take roots and acquire the stature of good governance.

Is It 'Union Government' or 'Modi Government'? Which Description Is More Appropriate?

In a presidential form of government, one can understand describing the government of the time by name of the President, as 'Obama government' or 'Trump government'. But in a parliamentary democracy, the government cannot be described as that of Manmohan's even though he was the prime minister. Cabinet of ministers are supposed to be jointly responsible for decision making in the government. Even when it was a coalition of over 20 parties, the government was often described as 'Manmohan government' and sometimes even as that of 'Sonia Gandhi'.

In the parliament, members of treasury and opposition benches often describe the current government as 'Modi government'. Chief minister of states and Prime Minister Modi talk inside the House and outside, in formal government programmes as well as party meetings, in 'I' or 'me' terms, like 'I did', 'I gave', 'I decided', etc. Only rarely 'we' is used in such contexts. Even if that is the case, protocol and public culture calls for restraint so that the public can develop ownership of government cutting across party lines and extend support to its policies, schemes and their implementation.

By describing a government as Manmohan government or Modi government, we are personalising the government as if the government is run by an individual. Instead, describing it as 'union government' or 'NDA government' would be gracious, which upholds the spirit of 'WE, the people' of our Constitution.

Most chief ministers position themselves in terms of 'I' and 'me' rather than of 'we' and 'us'. Is it insensitivity or arrogance or over-anxiety to take credit for everything? They do not seem to realise that such singular way of description could distance other team members and alienate larger public. A leader is expected to take along not only his or her team (Cabinet) but larger public too and inspire them, and motivate them for their support. Personality cult is what our political leaders tend to indulge in, may be unwittingly. Parties and candidates look for a 'vote getter' leader to rally around. They go along him/her and call an individual leader supreme. In most parties, this outlook is obvious when such a trend is not conducive for promoting good practices.

Desh Badal Raha Hai, Not Our Leaders

Countrywide celebrations of *Vikas Parv* in 2016 and in 2017 on the completion of two and three years of Modi government respectively made me wonder whether once in power, do our political parties ever learn from the past? I expected NDA to be more sensitive and restrained. Do such celebrations help prime ministers and chief ministers make a difference in the lives of people and in the functioning of the government? Not necessarily, if we go by the 'Decade of Achievement' of Mrs Indira Gandhi (1976), or the 'Shining India' of NDA (2004). Neither of those celebrations were so elaborate and all out as Vikas Parv was in 2016. But they all offer a lesson. Surveys, slogans, songs and ad campaigns on the accomplishments of a government of five years hardly guarantee a political future (that is, winning the election again). One reason could be that such events add to the complacency more than help in rededicating and reinforcing efforts of the party in power at different levels. Had the prime minister declared that NDA government is not creating a hype for the second anniversary, for example, as it was too early to claim achievements for sure, that would have won the hearts of people, particularly of those hard hit farmers, unemployed youth and the drought effected rural population. And would have saved the country a couple of thousands of crores of rupees. Governments of even a couple of years tend to claim that they have achieved what governments in the previous 60 years could not and that the government has removed poverty, provided drinking water everywhere, electrified every village, eliminated illiteracy, and so on, when in fact the reality was nowhere near such claims.

But then Modi's mark in 2017 was as no other leader earlier. His appeal was wide. His leadership and some of his programmes have an appeal to the extent that he no longer need to play to galleries. No one else recently has had so many opportunities to make a long lasting difference in the public psyche, political landscape and address the mindset issues. If only Prime Minister Modi had taken his own slogans seriously and also pursued them, his government would have made a long lasting difference even more tellingly. *Achchhe din* (better days) are bound to come if the idea of *Sab ka Saath, Sab ka Vikas* is taken forward. To achieve that, one sure way is 'minimum government and maximum governance'. And that is when one could say that an era of good governance of Narendra Modi is on. Rajeev Gandhi missed his opportunity despite impressive majority in the Lok Sabha.

Two years ago, on the eve of taking oath as the chief minister, the newly elected leader Pinarayi Vijayan promised the people of Kerala that he was elected to head the government that serves the interests of everyone in the state irrespective of their community or their current political affiliations and also irrespective of to whomever they had voted for in the elections. Of course, Prime Minister Modi did say something once to that effect while addressing the North Eastern Council meet at Shillong two years after he was elected. The impression that elected leaders in most states, irrespective of their political affiliations, give these days is one of outright partisan and confrontationist notions. Instead, taking people along, involving them and engaging them is a better bet for development, democracy and governance. This is what 'inclusive politics' is all about and a necessary feature for the success of development programmes. Prime Minister Modi can afford to exhort political cadres and leaders to such a course and see that a 'Team India' emerges as he talked of in his overseas speeches in 2015 and 2016. Many in the Modi government and NDA seem to believe that 'provocative politics' pays. Yes, to some extent and some time, not always, and unrestrained provocations could even boomerang as some ministers in the Modi government experienced in 2016.

There is nothing unusual in a democracy when a party in power tries to expand and consolidate itself. But it may amount to missing an opportunity to distinguish itself by focusing issues concerning the poorer sections, in the delivery of basic public services and in addressing their grievances. *Congress Mukt Bharat* rhetoric even after three years in government may amount to wasting time as Janata Dal did in 1977. There are more than a couple of such examples when such a preoccupation with trivialising the previous has harmed an incumbent more.

As chief ministers both N.T. Rama Rao and Narendra Modi had questioned earlier certain fundamental issues to do with federal character of the Union and control and command nature of the union government in New Delhi. That is how states are likely to react now when they are cornered on basic needs issues. States should not be treated as subordinates. Prime Minister Modi will be a reformer if he could also replace certain naming conventions such as 'Centre' with 'Union' and not expect states to adhere to Delhi-centric formulas and wishes all the way. Similar sensitivity to certain centralisation moves in a proactive way could prevent confrontation situations between union and states. Similarly, a liberal approach towards citizen activism in the context of development, anti-corruption and governance ensures harmonious relationships for governance and for the better, and take the governance to newer heights. Citizens should not think that one party replacing another makes no difference to their life and aspirations and the extent of their dependence on the government. If Modi could motivate over a million people in no time to give up their entitlement for subsidised cooking gas, he could as well call up on the society and citizens to partner in development initiatives as well in specific terms for good governance.

Narendra Modi is credited as a master strategist and an impressive motivator ('modivator'), yet certain perceptions about him as prime minister continue to be critical. They could be corrected. These include Modi as a 'poll-bound' leader, as a good 'event manager', and as 'pro-industry', and what he articulates is 'rhetoric more'. A shift in such perceptions should be much easier for Prime Minister Modi as his initiatives have the potential for much needed changes in governance scenario in the country as never before.

Some examples of specific efforts of achievement campaign relevant in this regard are indicated here. First, social audit approach should be taken in a truly independent and in a non-political way. Second, invoke rights provision (there are already several laws empowering citizens) whereby the society and the stakeholders could take active interest in the implementation of government initiated schemes. Third, an all-out effort needs to be made to digitalize and avail ICT tools for efficient and targeted reach in an interactive way. Modi has made a mark in using social media as a tool. A number of schemes could benefit with broadband connectivity catching up in a big way now, but the process need to be expedited by imparting skills on a massive scale at every level. Fourth, focus on 15 to 20 basic public services which a citizen is likely to avail at least once in a year but in a corruption free environment. Legislation for service delivery guarantee is already there in more than a dozen states which need to be linked up more actively now with other citizen empowering provisions.

Sab ka Saath, Sab ka Vikas could take any government to newer heights if only followed up in letter and spirit. Only then *achchhe din* would be evident. Celebrating the processes is a better bet than celebrating only the outcomes. Attributing achievements to communities and stakeholders instead of to an individual leader, however impressive and charismatic he/she may be, go a long way. Pre-emptive communication campaign is no better than proactive initiatives and correctives.

Prajala Vaddaku Palana (Government at the Doorsteps)

It is natural to expect that a government, which is closer to people in its concerns and policies, would do better in delivering public services. An often cited excuse for lapses or non-performance is jurisdiction not reaching out to people at the grassroots. Long distances from the seat of administration, differences in the climate zones, and economic conditions are the other reasons. This has been a factor in some parts of the country for the demand for new states and new districts. That is how Haryana came into being splitting from Panjab. Earlier, Andhra and Gujarat became states splitting from Madras and Bombay respectively. And a couple of years ago Jharkhand, Uttaranchal and Chhattisgarh have become states splitting from Bihar, Uttar Pradesh and Madhya Pradesh respectively. For the same reasons, more recently in 2014, state of Telangana was formed splitting Andhra Pradesh. The number of states has gone up to 29 in 2016 against 14 in 1951 and 22 in 1991. All of them have come into being as a result of pro-longed agitations and popular movements for or against such split so that the government could be closer to people and grievances could be addressed.

It was Chief Minister N.T. Rama Rao who initiated *Prajala Vaddaku Palana* (government at the doorsteps) in the undivided Andhra Pradesh in 1980 and made people realise the seriousness with which that programme was taken up, an area of difference from earlier governments. Not only the delivery of public services to the needy in the remote corners of the state was ensured but even redres-sal of people's concerns and complaints were attended to there and then. This gave a face lift, even if temporary, to the credibility of the government officers.

More recently (January 2018), the AAP government in Delhi initiated the proposal for 'doorstep delivery' of 40 public services. This scheme was devised after realising that kiosks for various such services were availed by only 8 per cent of the people even in the nation's capital and that over 25 lakh users of these services visited the relevant offices annually. Under this doorstep delivery, a 'mobile sahayak' (on contractual terms) will deliver the service needed once any citizen sends out a request or when it is due. This unique scheme, 'government at your doorstep', hopes to reach out every house to collect necessary documents, take photo and biometric details of the person, so that requirements can be processed quickly and the service can be delivered without requiring the citizen to visit any government office. These 40 services include certificates of all kind, driving licence, pensions, sewage connection, etc. Hopefully, this scheme is not poll oriented but the Lt. Governor of Delhi had his apprehensions despite allowing the experiment.[13]

Similarly, some states in turn have increased the number of districts by splitting big ones or by rationalising the jurisdiction of mandals within a district. The number of districts in the country has gone up from 356 in 1971 to over 700 in October 2016. Each newly constituted state has been increasing the number of districts. The state of Telangana for example had created 23 more districts over the existing ten. Andhra Pradesh with 13 districts after bifurcation, on the other, did not increase the number of districts nor the number of mandals or revenue divisions, going by its own priorities. Some of those districts have population of over three million. That there are increasing compulsions today for decentralisation all over is obvious. Recent 'clashes' between the state and the union in 'claiming' schemes has increased the demand for the decentralisation of service delivery apparatus. How far the new technology-based apps help this process need to be seen as states are still adopting new technologies and speeding up the process.

Recently, there have been demands for shifting the headquarters (HQ) of mandals and assembly constituencies either because they are located at inconvenient places and development takes place mostly around the HQ or the HQ has been for decades. The idea of shifting certain HQs of districts and mandals, which have been at one place so far, could be extended to many as part of the *Prajala Vaddaku Palana*. The idea of shifting HQs of districts and mandals could be looked into by states where their number has remained same for decades. That should not, however, lead to an increase in or expansion of government bureaucracy or increase in the layers of decision making.

A review of convenience of HQ locations of mandals, and even districts, could be conducted to explore the pros and cons of shifting to a new location so that it amounts to taking the government closer to people and extend the infrastructure development to hitherto undeveloped pockets. This should be possible now with the spread of ICT infrastructure and increased access to its outlets. Such measures could be considered as contributing factors for good governance, provided the evidence becomes obvious. This shifts of HQs and the split of big districts also help in reducing in equalities in access between different pockets with in a district.

Interestingly, while on the one hand the government of Telangana has doubled the number of districts and mandals to take the government closer to people, the Village Revenue Officers (VRO) Association demanded the government for a four-wheeler for their official duty (covering about 2000 households).[14] Such demands could vitiate the very idea of *Prajala Vaddaku Palana*, as distances to be covered by people were reduced remarkably, thereby requiring no four-wheeler to reach out as frequently as before. Moreover, their emoluments were already increased by 20 per cent.

Most Sought-after Public Services

Basic public services, which citizens seek or try to avail at least once a year, are the ones which determine the eventual perceptions about the government and the extent of corruption in the country. There are also some services which are availed less frequently, may be once or twice in years but the experience in availing services like police or house building or land registration go a long way in determining the people's perceptions about the government. CMS India Corruption Studies focused on some such public services for a more systematic study and time series analysis. These basic services include:

Basic Public Services	**Need-based Public Services**
• Public Distribution System	• MGNREGS
• Hospital (government)	• Land Records and Registration
• School Education (Public)	• Forest-related

- Electricity
- Water Supply
- Rail Reservation
- Housing
- Banking
- Police

Apart from these 12 public services, CMS India Corruption Studies covered five other services at least once. These are judiciary/ courts at different levels, driving license, passport, building permit and income tax. Being some of the most sought-after services, the way these services are organised and operated, and how easily could be accessed by public, determine the status of governance significantly. If these public services could be attended to and streamlined for making them zero corruption services, it would go a long way to consolidate governance.

Public Behaviour of Elected Representatives

Responsible public behaviour of those in power, particularly those elected representatives, sets the atmosphere for governance. Public expect their representatives restrain from availing discretionary privileges and not give scope for conflict of interest. Such behaviour is expected from all those in responsible public positions in judiciary, the executive as well as of those in mass media and society.

Prime ministers and chief ministers, starting with Jawaharlal Nehru and Rajaji, chief minister of Madras, have been advising colleagues in the Cabinet and elected representatives during their time to declare assets, but even after 60 years, hardly one-third of the elected ones share such information on their own.

Left party on its comeback to power in 2016 Kerala election advised its ministers to follow certain dos and don'ts. It even suggested that they should keep away from private functions. Many others too made such announcements but there is no evidence of compliance.

Prime Minister Modi was prompt in suggesting a revised code of conduct to the ministers, including their conduct on social media. Even Prime Minister David Cameron government in 2015 had announced a code for ministers.

Every parliamentarian has a code of conduct on receiving gifts, etc. As of June 2016, about 100 MPs had neither declared their assets nor declared any 'conflict of interests' on their own as they are required by the Speaker.[15] An interesting case was that of Chandrababu Naidu. As the chief minister of Andhra Pradesh, he used to release his assets periodically. But his declarations were either not taken seriously or they ended in rumours about his wealth because of 'conflict of interest' and allegations of corruption and his public image. People in such positions should informally allow 'access' and assessment by independent personalities like an editor or an academician or an analyst.

Prime Minister Modi during the celebrations of completion of two years in government at India Gate, New Delhi, on 28 May 2016, claimed that 'corruption has stopped ... not just for a year but forever ... this is just the beginning, a new dawn'. This assertion was never backed up or followed up by any in the news media.

Two years down as Prime Minister Narendra Modi came up with seven mantras or codes for his party functionaries across different levels in a Allahabad meet of the party executives on 13 June 2016.[16] These in fact are human values for daily life. Modi suggested these seven as guides for policy formulation, which obviously will determine the quality and concerns of the party, the government and the status of governance. Neither NITI Aayog (which has been 'rating' and ranking some public services without transparency in the exercise) nor anyone else ever looked into compliance aspects, except occasional news media.

These seven mantras of Modi are: (a) *Seva-bhav* (a mindset towards service), (b) *Santulan* (balanced or objective view), (c) *Sanyam* (restrained public behaviour), (d) *Samanvay* (coordinated efforts), (e) *Sakaratmakata* (positive outlook), (f) *Sadhbavana* (empathy towards the poor) and (g) *Samvad* (keeping up with dialogue with the public). If the senior functionaries in the government and in the organs of the state observe these behavioural norms or characteristics, good governance could be achieved on a sustained basis.

In the beginning of his taking to the office, Prime Minister Modi had described himself as 'first in the service of people' or *pradhan sevak*. In that spirit of the prime minister, ministers and Members of

Parliament should have set examples of their public behaviour, even if that is not their lifestyle otherwise. Such public statement will go a long way in sustaining good governance in the country.

Transparency in Appointments

Transparency in the process of getting elected or selected or appointed in the case of functionaries in the legislatures, the executive and judiciary makes a difference to the responsiveness with which they perform their roles. This in turn is a contributing factor in expecting better governance.

Those who get elected to legislatures go through a series of phases of selection process before getting to the position. And at each phase, they face open competition and are vulnerable to critical appraisal in the final phase by the voters themselves, no matter what the inducements were. There are of course some who get selected to contest an election without having any of the credentials for other reasons, which could be relationships based on business or some quid pro quo understanding. Even in the case of those who get to the positions in the Executive, go through certain selection process and, importantly, have to fulfil certain qualifying criteria and after getting into position, are expected to observe certain codes, guidelines, and discipline. The President and Vice-President of the country also go through certain electoral process before occupying those positions.

Not so in the case of Governors of states in whose name or pleasure the state government functions. A Governor is appointed 'at the pleasure' and without going through any process of any kind; nor are there any specific criteria or qualifications required and the public often is unaware of their credentials except that he or she perhaps belongs to or is a supporter of the party or the leader in power.

And even in the case of appointment of ministers in the Cabinets, both at the Union and states, people do not know much about them until after the appointment. Also, the basis for their occupying those positions with certain powers to effect the government and the governance—even after appointment—is not known. The appointment of ministers and even of the prime minister does not have any transparency (as in the case of P.V. Narasimha Rao or Dr Manmohan Singh). It is at the discretion of an individual or a party, which again means an individual, often without coming formally under any transparency process. Public comes to know who the ministers are first time as they take oath. Although it is the pleasure of the prime minister to recommend the appointment of a minister in the cabinet, on what basis or for what background he or she was appointed is not known. Credibility of Cabinet obviously depends on such transparency in the appointments. If someone with no connection with agriculture is appointed, for example, as the Minister for Agriculture, it obviously has its implications as to what is happening on the agricultural front or how the agricultural community perceives the government.

In the case of appointment of judges, both in the High Courts and the Supreme Court, the process is non-transparent or the public has the least idea until after appointment although their track record is known mostly only to a few in that field. The only condition for appointment to Supreme Court is 5 years' experience as a judge at a lower level and 10 years of practice as a lawyer. Despite that judiciary is viewed as the most sacrosanct, it is the least transparent. Since the Chief Justice of India is appointed by seniority, it is known at least before the announcement, although only to those who are familiar with the seniority or service register of court judges.

Good governance cannot be expected take roots without transparency not only in the functioning of the government and its various institutions but also in the appointment process of the key functionaries. When government takes root in various services and institutes and in the appointment of functionaries with transparency, the state could be said to be on the course of good governance. An important facilitator for good governance is that the criteria for appointments and credentials of those in important public positions should be in the public knowledge.

Hire- and Fire-based Appointments

In good governance scenario, executives of the state are not hired and fired each time there is a change in the government or in the head of the government. They are not purged because they were appointed by previous government. Of course, political appointees are more likely to be moved or shifted out each time the political party and/or the political head of the government changes. This shuffle includes not just individual functionaries in the government but also a working group or a committee even when the tasks dealt by them are of serious nature.

A civil servant, on the other hand, remains in the job in successive governments even if his/her position and functions differ or are changed. The problem of course is the tendency of converting some 'political appointees' as civil servants with continuity in the job. The extreme examples include setting roadblocks for the successor government in different ways, including misplacing/hiding or destroying of official files. In 2014, on the eve of transition of the UPA government, for example, there were reports of fire in Shastri Bhavan, an important headquarters for many ministries and also in Delhi secretariat when the incumbent lost the elections. The news media attributed motives in both instances to outgoing office bearers. Such instances signal uncertain times and delays in transition in the government.

I could recall instances where hire and fire culture had crippled smooth transition of the government. Two examples are relevant. Each one is of different type. The first is a high level social audit panel in the Ministry of Communication (2002–2005), which includes postal and telecom services, formed on my suggestion by the minister, Rajesh Pilot, with me as the national coordinator and headed by a former Chief Justice of India (Justice Bhagwati), also including a just retired Cabinet Secretary of India (B.G. Deshmukh). Two and half years later, Rajesh Pilot was shifted to Environment Ministry and was replaced by Sukaram of Himachal Pradesh. The government was the same and the prime minister also was the same and yet the new minister saw the Social Audit Panel as a political opportunity. I tried to explain the significance of social audit, which he did not understand and, instead, appointed two of his defeated political friends from his home state as members of the panel and thereby eroded the sanctity of a high level body.

Another example is that of a Task Force of Cabinet Secretariat for performance appraisal. It was a high level group going into 'Result Framework of Ministries'. This group consisted of senior bureaucrats who had retired as the secretary in one or more ministries. And this group was headed by a senior secretary in the Cabinet Secretariat, (Dr Prajapathi Trivedi). This group went into vision, mission, activities and the outcomes of each ministry in a transparent way for three-four years. In 2014, another party won the election and came a new leader as the head of the government. Soon this group was dissolved abruptly even though it was not a politically appointed group. Instead, its functions were shifted to the Prime Minister's Office!

Two implications of such changes are counter to good governance. One is the demoralising message that is sent out among the bureaucracy. Second, the government lost much needed independent insights and review on the functioning of ministries, which could have helped the new government as well. No one can deny the relevance of the role and relevance of such independent task force or social audit. A spill-over effect of such abrupt decisions in the wake of change in the government was that, for example, the workshops conducted by management schools for civil service functionaries of the Union ministries and state government too were discontinued. Sending out the message of a 'disconnection' with the past or spreading the climate of 'purge'.

Hire and fire or winding up of good practices each time there is a change in a ministry or party in power or the head of the government, chances of good governance taking much needed roots become bleak. When a government claims it is 'inclusive', one expects that it does not view with suspicion earlier appointments. Political appointees attached to individual ministers moving out under such circumstances is understandable but not so with the civil service. Change in political leadership in government should not disrupt governance. Institutionalising is a better and assured way of continuation or consolidating governance practices.

Institutions Sustaining Governance

A feature of good governance is a series of new initiatives by bodies, forums and institutes outside government. These should imply institutionalising good practices and precedents with a perspective for options and alternatives. Consolidation of good governance depends on how vibrant such outside government institutions are and how independent they are. Indian Institute of Science, Tata School of Social Science, Physical Research Laboratory, NCAER, IITs and IIMs, TERI, ASCI, CESS, and many apex bodies like FICCI, CII, etc. are a few examples of such bodies which enrich governance.

Many legislations make sense and also make difference when there are backed by independent institutions working outside the government. The legislation banning child labour, for example, becomes meaningful when there are outside agencies working to sensitize larger public on the issue or bring in an objective and structured feedback or impact analysis. Only then such laws could be implemented and can achieve targets. 'Swachh Bharat' cannot succeed without the society taking active interest and responsibility. Devastation by the hood–hood cyclone of Visakhapatnam some years ago could be overcome in no time because of efforts from senior citizens, resident welfare societies and the like who took initiatives and extended cooperation to the local government.

Wherever there are more independent and active institutions, as in the case of Ahmedabad, Pune and Bengaluru, for example, it leaves a distinct mark on overall prosperity and public life. Vikram Sarabhai, as a socially concerned scientist, established so many institutions, academic, scientific, fundamental and applied, in Ahmedabad. Those institutes continue to distinguish the city. Mokshagundam Visvesvaraya and a few others had made similar contributions to Bengaluru decades ago. By setting up Bharat Agro Industry Foundation (BAIF) in Pune 60 years ago, freedom fighter industrialist Mani Desai made a similar difference. He showed how a societal initiative can make a difference. These are only a few examples.

In 1954, Prime Minister Jawaharlal Nehru described the Bhakra Nangal dam, an early PSU, at its inauguration, as a modern temple of India. Twenty-five years later, Prime Minister Indira Gandhi was accused by her critics for not caring for the already existing PSUs. Some leaders in the government do not like to see independent institutes play the role of a 'watch dog' or take on a 'supervisory function'. But it is a critical and an essential feature of good governance. Think tank institutes engaged in envisioning, scientific outlook and sensitising the larger public have a special significance.

Over the years, successive governments have set up institutes controlled or overseen by individual ministries, and have funded them, although they were set up legally as a society or as a foundation. I have been an executive member of half a dozen such national institutes whose impact or contribution is difficult to describe even after 30 or 40 years. This is irrespective of the party in power or the prime minister. They neither appraised the functioning of such institutes nor did they think of repositioning the institutes in public domain or even encourage more of such institutes, bodies or forums to be formed.

There are institutes provided for in the Constitution to function independently of the government of the day, like the Election Commission of India, Audit and/or Controller General of India, etc. There are also institutes statutorily proved for without executive powers, like the Press Council of India, Law Commission of India, Medical Council of India, etc. Together, these institutes facilitate good governance. Then there are also foundational bodies like Audit Bureau of Circulation and Consumer Guidance Society. And when such institute and bodies are active and proactive in every field, no matter who is in power, they sustains governance mechanism.

Is a State Government That of a Governor?

A governor of a state describing the government as 'my government' in every formal address, including the state assemblies, is against the spirit of parliamentary democracy. How can a person who has been appointed as the governor of a state with no functions and who is not known to anyone until after his/her appointment, say 'my government'? Sooner or later, this deceptive view need to be reconsidered. It makes sense if an elected chief minister makes such a claim.

Not Without a Future Outlook

Concern for good governance does not come without a futures outlook in so many respects. Concern for future is more the concern for better prospects in the coming years, beyond one's own life, apart from equity, social justice and equal opportunities.

Harinder Kohli, who edited the *World in 2050*,[17] contends that the book strives for a more just, prosperous, and harmonious global community. Could we then take that as a goal of 'good governance'? That is, a just, prosperous and harmonious society. T.N. Ninan, editorial director of a leading economic daily, while speaking at the release of the *World in 2050*, reminded that the world was never harmonious and never will be. Should that mean that we give up many of the goals just because those cannot be static. Just and prosperous are not in terms only of economics and opportunities at a given time, neither are they about how reliably ideas have taken roots. Harmony, too, can exist at different levels and stages.

Looking from a different perspective, I am reminded of Prime Minister Modi and President Obama's joint communiqué at the end of the fourth visit of Indian prime minister to the USA.[18] The concept, 'inclusive democratic governance', never heard of in such joint communiqués before, was endorsed by them. The three concepts, 'inclusive', 'democratic' and 'governance', aim for the same outcome as that of Kohli's book. They offer a framework to explore the world of good governance. Prime Minister Modi should operationalize the idea and pursue it.

T.N. Ninan contended that the future should not be looked at with a linear perspective, because it often is a result of 'disruptive influences'. This very trend could change the course, and even the direction, of growth. It could either slow down or speed up the road to good governance. A good test and indicator for the state of good governance is how well such disruptive situations are coped with and the various options are differentiated, not just by the government but by other stakeholders too.

The world was never a harmonious entity and will never be one. No country can claim to be an exception. Should the pursuit for good governance end, then? Good governance is a constant desire and pursuit of any civilised society. This is also primary to prosperity and equity. It is a question more about narrowing the gap and divides and minimising the exploitation of a majority by a minority. How holistic and sincere such efforts are and what kind of institutions are there to achieve this is what matters. It matters more than the ultimate outcome at a given time. In this pursuit, 'We' is better than 'I'. Individual happiness and prosperity of the community cannot be only in quantitative terms. The state of mind—how restrained it is in terms of consumption patterns, greed, gratification and glorification—determines the road to good governance. 'Sharing' and 'caring' for each other while being competitive is what distinguishes good governance from bad governance, for 'happiness' is a concept that can only be realised in community terms, not at the level of only individual or family. Can one be happy if a neighbour is not and yet live in harmony?

Good governance expects envisioning the future on different indicators that differentiate the quality of life, harmony, equity, knowledge and access to ICT. Concern for both immediate and distant futures and how the various integral processes for a better future take shape are essential criteria for good governance. But such a concern and envisioning should be by the people at large, not just by the government of the day. Whereas, today, elected representatives as well as academics are more limited to a year by year or at the most a five-year outlook. Futurology or future studies is not merely a subject of academics. Such exercises are expected to envision the things to come or to know how the affairs evolve and mould the desired outcomes. Department of Science and Technology wound up a section on future studies two decades ago. Technology Information Forecasting Assessment Council (TIFAC), of course, was entrusted with the responsibility of forecasting the future in the context of the industry and technology. However, even the much famous book by Dr Abdul Kalam, *India 2020*, has not pushed the concept of future studies further. Six years prior to the publication of Dr Kalam's book, I edited a book, *India 2021*, based on a series of studies at ORG on different sectors. While research could be a support, the very orientation of a research has to be such that it deals with a concern of the people. The trend today is somewhat like 'today matters, even if at the cost of tomorrow'. A good governance does not evolve without minimal essential societal concern for futures. The idea of 'living in the now' is not in conflict with the idea of having and taking a long-term perspective. Such a perspective should guide today's lifestyles and living standards.

Data Is Essential, but There Should Not Be a Data Trap

Understanding good governance and development relies on measurements and quantification of inputs, outcome of benefits, changes, effects, influences, etc. of innovations, initiatives and interventions. In a good governance scenario, there would be credible and independent institutions whose data and analyses would be in public preview and shared for their potential usage by any of the pillars of the state and public institutions engaged in democracy and development and futures studies. Credibility of and timely access to such data is yet another aspect of equal importance. The traditional indicators of development, growth, behavioural change are not good enough in fast changing scenario, particularly with the availability of newer technologies and ICT tools. In such situations reliable data and objective analysis and transparency in the process is critical and detrimental.

A prerequisite for development, democracy and good governance to take roots is reliable, updated and comprehensive data about households, citizens, voters, consumers, users and non-users, beneficiaries and non-beneficiaries in an integrated as well as a desegregated way. Analytics facilitates such a view and helps remain focused and prompt delivery of public services. Census data available once in ten years was the sole basis for many policies earlier. Later came Central Statistics Office (CSO), National Sample Surveys (NSS) and Directorate General of Commercial Intelligence and Statistics (DGCIS). Some of these used different rounds but with the focus on specific themes and samples of different sizes in each round. NSS rounds still continue and its data is used but more to appraise or for a mid-course review of public schemes. There are many other NSS surveys. The 75th round already underway in 2017 takes family expenditure as the basis for agencies like NCAER, and recently ICRIER, with large sample surveys conducted independent of potential users. And yet conflicting data on the percentage of people below poverty, people who are entitled for subsidies, and targeted schemes, etc. has been found.

In the absence of reliable and adequate data acquired in a transparent way, recipients or beneficiaries of certain government services and facilities continue to be those who are not entitled. Delayed release of data could be more misleading. For example, the 2011 Census released, only in 2016, its much critical data on children (of 5–17 years) 'not in school' as 8.2 crore, as the census was trying to save the face of National Education Policy and how it was taking shape for the future? And finally when the data was released, it indicated that one-fifth of those children not in school were at work. Had this data been made available promptly, perhaps government intervention could have been different.[19]

From the very outset, policy planners felt the need to do post-implementation analysis more than the need for the very planning and design of welfare programmes. The PEO remained an important organ of Planning Commission until it ceased to be active nearly two decades ago, before the Planning Commission was rechristened in 2015.

Good governance requires taking into account the unknown aspects and dimensions of the yet 'unreached', far more than the immediate need-based requirements. The pursuit generally has been to look for more of the same again and again. A number of studies have been conducted about the delivery of basic public services but no study has ever brought out, for example, what percentage of the country's below-poverty-line population could not avail them as they could not afford to pay the 'unofficial money' or had no 'contact' to go to until CMS India Corruption Survey yielded the data, state-wise first in 2005 and then in 2007.

When data inconsistencies and contradictions are rampant, policies are likely to be bungled up and misleading. Also, that is when the key statistical indicators get reworked and data manipulated; and that is when base lines and definitions are changed to suit political interests and vitiate national debates as we see some time.

Now, in 2018, I see a big vacuum in the much needed analytical base and back up carry out an exploratory analysis to understand the current scenario and then explore various options. This is despite proliferation of research agencies, new analytical tools and access by people to newer communication technologies. And yet reliance on readymade tools from outside the systems and without ground linkages, has become the fashion of the day. Perhaps because our leaders are in a hurry to claim 'achievements'. In our anxiety we have rightly provided the budget for analytics. For example, over ₹1,600 crore were provided as a part of Digital India project but without an understanding of the pace with what software are advancing. This is particularly true for tasks and development missions in the social sector, as if an app by itself is a reliable solution while it is merely a tool to be adopted to the local situations. To what extent such efforts are going to facilitate good governance need to be seen. Girls drop out will not decline because of an app of a global leader in information technology. Nor the school enrolment will increase. An app will help if only it is designed for a specific purpose and in such a way that a particular section of our people could benefit from using it. To make a difference, digital economy, online payment, e-wallets and cash-less economy campaigns require a reliable baseline data and periodic appraisal and assessment.

The Smart Pulse Survey[20] (2016–2017) of the Andhra Pradesh government is another example for the government claims that it was to reach the intended public with all government services without middlemen. The chief minister addressed all district collectors more than once on the relevance of field survey and why they should be interested in conducting the survey. The survey was to be a census covering each and every aspect of government services and programmes to do with individuals and households. This survey was expected to link Aadhaar with all essential mobile phone applications. In this survey, 14 households were expected to be covered per day by the enumerator. iPads and other tabs were used for conducting the survey.

In my 40 years' experience in conducting large scale surveys, I can say that no outcome from such surveys could be reliable and comprehensive when the fieldwork was conducted by teachers on 'extra duty' and when the investigator covers more than ten households a day. No findings could be used without validation and verifications.

Every time there is change in the government, the leader in power comes up with schemes for certain sections of the people and claims some survey as the source to identify potential beneficiaries. The chief minister of Andhra Pradesh, for examples, claimed 20 yardsticks for this smart pulse survey. These include bank passbook, Aadhaar card, water bill, electricity bill, caste, income certificate, Kisan certificate, Dwakra certificate, scholarship, pension, etc. as applicable. Earlier, Telangana chief minister had conducted similar census survey. In both cases, the survey was conducted by various employees of the government and they were given a number of families to be covered in a day. For example, in Andhra Pradesh this quota was 14 households a day per enumerator. Claims are made of certain authenticity and focus in government functioning because of such surveys. The government is inundated with data of all kind and with different reliability to allow it to claim achievements. There is no evidence that analytical tools are availed to integrate multiple sources for making sense out of delusion and enable a futures perspective. (This is the same approach or strategy that agencies conducting viewership and readership surveys take so that data is not compatible for an over-the-years assessment.) Such surveys should not become tools for the *jugalbandi* phenomenon (justifying each other and echoing each other's claims). The exaggeration and hype about what is claimed as 'achievements' of the government gets away without being questioned with a credible argument based on analytics.

IVR driven surveys are relied more recently by chief ministers as a more reliable data source. Instant surveys for instant responses are not necessarily reliable. They are 'robo responses' without qualitative inputs and such data could be more misleading.

Analytics could come handy to save a state from a deluge of data which comes handy to the news media more than the people at the grassroots. Analytics could help restore credibility of claims and promises of political leaders. In the process, good governance claims are never consolidated or sustained. Also, in the process, people should not be reduced to numbers.

Slogans That Could As Well Be the *Mantras*

During the first three year of his tenure (2014–2017), Prime Minister Modi proposed a series of initiatives with lasting implications by way of public statements. They should not remain ambiguous slogans.

They deserve a serious follow-up with specific interventions. Three of these have special relevance to the prospects of good governance. Modi captured the imagination of the voters with such themes like *Sab ka Sath, Sab ka Vikas* and 'less government, more governance'. If these ideas are pursued truly and become evident in policies and in implementation, they would expedite the much needed shift in the paradigm.

On 15 August 2016, speaking from the Red Fort in New Delhi on the eve of the 70th Independence Day, he gave a call for *Swaraj to Suraj* by which he meant that we should work for good governance in the country and that only then independence makes sense to people. But neither he nor anyone else explained even during the year as to what *Suraj* comprises or consists of. In fact, subsequently, none from the cabinet or NITI Aayog or the ruling party has ever echoed the spirit of the prime minister's proclamation for *Suraj*. But it was good that the prime minister addressed the nation and committed himself to the idea of good governance on such a solemn occasion.

On 30 August 2016, addressing a public meeting in his home state Gujarat, the prime minister noted that 'by luring voters one may win an election, but cannot run a government'.[21] Whereas that is what has been happening for years as if that is the only way to come to power and form a government. Beyond paying lip service, nothing much concrete comes towards curbing the lures of all kind, formally through party manifestos and informally by candidates. With ever increasing and wide spread lures on the eve of elections, is it possible to unleash good governance? No one, including in the ruling party, ever responded to the prime minister's important address in Gujarat.

On 27 October 2016, talking to a batch of young IAS officers, the prime minister told them that 'politics should never override policy' and urged them to 'use two touchstones to help them in their deci-sion making'. What are they? One, the decisions under consideration should never be against national interests and two, the decisions should not harm the poorest of the poor. The prime minister rightly touched upon an ideal principle. That should not be forgotten by the politicians. Can anyone today say that many of our public policies are sans poll politics?[22]

Against such a backdrop, the prime minister's observations should have been promptly endorsed by other political leaders and the news media should have echoed the sentiments, particularly because the country is already in a 2019 poll mood and mode. The Chief Justice of India, T.S. Thakur observed on 28 October 2016 that offer of freebies from contesting political parties is tantamount to bribing voters. And yet what have we done? Can we better governance without tackling this much known phenomena?! This 'linkage' assertion by Chief Justice of the country should have revived a national debate. Observations of neither the prime minister nor the Chief Justice received any follow-up, not even in news media.

Addressing an important meet of NITI Aayog on Transforming India, Prime Minister Modi noted that 'step by step changes will not yield desired changes; what is needed is revolutionary reforms and changes'.[23] Echoing that observation of the prime minister, the then Minister for Urban Development and now the Vice President of India, Venkaiah Naidu wrote in an article that conventional approaches and methods will not do for development and are not good enough and that 'all sectors need to be thoroughly overhauled or reformed for achieving long-term solutions, not temporary solutions'. Prime Minister Modi have echoed some of these ideas in his speeches abroad.

The above propositions of Prime Minister Modi was echoed by any political leader not even by his cabinet colleagues. In fact, these have not been reiterated by any government agency nor has Modi come up with specific follow-up plans. On the contrary, the signals from others in the government were that these statements are merely populist. NITI Aayog could have come up with a plan of action or as a package of advises to the concerned government departments. Particularly since the prime minister has noted that 'revolutionary changes' should have been taken up. They deserve a serious national debate. The five fundamental topics Prime Minister Modi had articulated mean something significant if only they are pursued with specific proposals or action by the government, by the parliament and political parties.

But these five publicly stated ideas together can distinguish the Modi government from other governments and make him a harbinger of good governance. These could be guiding principles to change the very scope of governance and the future of the country. The five publicly espoused utterances of Modi that deserve to be followed up are:

1. Swaraj to Su-raj
2. Power, not by wooing voters
3. Politics should never override policy
4. Less government, more governance
5. *Sab ka Sath, Sab ka Vikas*

These are key fundamental shifts to get rid of the fallacy that the country is in today. The other shifts for good governance could follow if only these five ideas are seriously pursued, but these require to be operationalised. For example: How do we reverse the 'culture of bribing voters', as the Chief Justice of India had expressed? How do we depoliticise policy issues? Where do we start the process and who should be the ones to set an example? The party in government obviously should be the one which should initiate the process with examples. Regarding 'less government', the prime minister did take an initiative early on but it was limited to scrapping some outdated laws. The party in government should set example by demonstrating inclusive policies and programmes and also implement them with the spirit of *Sab ka Sath, Sab ka Vikas*.

These should not remain as mere Modi slogans, instead, they could become Modi's mantra for pulling the country out of the current divisive politics and populism. He has not even suggested a debate in the case of either of these important themes as he suggested in the case of simultaneous elections, for example. Speaking to journalists at BJP headquarters on 3 November 2016, he urged the media to encourage debate on constructive subjects and referred to the idea of simultaneous elections for the third time in as many weeks. He referred to none of the other more fundamental issues he himself had raised and which need more urgent follow-up in everyone's interest.[24]

These reminders of Modi deserve to be followed up seriously by the institutions of the country. These are the *minimum mantras* that Modi government should pursue towards ushering in good governance. By applying these propositions, Modi is likely to stand out for two things. One, he meant what he preached and stood for unleashing good governance. These five public statements alone could take his government to newer heights and distinguish his from the previous governments.

Notes and References

1. *The Pioneer*, 23 January 2018.
2. *The Hindu*, 8 September 2016.
3. *Business Standard*, 11 August 2016 (Nilanjan Mukhopadhyay, senior journalist who wrote a biography of Prime Minister Modi).
4. *Eenadu*, 14 August 2016.
5. *The Pioneer*, 8 September 2016.
6. *Times Now*, 30 August 2016.
7. *Times of India*, 27 July 2016.
8. Pradip Khandwalla, *Creative Society: Prospects for India* (New Delhi: Vikas Publishing, 2014).
9. N. Bhaskara Rao, 'Social Audits Are Real Performance Indicators', *Transparency Review* 9, no. 2 (June 2016).
10. Mohit Kumar Daga and Parag Mohanta, *The Wire*, Web daily, 13 September 2017.
11. N. Bhaskara Rao, *Controlled Mass Communication in Conflict Resolution* (Delhi: Chand Publishers, 1970).
12. N. Bhaskara Rao, *Poll Surveys in News Media* (New Delhi: National Book Trust, 2007). Pre-emptive nature of opinion surveys was discussed.
13. *The Pioneer* and *Indian Express*, 16 January 2018.
14. *Sakshi*, 9 December 2016.
15. *Times of India*, 13 June 2016.
16. *Times of India*, 14 June 2016.
17. Harinder Kohli (ed.), *The World in 2050* (New Delhi: Oxford University Press, 2016).
18. *Times of India*, 8 June 2016.
19. *Times of India*, 24 September 2016.
20. Smart Pulse Survey (2016) by Andhra Pradesh government is an example of how field surveys were being organised by state government to support policies and decisions of the government with unreliable field methodology.
21. *Eenadu*, 31 August 2016; *The Hindu*, 28 October 2016.
22. News X, 28 October 2016, news bulletins.
23. *Eenadu*, 30 August 2016.
24. *Times of India*, 4 November 2016.

CHAPTER 6

Rights Regime

In India, rights have never been provided legally for citizens as they are being provided for at present, but the big question is whether the public is aware of these rights. To enable citizens to avail these rights, several mechanisms or instruments are also provided for. Activists can make a profound difference only if they avail these provisions individually or as a group. But then there are certain rights about which successive governments have taken a lukewarm view and even tried to scuttle them, and in fact a couple of them have not yet come on board. If citizens avail these rights it would brighten the prospects of good governance and also deepen democratic traditions.

Major initiatives of the governments of last decades includes legalising rights of citizens in availing public services. The range of initiatives being comprehensive, it can be said that a rights' regime has set in. If provisions and objectives of these various rights are unleashed and also availed, the face of the country will change for better and chances of good governance taking roots will be as never before. However, that is not feasible without the next incoming government promoting the provisions. The pillars of republic have to be active, proactive, involved and participative in the process of asserting the rights by citizens.

Both society and political parties can make a difference in particular by taking forward the citizen rights from being mere entitlements to becoming enablers. The mechanisms that help citizens realise these rights have also been activated recently with continuous efforts. This brings out that mere the government promoting the rights even though they are all there, as in the case of consumer rights, has not made much difference beyond a 'deterrence influence'. Apathy and conflict of interest in the government has added to the dilemma in the case of education, making the rights like RTE irrelevant or of no consequence. RTI, on the other hand, reflects the lukewarm outlook or half-hearted efforts of the government instead of availing RTI for much needed paradigm shift and achieve a win–win. Operation level linkage of politics, or connection of MGNREGS to vote bank politics, has diluted and diffused the very futility of right to employment.

A review of the ground level scenario indicates that perhaps these rights and provisions have not made as much a difference as their potential can. Experience shows that the most potential RTI Act remained undiluted so far for 13–14 years because of citizen activism despite efforts of the government, the executive and even the judiciary's lukewarm approach across all levels—the Union, States, Districts and in the context of other state agencies and political parties.

Pillars of republic too often clash with them on one or the other issue. For example, in November 2016, the Attorney General reminded the judiciary of the *lakshman rekha* when the Chief Justice, T.S. Thakur observed that delay in appointment of Judges is only accumulating the pending cases. Occasions of such accusations were not rare between the judiciary and the legislature. On the Constitution day, 26 November 2016, the government had put out advertisements in print media listing 11 'duties' of the citizens under the Constitution. This is in the context of rights vs responsibility dilemma, but no leader of the ruling party or of other parties or any other agency took up the full-page claims with ground level realities. Schools should have taken up this task, for example. Accusations of not seriously taking up citizen duties and responsibilities are also frequent between political parties and media, and the government and the media.

Children not only have the right to be protected against ill treatment, there are several other provisions as well. Four main ones are right to survive, right to participate, right to development and right to schooling. Similarly, consumers have a separate set of rights in acquiring goods and services. What difference have we seen in the last decade despite these provisions? Why there has been no review and assessment of such provisions?

There cannot be an all-time valid formula for good governance. It has to be experimented and get evolved as per the local conditions. Good governance is a dynamic concept, but there could be a framework outlining the critical parameters with a potential to make a difference sooner or later. A formula that I have proposed (later in this chapter) should indicate the kind of interlinks among factors that make a difference in the relationships. Good governance is an outcome of effective or efficient linkages among variables and systems that matter in the process. Rights that citizens are entitled to and avail with transparency in that process, for example, are key variables for good governance, particularly in the context of basic public services that most citizens seek.

To facilitate the process, different instruments are provided for by the government over time. It is for the pillars of the state to ensure that these rights are availed by citizens. How well and reliably citizens avail these rights critical for a good governance?

The rights that a citizen is entitled to could broadly be viewed as the fundamental rights provided in the Constitution like freedom of expression, right to vote, contest in an election, etc., but even these fundamental ones have certain qualifications. To vote, for example, one has to be 18 years of age, to contest also one has to be of certain age depending on whether the election is for panchayat or assembly or parliament. There are some qualifications expressed by the United Nations conventions that various countries are trying to adopt. Not all of them were endorsed by every country. Right to expression, for example, is subject to the neighbour's privileges. There are also special rights that one is eligible for privileges, like the ones employed are eligible for provident fund, gratuity, or maternity leave if they work beyond certain years; those who are jailed still have certain rights like get a driving license or get a passport, etc. One has to qualify with certain conditions. The government of the day can change these conditions and the same have to be approved by the parliament. The government of the time endorses or assures access to basic rights like employment, shelter and food. Surprisingly, health is not indicated specifically as a right under any category, but government, and the party in power, take credit for providing health services as a part of the special entitlement of their regime.

A hallmark of good governance is the ease with which the rights' regime is in effect, where citizens enjoy a range of rights empowered, entitled and also treated in that process as equal. From a citizen's perspective, good governance is one which ensures such rights without discrimination or differentiation on grounds of political, economic, social or cultural origins and that majority–minority issues do not dictate the policies or there will be a scope for discretionary interventions.

There are, on the other hand, policies and practices which vitiate the citizen's freedom, rights and activism. Equality of citizens under Article 14 or 44 of the Constitution is an overriding provision. These could be political depending on which political party is in power or social evils like child labour, dowry, drugs, etc. or cultural practices like entry of women to certain temples, etc. Every citizen has fundamental rights such as the right of life, property and livelihood guaranteed under the Constitution. These rights are not enjoyed at the discretion of the ruling party in government.

Rights Regime and Mechanisms

Successive governments have realised that the days of government achieving massive changes on its own, based on its political power, are over and that public involvement or support is critical. Neither could claim success without the cooperation of the other, tacit or otherwise, and by offering support, sometimes by opposition even, or offering suggestions or making interventions. To achieve this, governments have been coming up with intervening instruments so that citizens can play an active and assertive role. In that process, public opinion and perceptions have become even more important factor for participatory democracy.

Some of the instruments introduced and in vogue for some years are given as an example for illuminating how they are languishing.

1. **Citizen Charter**

   Citizen charter for public services indicates what specific services could be expected from a particular department of the government and within what timeframe. This charter is supposed to be widely displayed in such a way that users and potential users of the services know about the timeframe for each specific service. Citizen charters have been in vogue for more than two decades making no difference. This is as potential as RTI to facilitate governance, but unlike RTI, citizen charter is not backed by an Act. This instrument needs to be revamped and repositioned. Citizen charter should be redrafted after consultation, both with users and providers of the service in a regionally relevant way.

2. **Grievance Redressal Commissions**

   These commissions are supposed to function independently to receive complaints of aggrieved citizens of government services and find out the reasons thereof and address or resolve the same in a transparent way. Thirteen states have such Grievance Redressal Commission set up. Similar arrangement is needed with public services provided by private organisations as well.

3. **Information Commissions Under RTI Act of 2005**

   These Commissions exist separately for the services provided by the central as well as state governments although each government appoints its Commission. They are supposed to operate independently and facilitate citizens to get replies to their queries on decisions and functioning of public funded services within a prescribed time. This systems are in effect for 13–14 years now. The Commissions are expected to see that departments supply the information sought by the citizen and also promote suo motto flow of information as an obligation. If a citizen does not get the information sought for, he or she can appeal to the Commission, which is expected to probe into and order the concerned agencies to provide information, even fine them if it is called for.

4. **Service Delivery Guarantee Act**

Since many basic public services are the responsibility of state governments, most states have passed in the last couple of years a special legislation to guarantee citizens with delivery of certain public services. Madhya Pradesh Government passed this Act in August 2010 and Bihar in 2011. Andhra Pradesh Assembly did it in 2018. The number of services that come under this provision range from 30 to 50 and the states are competing to add more and more services. This Act provides for penalising the officers responsible for the service in case of delay in providing the service. However, this Act by states has made no difference so far in any of the states and, in fact, it is hardly talked about after the concerned Minister announced it. This Act has not become a serious pursuit as it deserved to be and the governments do not seem to have promoted the Act and its provisions. Most civic activists are not yet aware of such a provision even after five years of the Act, when, in fact, they could have pursued better along with RTI. This should be a priority of active citizenry, otherwise this too will be forgotten.

5. **Social Audit**

Social audit has come to practice from an initiative of this author taken outside the government as an independent instrument to see that citizens benefit from the schemes, policies and programmes of the government and the schemes in turn get modified based on the experiences of the citizens. Except in the case of MGNREGS, where social audit has been incorporated as an obligatory arrangement, it is more talked about than acted upon. There is no legal sanction for a social audit. It is now being adopted by widely spread public services involving disadvantaged citizens or regions in particular. However, the methodology of social audit has not been grasped widely. For example, social audit panel wherever appointed comprises mostly those who are part of the project and responsible for its implementation. Social audit yields results only when the society is actively involved.

6. **Public Interest Litigation (PIL)**

PIL was formally recognised by Justice P.N. Bhagwati, former Chief Justice of India, more than three decades ago in 1985–1986. An aggrieved citizen or someone on behalf of the larger public could file an appeal before a higher court, which can have implications for the larger public. The court can also pursue a public cause on a suo motto basis going by a media report or some such source, including letters written to the judiciary by an agonised or a responsible person like a professor or an activist with a track record. Anuj Bhuwan well described after research in the only book on PIL, *Courting the People* (2017)[1] how PIL became an instrument of the Judiciary to even micromanage governance. The book refers to a dozen specific instances of PIL changing the face of Delhi in the recent decades.

7. **Rights Provision Under Various Legislations**

Consumer Act is one such act which is provided for. Many of the rights already provided for are hardly known to the larger public even after it's more than a decade-long promotion in the media by the government. In some cases, perhaps because the right provided for has not made any difference or perhaps that was not good enough to generate a ripple effect. The Consumer Act provides for a combination of rights. These include right to safety (from ill effects of the product), right to information on products, right to choice, right to be heard, right to seek redressal, and even right to consumer education. Organisational infrastructure is created at union, state and district levels with forums, redressal courts, and so on, to implement the Act. And yet even general awareness about it is hardly there. Only one out of five consumers has availed many of these consumer rights. Awareness is much low despite that a Consumer Week is celebrated annually for some years now as a campaign for consumer activism.

8. **Consumer Redressal Forum**

   These are available under the Consumer Act for any end user of a product or service available in the market, outside the government, but one needs to file a formal complaint. The new 2015 Consumer Protection Act seeks to replace the 1986 Act. Consumer protection authority is empowered to initiate complaints and investigate and penalise any lapse on the part of the manufacturer or the retailer of the product.

9. **Lok Pal Act 2014**

   Lok Ayukta Panel, appointed by the union government, has to deal with complaints against government services/agencies. All or most in these panels consists of retired judicial persons. Despite politicising of the institution, it has not become an effective forum for citizens. Although the law was enacted four years ago after considerable debate, governments including one of the Union, have not implemented and appointed a Lokpal, a chairperson and members. That should not undermine the potential of the idea of Lokpal.

10. **Whistle Blower Act 2014**

    Whistle Blower Protection Act 2014 is pending operationalisation with rules for four years. Despite over 65 killings and 500 threats across the country in a decade for asking questions under RTI, no protection is being provided to the concerned person(s). The whistle blower Act is only a first step in that direction. This Act aims to protect the people who bring to the notice of the authorities concerned allegations of corruption, wilful misuse of power against a public functionary or system, which they come across in the course of their work. With certain slackness, recently in the very momentum of RTI, more threats could be expected in coming months unless protection measures are provided at district, state and union levels. However, why the government is delaying its implementation is not known.

11. **Human Rights Commission.**

    This commission, created under an Act of the Parliament, is expected to act on the complaints registered by the aggrieved party or on a suo motto basis after even a news report. Despite of the fact that this commission is headed mostly by a retired Chief Justice and provided with budgetary support, some of the provisions are not given the kind of seriousness and promotions that they deserve.

Basic Public Services for Good Governance

Basic public services are those services which are essentially required and availed by most citizens of the country sometime or another. In a good governance scenario, what eventually matters is how well these services are catered and provided for without the citizens having to indulge in any deviating methods like paying bribes or using a middle contact. Broadly, basic public services that contribute to good governance could be universal or need-based but critical.

A. **Some basic public services include:**
   - Health
   - School
   - Water Supply/Drinking Water
   - Electricity Supply
   - Public distribution system (PDS) or Availability of Essential Food Items
   - Police Services
   - Basic Certificates Needed by a Citizen
B. **Need-based services include:**
   - Land records and registration
   - Housing
   - Banking
   - MGNREGS
   - Forest services
C. **Other public services that a citizen uses include:**
   - Municipal services
   - Phone
   - Railways
   - Passport
   - Income Tax

- Judiciary/Justice
- Transport services (getting a driving license, etc.)
- Postal Services

The provisions for complaints and redressal of grievances in availing these public services is of much consequence to good governance. Citizen rights in this process of availing facilities could make a difference as to the pride and confidence level of citizenry.

Six Pillars of the State

In the earlier sections, it was discussed that why and how the three systems—media, society and political parties—should be viewed as pillars of the state the same way as judiciary, executive and legislature are. Desired outcomes for the country are possible on a sustained basis only when these six pillars work in tandem and in a spirit of checks and balance rather than in a suspicious and a conflicting way. In a nutshell, the six pillars are:

1. The *Judiciary*, to uphold the constitution of the country.
2. The *legislature*, to pass appropriate laws to govern the affairs and economy of the country.
3. The *executive*, to implement the policies of the legislature within the framework of the Constitution.
4. The *media*, as nerves of the state and functioning independently as a watch dog for public affairs.
5. The *civil society*, comprising larger population of the country, go beyond elected legislators into organised groups and forums for an over-arching role in a self-motivated and sustaining way much beyond political parties.
6. The *political system*, comprising political parties, seek public endorsement for their agenda in an electoral process and come to the legislatures. Conventionally, political parties are viewed as a part of legislature. However, experience of 70 years brings out that as political parties they play more significant role detrimental to the very functioning of other pillars including the legislature. Moreover, they do not have accountability and responsibility compulsions.

Why Political Parties?

Political parties were much pampered and looked upon in earlier decades as some kind of umbrella organisations. Over the years, they have become overriding and overpowered institutions, but without any checks and balance, discipline and even without accountability. Besides, they dictate future course and directions of the country. Although carved out of civil society, political parties have become super-bodies, institutionalised and bureaucratised, imposing their own rules on citizens, candidates, poll process, legislature and the executive. In a parliamentary democracy, one cannot imagine a State without the active role of political parties. In view of such a situation, it is appropriate to view them separately from the legislature and society and as the sixth pillar of the republic.

The six pillars are expected to work in a checks and balance way to maintain an equilibrium to ensure that everything is going according to the Constitution and uphold it. They operate without intruding and eroding the role and responsibilities of each other but may be sometimes in a competition to get most out of their continuing relations. That is why I describe this phenomena as a six-pronged pursuit for governance, democracy and development. Right to education and Right to information are important legislations with lasting implications. How these rights are subverted in connivance of the government need to be talked about. If the governments themselves subvert the rights of citizens, what would be the fate of such legislation if citizen groups are not alert and proactive?

Dilemma of Right to Education

Education too contributes indirectly in sustaining good governance in a special way, especially the primary and secondary education. It holds the key to social transformation, future perspectives, knowledge quest of a generation and economic growth of a country. Despite constitutional provisions for compulsory and free education to all children, governments have failed to develop and manage schools and the parents too have failed to assert their right. The political parties did more harm, if anything, in pushing education to become a dilemma and allowed it to become a business proposition. It is only recently that the Supreme Court has taken some interest in this regard. They could have intervened suo motto much earlier. Today, education system too is a factor, as in the case of electoral politics, to determine the kind of governance we have. The question is, can we expect big changes without correctives in our education system?

The Constitution mandated compulsory and free education to all children for 10 years from 1950, but the government ignored it. Though we have better infrastructure today and there is RTI Act, which can be availed for Right to education as provided under Act of 2009, and parents to have a right and duty to fight for their children for quality and fair education. Initiatives of political parties and society are too few to make a difference in this regard.

On the contrary, Delhi Private School Association questioned the Delhi Government's enquiry about salaries of teachers and even protested it. Every private school has to give information under RTI Act about admissions and education be provided to 25 per cent students enrolled from poorer sections in such schools. Providing education is also a service under Consumer Protection Act, 1986, Section 2(d). But the question is, do we have any examples?[2]

All India Parents Association, when met in New Delhi on March 2016, demanded regulation of private school fee structure. Parents from 18 states who attended that meet demanded a law to regulate fees and other charges in private schools. The Association opposed the 'commercialisation of education' at the primary level and said that the quality of school education has been declining post liberalisation and has now reached its nadir. The rights have remained more as a 'bureaucratic exercise' and failed to focus on the 'holistic development' of school education. However, that concern has not been followed up in or endorsed by any other states.

The RTE Act 2009 provided that schools as public authorities are duty bound to provide information to local bodies and government agencies; even private schools should provide information under that Act. Main duties of parents and guardians include admission of children into a school. As per various sections of the Act, the duties of appropriate government include providing free and compulsory elementary education to every child, ensure availability of a neighbourhood school as specified with infrastructure, and ensure that any child belonging to weaker sections of the society is not discriminated from pursuing and completing schooling. Moreover, there should be a parents association at every level to secure children's right under Right to Education. But what is the extent of their concern? Why Parents in most parts of the country are not vocal of the decay?

Equality in accessing quality education is though a fundamental right under Article 14 read with Right to Life under Article 21, stories coming out from various parts of the country are contrary. No wonder why Allahabad High Court directed (in 2015) all public servants to send their children to public schools. Right to Education will be realised only when every child in India gets education as standard Kendriya Vidyalaya (KV), but huge advertisements across the sky in metropolitan cities continue to be displayed by schools flaunting international tags and luring parents and children to a superficial world.

Delhi Government made an attempt (2015–2016) to regulate private education by passing three Bills, which are stalled at different levels for political reasons. These schools are prohibited to interview a child for admission and charge capitation fees. Violation of this could be a fine up to ₹5 lakh and even imprisonment. Why such provisions are not considered in most other places?

RTI Crying Out for Revival

Unlike in the USA, where it took two years for Freedom of Information Act to come into operation, Right to Information Act in India took off almost immediately after it was passed by the parliament. RTI being a tool for good governance, delivery of public service matters more than mere giving information. An analysis of who is seeking what information indicates how well the Act is being availed. With Digital India in air, prompt supply of information should be possible to make RTI far more relevant and its impact much more evident.

Finance Minister Arun Jaitely reminded at the 10th anniversary convention of RTI (2015) that RTI is not only for transparency, but should also facilitate governance and make it citizen-centric. As he reminded that RTI has been a success story, the question arises how that success has been possible? First, although initially I opposed, appointing retired senior bureaucrats at the outset as Chief Information Commissioners had helped to quickly establish the Commissions at the Union and in the states. As a senior IAS officer, Wajahat Habibullah, the first Chief of Central Information Commission, for example, played a key role and set a good example in organising the Central Commission. Some of those Commissioners from journalism background in some states like Kerala and Andhra Pradesh, too had set good precedents.

It is also to the credit of activists and organisations that RTI soon acquired traits of a mass movement. A meet of commissioners that I organised in January 2006 in Hyderabad too helped expedite implementation process. This meet at Administrative Staff College of India (ASCI) discussed modalities of Information Commissions going about with priority concerns. Commissioners were appointed in eight states at that time but had not started working yet. They had the benefit of deliberating steps to quickly get going with the implementations of the Act. Ajit Bhattacharjea, Sekhar Gupta, Nikhil Dey, Maja Daruwala, Dr Jaya Prakash Narayan, Arvind Kejriwal, among others, were the key participants in that first meet on RTI Act. It was Kejriwal's first tour outside New Delhi. He and I met the local activists from various fields next day in the local CMS office and chalked out campaign plans for creating awareness about the Act and ways of going about availing the Act. Thereafter, many others elsewhere too picked up to scale up the momentum. Aruna Roy, whose pursuit has made the Act a reality, launched CMS's *Transparency Review* magazine in early 2006 to cover and analyse RTI implementation across the states. Initially, Information Commissioners wrote their experiences in this journal. I had the privilege of taking part in all the annual conventions of CIC over the years in New Delhi. I analysed the participation and deliberations of these meets for *Transparency Review*.

Professor Madhav Menon, chairing one of the sessions at the 10th Convention of RTI in 2015, rightly observed that 'RTI lost enthusiasm' of earlier years. This could be for two reasons. First many of the commissioners, including the Chief of CIC, were on the verge of completing their tenure around the same time as the first generation commissioners were on way out. Second, rather unusually, as compared to previous years, there was hardly any participation in 2015 Convention of activists, who played key role over the years in taking forward the rights regime in the country. Out of some 26 panel members, for example, only three were from outside the government and only two[3] actually attended and made good presentations. The 10th Convention missed an opportunity of being citizen-centric as there were hardly any there to mention their perspectives. Also the Convention should have regretted the killing of over two dozen RTI activists and threats to many more. However, delay in the Whistle Blower legislation was not even referred to and regretted. The 11th Convention supposed to have held on 12 October 2016 was held the following month after postponing twice and without the Prime Minister attending it. In fact, the Prime Minister did not even refer to RTI even as a formality and not even on Twitter or in his 'Man Ki Bat' radio programmes.

Although Professor M. Sridhar Acharyulu, an active commissioner of CIC, referred directly and indirectly to some of the issues crippling the RTI Commissions, there was no discussion on any of those issues facing RTI movement in the country, neither in that convention nor subsequently as a follow up. The activist model that Acharyulu demonstrated at Central Information Commission (2014–2018) offers hope for revival of the rights regime in the country.

The Information Commissions, including the CIC, suffer today on account of subdued compliance of their orders. Political parties' refusal to come under RTI preview is one of the glaring examples. The backlog in Commissions with piling of applications and appeals is due to lack of staff, delays in appointing commissioners, reduced budgets, government appointment of those whose support record was against the very spirit of transparency are some examples of that uncertainty. Implementation of Section 4 of RTI Act on suo motto continues to be a low key concern and no correctives have been specifically taken up despite recent spread of communication networks and increased resource allocations for that specific purpose and priority of the government for e-governance. One-fourth or more of the applications received continue to be rejected under the excuse of 'privacy', the excuse of 'exemptions' is being accepted more and more by the Commissions.

Every annual convention deliberated digitalisation and RTI, but there were no pointers for taking on or to expect qualitative change in the implementation of provisions of RTI Act. Most panel members at the annual convention were former secretaries of IT Ministry. Many participants referred to delays in giving replies and how that vitiates the very purpose, but how digitalisation could bring relief was not talked about or taken up for a follow-up. Do we, in digital age, need 30 days to respond? Why the number of applications does not increasing? Why a majority of RTI applications come from the same people? One would expect that information technology would have made a difference in reviving enthusiasm in RTI movement. Websites of these commissions, on the other hand, are not even active and updated in time when new media should have come handy for sustaining the movement for transparency. Video conferences are hardly held or not at all by some commissions. Applicants need not come from all the way and all the time to the State Commissions to its capital for filing the applications. Why do women constitute hardly 10 per cent of the applicants even after a decade?

The need in 2018–2019 is to think 'beyond information' so that people avail other instruments and measures currently available. For example, Service Delivery Guarantee (SDG) Act, which more than a dozen states have adopted, has penalty provision for officers responsible for refusal or delay in ensuring delivery of the service. This could be linked to RTI. Similarly, both Citizen Charters (CC), which most public services have adopted with specific timelines set, and Social Audit (SA) for some public services with the involvement of citizens could be linked with RTI. These measures together with RTI add to the potential of each to achieve good governance. A few years ago, I suggested to activists in the field, who are somewhat desperate or disappointed with RTI implementation, to go the extra mile and take a holistic view of their pursuit. The delay in the implementation of whistle blower act and increase in threats to the activists have added to the situation. The good governance (GG) formula I suggested is

$GG=RTI+SDG+CC+SA+ICT$, which acts as a helping hand in taking rights regime forward. Activists and organisations should adopt these enablers together in their fight against corruption; only information is not an end in itself. ICT facilitates this process further. National outfits like the Human Rights Commission should take on RTI route rather than merely relying on information in public purview.

I am convinced that RTI has a long way to go to get firmly set in the country. At the time of its 10th anniversary (2015), I circulated and also published an article 'RTI need to be saved from becoming archaic'. Although the role of the government and the commissions in the task of reviving RTI is significant, in 2018 it should not be limited to them. Society and its various organs too have to play a key role. For, the seriousness that RTI Act enjoyed in the last decade is no longer there. On the contrary, it has come to be viewed by many in powers as an 'inconvenient law'. By the end of the first five years of RTI, CMS had brought out that hardly 5 per cent of applications were from women and very few came from poor and from people living far away from the district headquarters.[4] Moreover, there were fewer applications for information on social schemes and the concerned departments in comparison to applications that were for urban development, infrastructure, and the like. Ironically, most applications were from people in powerful positions, including employees themselves. We have not come a long way in the last couple of years in strengthening RTI regime in the country.

RTI today, as other citizen rights, requires to be revived from certain slumberness within; activists need to be re-enthused; threats from multiple sources of establishment and those in power need to be exposed and even resisted by civil society groups. Only then citizen rights could catch up with the aspirations of people. Academics, researchers and news media need to change their gears too in this context in collaboration with activists. If the Prime Minister could reiterate government's resolve, for example, in support of RTI, it will go a long way in restoring RTI. Those leaders in the government should periodically reiterate their resolve to implement legislations and the provisions for citizen rights.

Notes and References

1. Anuj Bhuwania, *Courting the People: Public Litigation in Post Emergency India* (New Delhi: Cambridge University Press, 2017).
2. 'Revolutionizing Education Not Possible with Fee Tabs', *Times of India*, 2 November 2016, https://timesofindia.indiatimes.com/city/bengaluru/Revolutionizing-education-not-possible-with-fee-tabs/articleshow/55196892.cms? (Accessed 27 August 2018).
3. Those were Venkatesh and Anjali of Common Wealth Human Rights. Both have been active last decade with analysis-based advocacy and contributed in keeping RTI Act as a dynamic instrument of transparency. Anjali is also the founder of Satark Nagrik Sangathan.
4. N. Bhaskara Rao, 'Saving RTI from Becoming Archaic', *Transparency Review* 8, no. 2 (June, 2015); *Idem.*, 'A Decade of RTI: Information is Not an End in Itself', *Transparency Review* 8, no. 4 (December, 2015); *Idem.*, 'RTI Best Bet for Political Parties', *Transparency Review* 6, no. 3 (August, 2013); *Idem.*, 'Right to Information: Six Years of RTI', *Transparency Review* 4, no. 3 (July, 2011); *Idem.*, 'Agenda for the Third Year of RTI', *Transparency Review* 1, no. 1 (January, 2008).

CHAPTER 7

Could There Be a Formula to Go About?

There is no formula to a way out from the current impasse in the development and functioning of democracy. The scene is somewhat like Rubik's cube: one has to go through a series of steps in the process to have a single colour on each face of the cube. Without political intervention, these steps will yield only incremental change. It is in taking up these various interventions in the case of each of the six pillars together that matters. Apart from this, schools and ICT matter too. Of the few examples given for each of the six pillars and the schools and ICT, even if a few interventions are pursued seriously and in parallel, we could expect to be on the course to achieving good governance and rejuvenating the republic.

A formula is one which helps to identify key intervening factors and understand the relationships and the interplay between the options and outcomes. A formula indicates that value of an individual factor multiplies when it works in combination of other factors. In a combination of the same factors, results differ, many times more than what individually it adds up to. A formula is a simplistic way of explaining the process of change and outcomes and linkage between factors. Good governance is a complex outcome, result of a series of developments on several fronts, over time. It implies much more and much beyond decisiveness and popularity aspects and what the government does at any given time. A few interventions or initiatives taken up together can unveil an environment of good governance, but by themselves alone, they may not amount to good governance in the same time frame.

Good governance is the result of how citizen-centric governments function and how well the rights of the citizens could be availed without having to bribe or go through a contact, how well complaints are redressed and attended to, how inclusive the government policies are and how involved is the society in moving things forward.

Activists, particularly those engaged in RTI, were recently somewhat disappointed with the lukewarm outlook of the governments about RTI and certain recent slowdown in the transparency movement in the country. From my field visits over the years and interactions with activists in the field, I have found that activists pursued RTI as if by itself it would result in the decline in corruption, that government would become more responsive and problems would be redressed. Based on extensive interactions in the field and a series of studies of CMS over 15 years (2000–2018),[1] I have realised that unless their crusade is integrated with others' crusades for rights, the desired difference will not come through and be evident. For this vacuum, I suggested the activists and potential whistle blowers in the field to take on multiple activities including the provision of other rights as one integrated package and use instruments that are already available in a sequence or are parallel. Such an approach is also an effective way of pursuing good governance, reducing corruption and enhancing the transparency in the processes.

Dr Bibek Debroy, before becoming a member of the NITI Aayog, proposed a formula for corruption free governance, which is equal to (Monopoly + Discretionary power) − (Accountability + Integrity + Transparency). According to this formula, monopoly and discretionary practices of the bureaucracy neutralise accountability and the transparency features of a government.

My concept of good governance is much more than the government and its officers. Citizen-centric good governance formula, in my opinion, could be: RTI + (CC + SG + GR) + (SA + ICT), where SA is Social

Audit, CC is Citizen Charter, SDG is Service Delivery Guarantee, GR is Grievance Redressal and ICT is Information Communication Technologies. I also found certain negative features or stumbling blocks that need to be addressed simultaneously.

Some negative trends in the process of accomplishing good governance are:

- Discretionary opportunities of the executive
- Electoral compulsions of the political parties
- Pro-monopoly view of the government agencies
- Public opinion mobilisation or formation trends of news media
- Passivity of citizen and society, particularly the academics

Initiatives and Instruments

From a range of instruments that are available, some critical ones to make a difference for citizen are: citizen charter, social audit, PIL, news and other media and society networks, e-governance, RTI, etc.

With information received from RTI application, one could file a PIL, or go to the consumer court or seek redressal from one of the redressal forums. Under the Service Delivery Guarantee Act of the state, punitive action could be taken against the official responsible for the lapse in the delivery of the service. News and media could expedite this process in the larger interest only if they are proactive in their coverage.

These interventions could be pursued simultaneously in the context of availing basic public services. In this process, all six pillars of the State have a role to play. The Judiciary is expected to uphold the legal rights of an individual. The constitution is for equity and social justice without intruding into the rights of other citizens. The Executive is expected to work in a way to avail the opportunity to win back the respect and credibility they once enjoyed. The news media is expected to come under the purview of RTI on their own. The political parties and leaders should view this as an opportunity to rejuvenate their standing among people by coming under RTI coverage. Society, particularly the academics, could help build an atmosphere for good governance by taking to independent appraisals, as to who is taking advantage of the new rights regime and era of transparency. News media and communication technology could make considerable difference in shaping, speeding and scaling up the process of good governance inclusive of development. Together they could even expedite the process and deepen the democracy.

The formula indicated here is only an example. The pursuit of good governance is to sustain the status as an ongoing concern, irrespective of who wins or loses in an election and which leader is at the helm. This, however, does not mean that the party elected or the leader at the helm prefers status quo. On the contrary, good governance as a framework is expected to facilitate achievement of the basic goals ahead of the concerns of the political parties.

Initiatives That Could Usher in Good Governance

No initiative or correction in any of the six pillars of the State will usher in the claimed good governance in India; they may not even expedite that process. The need is a series of urgent initiatives in each case. Good governance will never be in sight without a series of interventions inter- and intra-sector. Only then one could say that a situation for good governance would be available and the government could claim to offer good governance. Based on the discussions in the earlier chapters, an effort has been made in this chapter to sum up about 50 interventions that could be considered as a 'package' across the six pillars of the Republic, which could make a difference.

The combinations of options that need to be pursued, at a given point, are difficult to envisage fully and to realise their outcome is also difficult. But it is essential to make significant differences in a few years, or at least in a decade. A concern-based perspective for the future of the country is necessary. The ruling party at the Union and even the senior most bureaucrats have to show their grit to pursue a course with timely interventions. The citizens and the society should support the package of initiatives and vice versa. There will be at least two general elections in the next decade. However, there may or may not be a changeover of the party in power. Not all interventions suggested here require repositioning and constitutional amendments, but offer opportunity to the parties to take over. Over the next couple of general elections, it should be possible to take many of the corrective measures and bring in the kind of changes, alterations or initiatives that scale up India's quest for a just society and more equitable, inclusive and accountable systems, which is essential for good governance.

It is not a control and command view at the Union level, but a checks and balance approach, where each pillar tries to do better for a more efficient overall performance without intruding into the domains of others and without seeking a homogenised view of the country. And in such a way the role of the six pillars becomes evident for a sustained equilibrium situation of governance.

Isn't Having a Vision Good Governance?

NITI Aayog's urge 'to align their planning to that of the Centre' and the advice to the chief secretaries of states to be in sync with the 'Centre's 15-year vision document, strategy and the action plan', is counterproductive to the very spirit of federalism. Expecting the states to ask for permissions of NITI Aayog and go by the advices (or confine to) of Union Government strictly is counterproductive to the very spirit of federalism and union–state relationships.[2] This idea of a 15-year plan, in place of the earlier Five Year Plan itself, expecting all states to follow a pattern, goes against the very mindset of federalism. We do need a long-term perspective and long-term goals. But these has to be that of the people, not of a party or a leader. Such a plan needs to be promoted so that the adopted goals become those of the states, not just of the Union government in office. This requires an exercise first at the state level. The Union plan should take into account aspirations and priorities of the states, particularly those which have remained static in their development over the decades.

NITI Aayog or any other body could make a 15- or 50-year plan for the development of the country, but that should be discussed and debated amongst the masses and the process should be transparent. Describing a document made by a few officers in New Delhi, however, capable they may be, as a 'vision document' for the country, is questionable. For, a long-term vision of the country, the states and the people should be involved transparently. Any such vision has to qualify as to 'whose vision' so that the document reflects for whom or for whose advantage it has been prepared. Any formal official engagement, as routinely by those whose mandate is for five years or less, becomes a hindrance in creating such a vision. Again, any agency which does not have a legal standing creating an action plan for 15 years is also not an ideal situation. How irrelevant it is to ask the states and state chief secretaries to 'formally align to a 15-year plan' without acquiring the states' input in the matter? Such a document could, however, be sent for a discussion as a proposition for ideas to think about and debate upon certain critical and contentious issues.

Some 15 years ago, the Planning Commission conducted an exercise for India 2020 without generating any visible outcome. Earlier, two publications had come out, both of which talked about the long-term perspective of India. The first one was a book I had edited, which was published in 1986 as *India 2021*, based on analytical work I was involved at ORG based in Vadodara. Even earlier, in 1978, ORG had conducted an India 2001 exercise and published the same in four volumes. In the introduction of this book, I argued that the concept of five-year plans was outlived and that India's basic problems were not amenable to a five-year perspective of the Planning Commission. But a more popular and much discussed pioneering exercise was *India 2020* of Dr A.P.J. Abdul Kalam and techno-scientist Dr Y.S. Rajan. It was before Dr Kalam became the President. It was through this publication of Dr Kalam and Dr Rajan, the idea of a long-term strategy for development received a boost even in the various states of India. The exercise I did for the Andhra Pradesh Chief Minister Chandrababu Naidu in 2000, 'AP Vision 2020', triggered a similar kind of exercise in some other states too. But neither the India 2020 nor the AP Vision 2020 considered 'future's perspective' a serious pursuit at any level, including academic. Chandrababu Naidu was the only leader who kept talking about such a 'vision' for two long decades, but without involving the state and its people in any of the exercises and at any stage that such an exercise requires. The suggestion here is that long-term plans for the country (or even for a state) should preferably be formulated with equal contribution of the government and the people.

It Is a Six-pronged Pursuit

Prime Minister Narendra Modi is already a change maker and has shifted the very paradigm of politics in many respects. He will be in a better position to go way beyond and set new records in the annals as the leader who pulled the country out of a certain stalemate and the state of stagnation in the mindset and outlook of the public at large. He can risk taking initiatives to decentralise the affairs. If he could change the name of a 65-year-old institution from Planning Commission to NITI Aayog, if he could come up with a 15-year plan instead of a five-year plan, if he could come up with a proposal of having simultaneous elections to Lok Sabha and state assemblies and get across the parties in Parliament, pass a contentious uniform tax (GST) requiring constitutional amendment, he could as well go all the way to reverse the centralisation model in vogue to a pyramidal structure without eroding the sovereignty of the republic. Such an initiative will set a base for transforming India and help it leapfrog to greater heights. This also means that India will not only become a truly democratic country, but will also serve as a working model for a decentralised and participative democracy with inclusive development.

It also means rejuvenating and renewing the federal character of the country. This has to happen at three levels. In the mindset of the political leaders, in the public policies and in the mandate of the institutions. As a first step, we should replace the nomenclature 'Centre' with 'Union' and change the perception that Union is a 'big brother' in New Delhi. Union government should not position itself in a 'control and command' position but function with in a 'checks and balances' framework.

In this framework, the Union government should focus on the core responsibilities, having to do with defence, external affairs, monetary issues, natural resource management, infrastructure, etc. The usurpation of the responsibilities of the states by Union over the years, particularly in the context of basic public utilities and services, should be reversed, and this will not happen unless the Union winds up some ministries that duplicate the responsibilities of the states. Only then it could be a less government and more governance.

Good governance is a six-pronged pursuit. It is a key feature of parliamentary democracy. Each one of the pillars matters and needs to move in tandem, in a measured way and in a checks and balance framework. Neither could claim achievements without cooperation and support of one another. Political power alone will not be sufficient. Gone are those days, when public opinion and peoples' involvement from bottom up didn't matter. That is a holistic approach to transform India.

The interventions suggested here are specific but not detailed. It is not some of these suggestions but each and all of them in the case of each of the six pillars that need to be taken up for optimising the governance–democracy–development trajectory.

Political Parties

Without correctives in the functioning and role of the political parties, no change for the better could be expected in India initially, on any front including governance. Some such initiatives needed are mentioned here. Only a separate and well-defined exercise could do justice in crystallising these correctives. These are outlined here, not necessarily in a sequence.

Without political parties coming under or confining to basic democratic principles and a regulatory frame work, there cannot be a distinct change in the country for good governance. This is indeed necessary in the long-term interest of political parties and also of the country's democracy, development and governance. The unleashing of true spirit of democracy is possible only then. Their functioning need to be transparent and they should be accountable to people within the confines of country's Constitution.

The process of the formation of political parties, their functioning and continuity from election to election cannot be undertaken without falling under minimum accountability provisions. The agency (ECI), which registers parties and expects their confirmation to codes from time to time, cannot do so without the power to deregulate or curb certain electoral practices. ECI should be empowered to initiate proceedings to that effect.

No political party should be allowed to be a player without confirming to the internal democracy and whatever rules the party has set for itself as required at the time of registration. Moreover, no political party should be allowed to function without a commitment to uphold the Constitution of the country. And, equally important, a party could continue to be a player in electoral politics only as long as it endorses and confines to free and fair and transparent codes of ECI, particularly and specifically concerning its revenue and expenditure aspects.

A party's poll time manifesto should be an accountable instrument and a basis for seeking votes and campaigning. This should be explicit and provided for in the books of law on a priority, so that ECI could restrain lures offered in it.

One-person, one-post-at-a-time in the party, for three consecutive terms or a 15-year ceiling should be a desirable feature. Political parties should ensure such a limit accordingly and incorporate the same in their constitution. Contesting in elections need not be a criteria for being a political party (ECI had issued notice to some registered parties which never contested an election). As Ramachandra Guha has observed, democracy is much more than elections. He reminded that ours is not an 'election-only democracy'.[3] Some parties may exist for pursuing a cause or facilitating service to people, but transparency in the revenue and expenditure aspects of the political parties should be an essential and obligatory criteria for the renewal or continuation of a party, enrolled with ECI.

Irrespective of the extent of support from the state, political parties should come under RTI. ECI should take necessary initiatives to put forward Central Information Commission's order to the Supreme Court. Such an intervention is necessary and the government should not come in its way. RTI should apply to all political parties, not just to a few major parties. RTI is a good opportunity for political parties to save themselves from their declining credibility.

Polls

We cannot afford to delay the much needed electoral reforms any longer. Parties should realise that by luring voters they might win an election but won't be able to run a government. This is what Prime Minister Narendra Modi himself had aptly remarked.

Simple majority-centric elections, with even a one vote majority to key democratic institutions, particularly Lok Sabha, assemblies and municipalities and other such bodies, need to be reviewed. If the 'first-past-post system' is not replaced with 'proportionate representation system', necessary legal provision should be made for at least a winning margin of 2 to 5 per cent. Over these 70 years, with 15 general elections, and over 400 assembly elections, has any improvement been seen, in the functioning of the Legislatures or in the representative character of the elected ones? Once political parties are brought under some kind of regulatory system, we should consider implementing a proportionate representation system sooner or later, but in the meanwhile this simple majority provision needs to be legally provided for. CPI has been advocating proportional representation system.

Both political parties and candidates contesting elections should come under electoral codes of ECI and accountability and transparency laws of the land. If 45 legislators in a non-democratic country like China could be disqualified in one go for electoral fraud,[4] why a democratic country, which boasts of free and fair polls, has not disqualified even a dozen members in 70 years for the violation of poll codes? (Only one member has been disqualified so far—that was in 2016).

It is time we consider and experiment with 'primaries' for potential candidates, to start with Lok Sabha seats, for instance. Political parties can experiment on their own with some kind of preliminaries so that a person, who is more aware of the local issues, emerges for nomination by the political party to contest an election (at least by a thousand party members spread across the constituency). This is a desirable initiative which may not be feasible in a short term. Independent candidates should be required to get their nomination endorsed by at least a hundred voters spread across the constituency. In the meanwhile, different means of voters knowing more about the respective candidate should be thought about (the current arrangement of a candidate declaring assets, criminal and education background at the time of nomination has not made much difference in the previous many years; nevertheless, that practice should continue). Can the responsibility of voters knowing about candidates be that of the candidate him/herself? Why can't it be obligatory for a candidate to indicate on all publicity material about certain basic elements, including with the areas concerning the aspects of 'conflict of interest'.

Section 123(3) of the Representation of the People Act should be strictly enforced. This provides ground for disqualification of a candidate if he/she or his/her agent or someone in his or her knowledge misuses religion, caste, community or language to garner electoral benefits. A seven-judge bench of the Supreme Court in a majority judgement held that an appeal for votes during elections on the basis of religion, caste, race, community or language will amount to 'corrupt practice' and will call for disqualification of the candidate (3 January 2017).[5] This should be converted into 'do's and don'ts' in consultation with political parties as well as some independent activists.

Those who are convicted in lower courts should be disqualified to contest any election. It needs to be considered that no one should be eligible to contest an election beyond three (15 years) consecutive terms from the same seat.

Those who violate the ECI codes, particularly indulging in unnecessary expenditure and misuse of public money for party campaigns or politics, should be disqualified and enquired into. The ECI should clarify and remove any ambiguity from its orders in this regard. Parties at the state level should be encouraged. Similarly, state funding and joint campaigning by candidates at the constituency level should also be encouraged. Corporates should channel their donations through ECI or designate an agency for further distribution transparently.

Bribing voters should be a cognizable offence. But what constitutes a 'bribe' needs to be specified. Can anything offered to voters outside of a formal manifesto by a party candidate be considered as bribe? Yes, ECI should try to formalize this. An example of such an activity is Aam Aadmi Party's debt *mafi* promise to farmers of Punjab in 2016, taking from farmers in writing about their debts, giving a receipt.

Election commission should have punitive powers over candidates as well as parties, beyond issuing multiple notices on poll violations.

The present provision, which states that a voter can contest from any constituency in the country in the case of Lok Sabha and Assemblies, has not made any difference to national integration. On the contrary, the number of non-resident members of a constituency have multiplied. Local residency should be a prerequisite for any candidate to contest and it should be legally provided for.

In an all-party meet of Election Commission of India on 27 August 2018, the ruling party argued for doing away with any cap on poll expenditure by parties and candidates.[6] Whereas all other parties in that meet advocated continuation of cap as that only ensures level playing field.

On electoral expenditure and funding we seem to be grappling with contradictions. It is known by now that note for vote phenomena has multiplied poll expenditure and the need is to curb and curtail the expenditure. Whereas, what is being done is to open up or loosen poll-funding rules. Earlier there was ceiling on what the corporates could contribute to political parties out of their profits. Now that ceiling has been removed. And when the need is transparency in poll funding, electoral bonds have been introduced in 2017 budget assuring confidentiality on such donations by bonds. There are doubts whether electoral bonds would in fact reduce black money into poll expenditure or increase? The Election Commission's efforts in this regard too seem have received a setback recently with court scuttling the ECI's disqualification of an elected MLA for not accounting the poll expenditure as required.

Holding simultaneous polls for Lok Sabha and Assembly elections goes against consolidation and deepening of democracy. Can't we go back to the practice of having 'party-less polls' for zilla parishads, mandals and gram panchayats? This needs to be explored in consultation with political parties and activists, even selectively. As the President Pranab Mukherjee suggested in April 2017, it is time that number of Lok Sabha constituencies are increased to reflect an increase in population over the last 20 years.

Legislatures

Why the chief ministers and the prime minister are not elected by all members in the House, the same way the Speaker is, in both Lok Sabha and in state assemblies. That means, all the elected members of a state assembly and Lok Sabha elect the leader of the House, cutting across the party lines, even when it is a formality after the election of the leader in the respective legislative party. Whether electing the CM and the PM should be by simple majority or by two-thirds majority present in the House could be decided by two-thirds majority of the House itself at the very first sitting of the House. This can be done without constitutional amendment under Article 86(2). The President can ask the Lok Sabha to elect the leader of the House, who can then be appointed as the Prime Minister by the President.

No confidence motion against a party in government should invariably be accompanied with a confidence expression resolution as an alternative option, so that there is no need for President's Rule or conducting a fresh poll. If a confidence expression resolution is not possible, it should be made obvious before the voting is done.

Another change in the present system suggested is regarding the system of whip. Our legislatures have functioned with the system for 70 years. An analysis of its use and ramifications gives the impression that it has suppressed active participation and representative character of elected legislators. The whip application should be limited to a no confidence situation but may also be used while passing the budget. Whip issued by the legislative parties on other occasions should not be binding.

A third intervention needed is in the context of floor crossing or defection from one party to another after swearing in. Except in the case of proven split of parties with simple majority (instead of present minimum one-third of the strength) as on the day of election, there cannot be any other exceptions for allowing such defections. Neither the anti-defection law nor much debate over the decades has made any difference. Disqualification of anyone who has left one's party from contesting a by-election may work as a deterrence. The anti-defection law should be replaced or amended for clarity and specifies.

The fourth suggestion is live video coverage of proceedings of the House and of its committees. Citizens should have the opportunity to be aware of and know about the deliberations among the legislators. It should be an obligation for all members of legislatures to file to the speaker their assets and revenues annually, without delay, and also declare 'any conflict of interest' in serving as a legislator with any family interests and benefit from public revenues or resources. On failure to file this, the Speaker (on his/her own or on recommendation of the Ethics Committee) should be empowered to issue notices and then suspend the defaulter from taking part in the proceedings of the House.

Fifth corrective is that voting in any context in the House should be transparent and voting of every member every time should be recorded and be made known to public as well, instead of passing bills by voice vote.

A sixth corrective is extending the disqualification of a sitting member under 'office of profit' to interests outside that of government. Or, as an alternative, the oath taken by newly elected legislators should include 'conflict of interest' disclosure aspect both within and outside the government.

The seventh initiative is a difficult one, but would go a long way for a much needed mindset. Going beyond the substantially increasing 'salaries' of the Members of Parliament (MPs), the Finance Minister in his 2018–2019 budgets announced inflation-linked salary revision and its review every five years. Elected MPs and members of legislative assembly (MLAs) should not be 'on a payroll with salary and pension' like employees of the State. Instead, they should be reimbursed for expenditure incurred in attending the legislature and service to the constituency in a transparent way. They could be provided necessary facilities for that or an honorarium, not 'salary', unless elected ones are viewed as 'employees' of the government.

The final requirement for effective functioning of legislatives is the need to strengthen the committee system with (non-political) subject specialists being included, so that bills could be more inclusive, realistic and futuristic.

The Judiciary

Despite the recent (2018) setback within the judiciary, it continues to be the hope of many and is viewed as a reliable institution. But the need to disperse the clouds is far more important. The issues involved have to do with reach and access of judiciary, its efficiency in the functioning, delivery of justice, transparency in the appointments, postings and pro-activism of the judiciary on public issues without stepping into the domains of other pillars of the State.

There are four areas that need to be sorted out with clarity among the stakeholders. These have to do with the process of empanelling appointments and tenure of judges, and formalising complaints–enquiry against judges. Second, transparency in the process of delivery of justice system availing newer technologies like digital videography of court proceedings and use of other digital and analytical tools. Third, expand and strengthen ways of resolving disputes outside the courts, and fast track avenues. Fourth, bar council, associations and such other professional and functional bodies take stringent view for judicial standards and practices, including prequalification's for judicial services.

The court secretariat at different levels (Munshi system, copy section, etc.) need to come under scrutiny and supervision of a panel of the Court Registrar, and CC camera should be installed. More than one-third of corruption complaints originate at this level.

Reach and access to judicial outfits, and at different levels, need to be expanded beyond 3000 towns in the country with subordinate judicial outlets, including fast track courts. Long waiting time for hearings and the costs involved to avail judicial services are detrimental for the people.

Thirty million cases are pending in the Indian courts due to shortage of judges, according to an SC Judge.[7] Several committees have in the past made several suggestions on each of these aspects but no evidence of any of them made a difference. Gram Nyayalayas, for example, were expected to usher in a breakthrough years ago but have made no headway because of the issue of sharing the costs between the Union and the states. An idea of e-courts taken up in 2007 is going slow with shifting deadlines of implementation. Even online filing and e-adjournment functions are still in experimental stage even after a decade.

Chief Justices of the Supreme Court and the High Courts retire hardly serving a couple months, leaving behind piling up of issues and even judgements. As the retirement age has not been increased for years, pending cases are mounting. To cope with these, retirement age could be set at 65 years for next ten years and the tenure of the Chief Justice of a High Court and the Supreme Court should be minimum two years.

PILs, despite several face-saving judgements, continue to be questioned at highest level as having threatened the potential of the system. Alternate Dispute Resolution (ADR) is hardly talked about, when the need is even more. Both these instruments (PIL and ADR) need to be strengthened with seriousness. Mediation and compromise outside courts need to be encouraged, organised and even promoted.

ADR system should be expanded, strengthened and simplified. Teams of advocates with certain track years as active practitioners should be allowed to take the burden of country.

Plans to digitalise the court proceedings and judgements, etc. should be implemented much faster, widely and extensively and at all levels. All Courts at different levels should be equipped with CCTV to record the arguments and proceedings. Transparency should be evident.

The Judicial service needs a thorough charge in inducting new judicial staff at various levels. First, to be eligible, one should have at least five year of active practice before qualifying for judicial service and ten years active practice in the case of higher judiciary positions, both at High Courts and Supreme Court.

The Supreme Court should not be allowed to be preoccupied with government cases, bank and bail appeals. The collegium proceedings should be in writing and transparent on appointment, elevations, etc. and on the basis of specific assessment of the performance of the judges by the collegium.

Some judges of the Supreme Court, and many more of the High Courts, do not declare their assets annually. There is no evidence that even specific complaints against judges and judiciary are being looked into nor procedures are in place for taking up such specific complaints. One instance is a recent (2017) case of a senior sitting judge of the Odisha High Court engaged in hospitality business with barrowings in his name from the government banks even as being a party to judgement involving his conflict of interest. Despite such examples, Standards and Accountability Bill could not pass through. Online monitoring of adjournments, judgements, etc. including those of lower courts should be reviewed for quick correctives.

Delay in justice and adjournments of hearings should be exceptional. The load has to be reduced. Government litigations and extent of cheque dishonour and similar cases are on increase. They should be dealt elsewhere, like in departmental Lok Adalat. Number of fast track courts could be increased. Equally important, Bar Association and similar bodies should have a code of conduct so that the lawyer's role becomes more honourable.

Disregard of Constitution by any of the pillars, including the judiciary and individual lawyers, should be exposed or the reasons be explained. Idea of a national judicial commission for the appointment of judges could be revived but the process has to be transparent.

Mass Media

What are the interventions required in the case of the fourth estate, the media? What could be the changes that could make a difference as to the kind of the role media is currently playing? A few are mentioned here, only as an example for the much needed shifts or initiatives or correctives. Initiatives and correctives in political system alone will not yield the desired paradigm shift needed for good governance. A holistic approach and parallel correctives are needed in all critical sectors of democracy and the pillars of the State as in the case of media and society, the fourth and fifth estates of the State.

Mass media, more specifically the news media, should come under the purview of RTI and then only could we expect media's accountability and responsibility to readers and viewers. This by itself is likely to bring in the much needed sensitivity in the content priorities of mass media.

Annual declaration of responsibility for content and ownership pattern should be obligatory in the case of television channels, particularly news channels. The newspapers are already making such declaration under the Press and Newspaper Registration Act. This practice should be taken seriously both by media and the regulatory bodies inside and outside the government, so that a quick analysis is possible as to who owns or controls the media and conflict of interest aspect should then be evident. Content source aspects should also be declared in a suo moto way. Such disclosure should be part of licensing conditions for channels as an obligation.

Mass media should not become marketing media, catering primarily to markets and investors. They should not lose track of their primary concern for the society and citizenry. This means a desirability condition of putting some checks on the extent news media, in particular, depends on advertising. A regulator should propose restrains on the proportion of and/or types of advertisements, including 'paid news'. News media should take initiatives for such declaration.

Instruments of market forces with a grip on the content strategies of news media, like TRPs, should be restrained, regulated even by an independent regulator. So that the fourth estate stature of media is not questioned and diminished. TRAI has recently taken initiatives in this regard. But these efforts cannot go half way only. TRAI should also consider the impact contents of television channels have, particularly on children.

Monopoly of media should be restrained, particularly in the case of news media. TRAI has already issued a consultation paper on this contentious issue more than a couple years ago, which didn't have a logical conclusion or recommendations. No media house should own more than 40 per cent of any media singly or in combination. Media ownership in the country should not be concentrated in the hands of a dozen profit maximising business houses.

Even foreign ownership of the news media should be in public purview. The policy in this regard should be transparent and unambiguous. Controlling rights as regards the content is should pertinently be in the public domain.

Equally pertinent is the French model where channels linked to foreign countries (in terms of investment, management or content source), for example, are expected to carry a certain minimum per cent of content which is produced locally and in local language. This should be a condition in the licensing itself. The regulator should ensure implementation of such license conditions.

Regarding film censorship, the report of the Shyam Benegal committee appointed by Modi government should be the guide. The government should reconsider its role, or exit from overseeing creative artefacts of whichever medium or minimise and encourage ombudsmen type arrangement.

Advertising Standards Council of India (ASCI), outside the government and as an independent body of advertising industry, has been a good model for self-restraint and self-regulation. The same methodology could be the basis for media to evolve their own way of upholding standards and accountability.

No shift in the paradigm could be expected in the media as long as the Ministry of Information & Broadcasting exists in its present form and works as it does. I have been saying this for two decades. The logic is simple. What is more pertinent is creativity and credibility of the strategies and messages of the government of the day than a command and control view of its role. A professional approach is better and durable than the one based on political and electoral compulsions.

This requires that the 'broadcasting' be shifted from Information & Broadcasting Ministry to the Ministry of Communication and Telecom and 'Information' function be grouped under an independent Board somewhat like the Railway Board staffed by professional communicators. Prasar Bharati should be allowed to play an independent role as per its mandate. A minister could be there as a coordinator and to report to the Parliament. There is no need for so many departments and an ever expanding Ministry unconcerned of new and emerging communication technologies and application packages and credibility aspect.

Citizens and social bodies should be encouraged to take on certain overseeing responsibilities on their own and at their end, and share the findings or experiences with the larger public. Without active concern of the citizens and content consumers, not much change in the paradigm could be expected. Hence, agencies such as ASCI, PSBT, CMS and CSE should be allowed to play an active role. They should also take on media literacy initiatives.

All India Radio and Doordarshan should be ensured to remain as public broadcasters under Prasar Bharati, and the government should allocate annual budgetary support from the consolidated fund of India. Public broadcasters cannot be exposed to competition with unregulated private channels.

Promotion of content standards and concern for quality and impact of media is inevitable and should be more looked after by citizens, academics and consumer groups. Social bodies should take on this responsibility rather than expect the government to do so.

The impact of various media, particularly the television channels and social media, should be taken up by social bodies with periodic monitoring and evaluative studies. These reports or findings should be in public domain. Regulators like TRAI should ensure that such studies on the impact of media are independently and periodically available.

Decentralised media is better than centralised one, given the diversity of languages, cultures and climate zones. The government should not pursue economic policies which amount to encouraging centralisation and monopolisation of the media operations in the country.

The Executive

There is no central legislation to ensure the accountability of the Executive. More often, it is difficult to pin down the responsibilities as the appointment order does not spell out exactly what functions a functionary is responsible for once in office. Every time a senior government employee is appointed or transferred, the government should indicate the functions he or she is responsible for. A recent classic example is Supreme Court proceedings on a PIL on Chikungunya outbreak in Delhi. Even the Health Minister could not name which specific officer is responsible for fogging in Delhi. Then how anyone could be held accountable? Of course, in this case the Minister himself was fined by the court. The government should first identify and describe the responsibilities of the functionaries before or while posting them. That would also make the service delivery guarantee provision more effective.

RTI Act should help restore the unique independence of bureaucracy. In a limited view, RTI is seen by executives as an inconvenient law as it adds to their workload and even could put them in vulnerable situations as they have to record on file the reasons for certain discretionary decisions. But in the long run, RTI helps them disassociate from the discretionary favours of their political bosses and also reduces the workload and/or makes their functioning easier. Once Section 4 of the RTI Act is taken up seriously, respect for the officers will go up among people. If sincerely implemented, citizen charter compels the government offices to comply with deadlines and organise themselves better. Payoff from sincere implementation by the Executive is critical for good governance.

IAS and cadre officers should declare their assets and also conflict of interest, if any, in their functioning annually or in each different posting. If they could take bold decision about, like sending their children to local public schools (as suggested by a recent [2016] judgement of the Allahabad High Court),[8] it will enhance not only the credibility and respect of the people but will also add to their control on administration and even respect of colleagues.

Allegations of corruption against senior officers should be dealt by ACB as a priority so that the case is not prolonged at the cost of the public image of the officers.

Postings and promotions of the officer should be far more transparent than they are at present. These should not be linked to a change in the party in power and in the approach of political parties to polls. The way these transfers are reported in media should indicate the reasons rather than spreading belittling perceptions.

Officers need to be protected against arbitrary and politically motivated transfers and postings as well as trying to exclude them from the existing enquiry forums or making the government's permission a requirement for the enquiry. A parliamentary panel has supported a move to bar anti-graft agencies from probing bribery allegations against public servants without an approval from the government. This was despite opposition from the CBI. They cannot be tried without the government's sanction. Why is this retrograde step? Has this provision out lived already?

Tenure of officers posted in certain functions should not be too short. Minimum three year should be possible in social sector and public services delivery departments as the tenure. The Indian Administrative Service should not remain a 'generalist service'. It needs to be strengthened and made attractive by encouraging specialisation in different sectors. Different ways and means should be put in place to restore the pride in the service and in its stature by bringing in specialised persons into the service.

Civil Society

One of my own insight from reviewing citizen charters, conducting social audit at different levels and dealing with several citizen groups and RTI activists over two decades is that 50 per cent of citizen grievances could be redressed by allowing them to ventilate their grievances at someone with functional responsibility. The process of governance can be better facilitated with such initiatives as media giving space to the civil society and citizen grievances. As Dr Subhash Kashyap described a decade ago, quality of governance is dependent upon the activism of citizens. Good governance can never take shape without active citizenry. And this should be evident as much.[9]

Government and senior functionaries should acknowledge that implementation of many public services will not be satisfactory without the cooperation and support of citizens, individually and as groups. Instead of giving an impression that citizens are at the 'receiving end', governments should treat them as 'partners in progress'. Citizens and (non-political party) society players should be encouraged. Such an approach would never be futile for sustaining governance. In that spirit, the following initiatives would go a long way.

Encourage participation of citizens in decision making at different levels of public services delivery. Visible involvement of non-political society representatives in advisory committees, consultation process and in governance forums is a better bet than trying to keep them off and alienate them. Information on various issues could be shared with public as often instead of keeping off. Suo moto provision, as Section 4 of the RTI Act, is one sure way. Consultation process with general or concerned public should be kept open and ongoing. Provision should be made in every public service for taking into account grievances or dissatisfied voices. Instruments like people's tribunals, websites, feedback outlets, etc., should prompt user interactions and bring in efficiency in the system.

Provide for obligatory public hearings for frequently availed public services. They could be videographed, even selectively, to promote best practices. Open house with the concerned functionaries is one way. As a national convenor of India's first Social Audit Panel (1992–1997), I tried open house with visible and immediate results. Stakeholders, end providers and supervisory and policy level executives were assembled for an open door meet for a face-to-face interaction along with independent members of the panel. An anguished citizen puts forth his or her problem first, the concerned functionary responds there and then and gives a timeline for follow-up and corrective. If such public hearings are made at least once in two years in each district, it would make much difference.

Social audit by independent professional and or user groups for massive and distributed public service schemes would go a long way for the citizens to become partners in progress. Social audit with the participation of society representatives should be obligatory for large and massive welfare and public service programmes. Social audit by service providers themselves (without citizen participation) will be perceived as deceptive (as in the case of MGNREGS). Swachh Bharat would go a long way and make the much-needed difference if it gets the benefit of social audit at different levels instead of relying on the government's own feedback, surveys and rankings.

Civil society has to work within the provisions of constitution and legislations and not engage in activities threatening the very security of the country in such a way that they do not engage in raising passions between communities and regions.

Registered civil society organisations should also be made to pledge at the very outset their allegiance to the Constitution and to comply with the laws of the land. The conditions and codes that registered society groups are expected to comply should be known to the public. Every time a new political party comes to power, the society cannot be expected to change these codes.

Citizen volunteerism should be encouraged and provided for towards better delivery of public services in the implementation of massive schemes.

Citizen should be encouraged to form groups formally or informally on the basis of some common interest and the local governments in turn should entrust them with the responsibility to take initiatives. This is being done by some officers in an exceptional way. Sheila Dikshit[10] as the Chief Minister of Delhi encouraged *Bhagidari* and entrusted them a series of local community services which were administered by the officials earlier. There are many such experiments elsewhere too at different levels. It will be useful to conduct an analysis of all such initiatives and experiments around the country and pursue the best examples. Some such examples were indicated by *Janaagraha* in Bengaluru.

Enhance resident participation in municipal governance. Advocating of rights within the constitutional framework should not be curbed. That is, clamping down of dissent should be dealt promptly and transparently before taking the extreme step of curbing or preventing it. Local governments should provide space in the cities and villages where the concerned people can hold meets in various contexts as and when they like.

Education

As good governance is an evolving phenomenon, the scope and structure of governance constantly undergoes revisions based on experience, outlook and aspirations. This process is shaped to a large extent by the education of the people. That is why education system too need to gear up for good governance to be a reality.

What are the critical shifts that education system should go through to spread the idea of good governance, its scope and also sustain it in practice? Interventions in six pillars alone are not enough and reinforcement from the education system too goes a long way in achieving it.

First, an outlook towards good governance depends to some extent on what kind of education system we have and from what motivational stream our education comes from. For example, if someone has an understanding that education is a profit making service, his or her priorities would be different in the case of idea of equity, inclusiveness and his/her sensitivities would be different. If one comes from co-education background, the outlook towards gender equity is likely to be different. Today, we have two (public and private) streams of education at the primary level and each has different motivations, standards and cultures. This dichotomy should end. If the government thinks that it would not be able to cater to the need of education for all children (!) and/or that it will not be able ensure the kind of standard it requires, it should foresee the implications of the available alternatives. Should we then ignore constitutional obligations and the legislations, as prescribed in the Constitution? Should the directive principles remain 'mere pious declarations' as Dr B.R. Ambedkar cautioned. This is what is happening today without a public debate. This dilemma needs to be addressed. Parliament and the state assemblies should come up with a policy. Article 45 of the Constitution provided for free and compulsory education for all children up to age 14. In 2002, 86th Amendment made education 'a fundamental right' of children aged 6–14 years.[11]

Since the dichotomy between public and private education at primary and secondary levels is too obvious, we need to find a midway. We need a specific policy and declaration concerning fees, syllabi, infrastructure, teacher–student ratio, teaching standards, promotion methodology and the responsibility for enrolments, dropouts, learning outcome, level playing expectations, use of ICT, etc. Equally important and a priority is quality of education at different grades, criteria for passing out or promotion to next class, etc. the ambiguity on each of these should end.

Why we are not able to fill in so many vacancies of teacher posts in so many public schools (even after Supreme Court's observation) even when so many teacher trained remain unemployed? Why this vacuum remains a continuing one? Is this to facilitate privatisation of education? This dilemma needs to end. Whether State has responsibility for primary and secondary education or not need to be reiterated.

For a knowledge society, for a more productive society and, even more, for ensuring and sustaining good governance of the country[12] schooling for 4 to 6 years in the age group 7–14 years is critical for the future of a generation in a country. If we could sort out the dilemma confronting education at this level, only then the nation could be said as on the safe and sure course.

The syllabus should include social studies and basics on governance, good enough for an adolescent to be an active citizen and be familiar with the socioeconomic realities. This cannot be expected without a child growing up reading a printed book first before taking to other media, including the new media. Book reading by itself is an experience that makes a difference and even more so when it becomes a group activity in the class room or in the family and followed up with writing and talking skills at the high school level. Any initiatives in this regard will go a long way in ushering in a new education scenario. I say this based on the insights I derived from the BREAD experiment[13] in the last decade of operating children's library in more than a thousand government schools in two Telugu states, where we made provisions for children to read books on a wide range of non-syllabus topics. If children in the age group of 7–14 years take to reading the lives of great people as well as folktales and stories, it makes a difference in the values they acquire. This, in turn, could determine the kind of role a citizen is expected to play in governance, as this could influence them to take wise decisions while selecting people's representatives during elections.

If education at primary and secondary levels is streamlined first as a priority, education at other levels and of other kind like vocational and technical becomes creative, more productive and value-based.

ICT—A Differentiator

Ease with which citizens can avail ICT reliably and affordably to get public services as and when they need without having to pay bribe and repeat visits to a government office is a proof-of-pudding aspect of governance. Dangers of continued centralisation in government and dependence of citizens on government are two possibilities that need to be watched out with increased access to ICT tools and networks.

Unless e-governance is expedited, scaled up and extended to more and more public services, ICT remains a big talk, a promise and a claim. Claims of Andhra Pradesh Government (2017–2018) to connect every house with high speed broadband to access telephone, Internet and a number of television channels for ₹150 a month could expedite the shift. But that should demonstrate e-governance in a two way communication mode. That amounts to empowering people. Empowered people stand on their own feet instead of looking for dole-outs from government, patronage and election-time lures. IEC (Information, Education and Communication) should also mean more and more decentralisation of decision-making closer to people.

Application packages in the local languages that could be availed for multiple public services should be in vogue, particularly in matters related to health, education, basic skills and availing citizen rights without having to pay any bribe. Digitalisation should facilitate suo moto disclosures by various public service functionaries. And, ICT should mean more transparency in public services, political decisions and government operations. Connecting devices should be inter-compatible and upgrades should not be necessary to retain connectivity and continue the service. The focus should not be limited to digital money transactions. Online and real-time governance should be the next big step when the very scope of governance itself should undergo change.

Real-time governance is possible with reliable and affordable online infrastructure. More specifically, speed and reliability of broadband and its access and availability is critical for differentiating from the past. Availability of application packages, which require minimal operating skills at the user end, in local language should be a priority concern. Interoperability of devices like set top boxes (on way out) and mobile SIMs help in upgrading the process. Once digitalisation becomes a reality, e-money transactions will become a reality, e-voting too should be possible. For the real-time functioning of government, extensive orientation and sensitisation of citizen is a prerequisite.

ICT is changing the very structure and scope of how people communicate, interact and relate with each other. As importantly, ICT is a differentiator for how the governments function. It determines the kind of relations that need to be kept with people, citizens, voters and the targeted sections. With every function added to the existing devices or a change in the ICT architecture, as in the case of smartphones, governance too is changing its scope and structure. This should be felt by the citizen.

Technology anywhere anytime has a double edged potential. It could be a facilitator or dampener in socio-political and economic situations and scenarios. Critical issues related to governance include centralisation vs decentralisation, depriving vs empowering citizens, inclusive vs exclusive nature of policies, participative vs non-participative, integrating vs disintegrating privacy vs transparency and discretion vs indiscretion.

How or in which direction ICT works depends on the kind of policies, user end sensitivities, citizen activism, concerns of the society and how the checks and balance culture is understood. To the extent such concerns are there with the citizen, the civil society and the government, positive effects of ICT are likely. Overseeing and an independent tracking of such trends would help prevent negative effects.

Notes and References

1. CMS studies over two decade on governance, public services and corruption.
2. *Economic Times*, 20 July 2016, New Delhi, https://economictimes.indiatimes.com
3. Ramachandra Guha, 'We Are More an Elections-only Democracy', *The Hindu*, 16 October 2016, https://www.thehindu.com/news/national/%E2%80%98We-are-more-an-elections-only-democracy%E2%80%99/article16073922.ece (Accessed 27 August 2018).
4. Rajya Sabha TV, 12 September 2016.
5. https://www.thehindu.com/news/national/Seeking-votes-on-religious-basis-a-corrupt-act-SC/article16977220.ece (Accessed 28 August 2018).
6. 'Remove Poll Spend Cap: BJP', *Times of India*, 28 August 2018.
7. Supreme Court Judge Gopal Goud, *Sakshi*, 18 September 2016. Goud, the retiring Chief Justice of Supreme Court, reminded to this fact on 4 January 2017 in his farewell reception.
8. Allahabad High Court (2016) suggested in one of its judgements on school education that public servants should send their children to public schools. See: https://indianexpress.com/article/cities/lucknow/govt-servants-must-send-kids-to-govt-schools-allahabad-hc/
9. Subhash C. Kashyap, *Crime and Corruption to Good Governance* (New Delhi: Uppal, 1997).
10. Sheila Dikshit, as chief minister (1998–2013) of Delhi, encouraged *Bhagidari* scheme. This scheme provided for participation of local resident organisations in taking local decisions which the government was taking until then.
11. Subhash C. Kashyap, *Our Constitution* (New Delhi: National Book Trust, 2015).
12. N. Bhaskara Rao, 'Children of Government Servants and Peoples' Representatives Should Study in Public Schools—Allahabad High Court', *Transparency Review* 8, no. 3 (September, 2015).
13. Basic Research Education & Development (BREAD), a 28-year-old independent initiative (implemented from 2005 to 2018) has proved how school education could be rejuvenated with the help of non-syllabus book reading in a non-structured reading environment in government schools. See: www.breadsocietyindia.org/

CHAPTER 8

Big Change with Citizen Initiatives

An assumption of this book is that the good governance paradigm being a complex and an evolving phenomenon, the much-needed interventions or corrections to achieve it should be taken up all together and in parallel rather than bit by bit or step by step. The latter will not facilitate the momentum needed for the kind of change or shift that is envisioned in this good governance–development–democracy model. Even an 'incremental approach' does not lead to it. How much radical or critical interventions may be in any of the six pillars of the State, their potential can be realised only when such adjustments will get linked to it.

The situation is complex and reminds us of a Rubik cube. Matching the colours on all faces of the cube requires patience, focus and a strategy. The combination of colours in the Rubik cube being many, matching them every time is a challenge and requires sensitivity and skill to optimise the time each round takes to complete. A general observation of experts is that given the kind of complexities under which these pillars function, the kind of package approach I am advocating is unrealistic in expecting the outcome and that may never even be possible. But I know that some of the landmark interventions of the last two decades have been possible because of the efforts of distinguished or disgusted people. A dozen such examples, each one displaying a different model, are recalled here. There are many more such examples across the country.

Dr Subhash Kashyap is an eminent expert and a research officer in the library of the Parliament. Dr Kashyap, started with conversations with Dr B.R. Ambedkar, became an authority in constitution and an adviser on many contentious issues and debates in the Parliament as its Secretary General. It was his convincing arguments with Prime Minister Rajiv Gandhi that led to the reduction of voting age from 21 to 18 without much public outrage. Dr Kashyap was also responsible for suggesting the idea of ministry-wise Parliamentary Committees. If one man with credibility can do so much, why not a team of dedicated ones can do more?

That was how Arvind Kejriwal with no significant background could launch a pan-India movement against corruption, of course under the umbrella of Anna Hazare and some eminent personalities on the national scene. In a short period of a year, this group galvanised concerned the youth across the country and changed the public discourse in such a way not seen in the previous decades. The change was more in the mindset of people at large and priorities of political parties and leaders in several respects.

I remember how Professor N.G. Ranga, whom I knew personally, stalled Prime Minister Jawaharlal Nehru and Congress President's proposal at the Avadi Congress to adopt cooperative farming, much earlier in 1956. Professor Ranga could not convince the Congress meet, but with a post-card campaign, he made Jawaharlal Nehru rethink and then withdraw the proposal. It was the power of an idea. Pursued strategically, and sincerely, an idea could make the difference.

Dr Jayaprakash Narayan (known as JP), taking early retirement from his position as a senior IAS officer in Andhra Pradesh, started Lok Satta in 1996 as a voluntary organisation and made a mark in articulating, crusading and sensitising the people about the evil in politics. His key theme was that systemic changes are far more important to achieve national goals, not the change of a party or a leader in power. For over a decade, he and Lok Satta were well regarded in public circles. At the height of that movement, he converted Lok Satta into a political party and adopted electoral politics with the belief that it was a sure and faster way to bring the much-needed change in the political system. But that reversed fortunes and, more importantly, the momentum he had built up for structural changes was somewhat lost. The agenda he pursued was pertinent, and appealing too, yet he could not mobilise a larger support despite reaching out to young and educated elite sections of the society. That was because of the prevailing perceptions about political parties. JP made more impact as an activist than being the leader of a political party—a reminder of the declining credibility of political parties. On the other hand, a young lady, Trupti Desai, in the Shani Shingnapur temple near the famous Shirdi in Maharashtra, in a matter of a year (2015–2016) could bring a change that should have been there decades ago: the right of women to pray inside any temple. In a matter of one year, the number of local activists increased from 500 to 5,000 for taking up the course of protest—without going far away from the home district. Despite having a women as a Sarpanch there, women were prevented from entering the inner temple. Haji Ali in Mumbai is a famous *dargah*, where women are not allowed to even enter the mosque since 1919. All that has changed in no time in months. The Ayyappa temple in Kerala too has agreed to allow women to pray inside the temple. All this has happened because the citizens protested locally and filed a PIL.

In 2016, practically unknown 23 years old Hardik Patel in Gujarat galvanised unusual numbers in no time in Surat, Gujarat, under the banner of Navnirman Sena and forced the state government to the negotiation table—the same way that Anna Hazare–Arvind Kejriwal did in New Delhi in 2011, when India Against Corruption (IAC) at its heights was part of such a group of Union cabinet ministers. Although the issue young Patel took up was inclusion of two sub-castes (Kadva and Leuva) out of the three Patels are composed of as OBC, his movement acquired larger base among Kisans cutting across states.

In the earlier decade, a farmer leader Sharad Joshi in Maharashtra crusaded for the farmers' rights and issues. Once he became a political activist taking political sides, his movement, which was going good for decades, declined. An impressive and disciplined rally on foot (in 2018) of over 30,000 farmers in Maharashtra was 185 kilometres long and which accomplished in seven days what farmers were demanding in the earlier years. In the process, they won the hearts of Mumbaikars, their support and compelled the state government to heed to the farmers' demands. They could achieve this with no involvement of any political party until after the success was evident. This rally also demonstrated how people can make a difference by coming together.

Bachpan Bachao Andolan of Kailash Satyarthi, a Nobel Laureate, is another example of an individual pursuing a cause, getting the existing legislature implemented and new laws to form for the rights of children. He focussed on identifying the children on the run, away from home and came up with laws in the interest of such children in distress. He has remained a non-political crusader.

Dr Subramanian Swamy, currently active in the ruling party and a member of Rajya Sabha, was a faculty of IIT Delhi and a US university. He has been making people at the helm of affairs think critically and differently. As a crusader mostly taking the legal route in the last couple of decades, he has made decision makers and opinion makers think twice, and even reconsider policy issues. After becoming a part of a political party, however, his role has not been as distinct as it was as a crusader.

How did the landmark RTI Act has become an Act without even being deliberated in the Parliament nearly two decades ago (2005)? Thanks to Aruna Roy's grassroots movement in Rajasthan involving illiterate women, mostly casual daily wagers. The crusade for local issues by local people was critical in ushering in this transparent law for the country. The social organisation she had put together (Mazdoor Kisan Shakti Sangathan—MKSS) mobilised the poorest of the poor in one interior pocket of Rajasthan. Aruna Roy and Nikhil Dey inspired many others by demonstrating what is possible.

V. Kurian is another unique example. Dairy movement or the white revolution has become legendry. He converted an employment assignment that came his way into a movement that changed the face of the farmers and their prosperity and health of the nation. He realised a cause and showcased what had failed until then by organising the farmers. Starting from a district in Gujarat, the movement expanded to many other districts and states. Using organisational methods, convincing logics and linkages, he availed the best of advertising skills to reach out and demonstrate the outcomes relatively in a short duration.

Dr Pai Panandikar is yet another example. He has advised Prime Ministers over four decades, starting with Morarji Desai and including P.V. Narasimha Rao, I.K. Gujral and Narendra Modi. He had the benefit of the experts of CPR and of debates involving several more experts, including political leaders and senior bureaucrats. Today, unlike Dr Subhash Kashyap, Panandikar is a disappointed professional and thinks that India has not accomplished the much-needed systemic changes which could have made a bigger difference. He thinks that it has been because of 'system failure', 'control view' of governance, lack of 'political will' and 'fraud and flawed system of governance'. But one limitation in his view is that he hoped only for 'incremental advantages' and looked for the change in a disjointed way and from more of the Delhi perspective.

Common Cause, founded by S.D. Shouri, has made a significant contribution to the society over four decades, taking the PIL route and focussing on New Delhi, with hardly a dozen activists involved in its activities. Shouri left behind a model for citizens for change and in the mindset of people in policy making. He demonstrated what one sincere individual could accomplish in the capital city of India with impressive nationwide implications and how support comes from other citizens impressed by the honesty once the success of the cause becomes evident. His simplicity, sincerity and transparency made Common Cause a unique model.

Research backup and analysis can make all the difference in boosting a big cause and idea and change by sensitising the stakeholders and convincing the opinion makers.

CMS has demonstrated with its initiatives on curbing corruption, creating environment awareness and sensitivity about social development issues. Parliamentary legislative studies (PLS) took the much-needed impressive initiatives with hardly two or three professionals engaged and in much short span of time. They showed the rhetoric-ridden character of debates in the Parliament and showed how debates could be focussed, motivating and productive. Commonwealth

Human Rights Initiative (CHRI) of Maja Daruwala and her team has crusaded over a longer period involving stakeholders, sensitising them on several issues like police reforms. Venkatesh of CHRI highlighted how RTI implementation was lagging, an analysis of which could bring change in the very outlook of stakeholders about the RTI Act and its implementation. They showed what difference independent research and analysis could make and how.

As a spiritual preacher of repute over a quarter century, Jaggi Vasudev of Isha Foundation, Coimbatore, has made a qualitative difference in infusing concern, sensitivities and urgency to address water crisis. In September 2017, he started a month long campaign, reaching out to most states across the country. Four features of Rally for Rivers (2017) deserve notice. First, the campaign was based on a visible linkage between water crisis and lifestyles and public policies. Second, he brought on one platform chief ministers and the government machinery (without it being viewed as of the governments), journalists, media houses and society as a part of the campaign. Third, he linked a national issue to his own concern for nature, spiritualism and the mounting water crisis. Fourth, ICT was effectively used to reach out and involve large sections of people and to network them for prompt action locally. But it needs to be seen how far such one-time campaigns can sustain the cause. As against a campaign of this magnitude, there is an individual in Kottagudem in Khammam district of Telangana who, on his own and with his own money, and by just using a bicycle, has been campaigning for about two crore plantations. He just used every social occasion—death, birth, marriage to reach out for his plantation drive. He never sought any support from the government or the corporates. After CMS recognised him as a role model in 2005, and awarded him in Delhi, he was awarded Padma Shri by the government in 2017. He continues his mission notwithstanding his advanced age.

Many sincere advocates of change have missed that the process has to be sequential.

These are only examples of many more such initiatives that have taken place in the country. Initiatives like these are there in every part of the country and which have become mass movements and truly led by citizens. These include how citizens could individually make a difference and bring big changes even when news media, even the local ones, hardly give them space. They, however, have never been scaled up for making people realise their power to change things around them.

Political parties ideally should be the ones which should take on the challenges of change and scale up the movements. However, the performance of various parties in parliament remind how much political parties are in a status quo or more of the same types rather than taking key concerns strategically and on a sustained basis beyond electoral compulsions.

Networking

I have been pursuing three issues as a part of political reforms. First, having seen first-hand how candidates in an assembly election distribute money (1972 assembly poll in Andhra Pradesh is an instance), I realised early on how it vitiates the democratic process as well as the outcome. I wanted to establish the phenomenon and its linkage with the democratic process far more reliably; hence I structure that research enquiry in the next election. The experiments in 1977 and 1980, researching how 'note-for-vote' has become a feature of our elections, thus became the background for the first ever quantitative study in 29 states conducted by CMS in two phases in 2005 and in 2007. The second was the way the news media covers poll campaigns, depriving some parties and candidates of level playing opportunities, and causes low voter turnout and dampens the enthusiasm. This concern brought to the fore that more coverage of polls is not merrier and how structure of coverage tend to trivialise issues and create hype for individuals at the cost of core concerns and sustains the note for vote feature of our democracy. The third concern has been for better candidates to contest the elections and transparency in the parties' process of selecting candidates.

These pursuits exposed how citizen activism and the spirit of society are traded and governance issues are sidelined. This pursuit also exposed fallacies in the development paradigm and the notion of inclusive governance.

As a part of my pursuit of these concerns, I took the initiative of putting together the trends (during 2003–2006) for a discussion with over 50 social groups identified from across the country. They were known both locally and nationally for their pioneering initiatives in poll reforms. Two important players by then were Dr Jayaprakash Narayan of Lok Satta in Andhra Pradesh and ADR system and its founder trustee Professor Trilochan Sastry, who just then shifted to IIM Bengaluru from IIM Ahmedabad, and Dr Jagdeep Chhokar of IIM, Ahmedabad. ADR at that point had a PIL pending in the Supreme Court for revelation of candidate's background concerning their assets, education, and criminal record. Candidates, and even political parties, were not enthusiastic of such disclosure but that was made obligatory at the time of filing nomination and the Election Commission has been making that candidate declarations available to public. That is how ADR could spearhead a series of initiatives, which has changed the scope of transparency in the electoral politics of the country.

At this point, more than 50 activists and social leaders, who were already crusading for poll reforms, were invited to CMS campus in New Delhi for a day-long deliberation. For the next month, Admiral Tahiliani, former chief of the Navy and ex-Governor, and I teamed up to meet political leaders, party-wise, after prior appointment. Other activists like Pramod Chawla and Maj. Gen. Vinod Saighal too had joined us. With Supreme Court concurring with the appeal filed by ADR and supported by CMS, Lok Satta and Common Cause, the government wanted to issue an ordinance against bringing required change in the Peoples Representation Act and send it to the President Abdul Kalam. We appealed to the President not to sign the Ordinance and about 25 of us called on him in Rashtrapati Bhavan. After listening to us, President Kalam returned the file to the government without signing, which was one of the rare occasions.

This experience reinforced my faith in the system, in the power of an idea and also in the belief that if you take on some cause, taking along other activists around the country, any efforts do not go waste. The logic of an idea and unity in civil society groups, however, is an essential aspect for the success of such efforts. This is also something that I learned from the experiences of Martin Luther King, Jr, who had set up the Upland School of Social Change (1966–1968), now known as Martin Luther King School of Social Change, in Chester at the outskirts of Philadelphia in the USA. I was a fellow at this unique institute in Crozer Theological Seminary campus where Martin Luther King Jr did his graduation and had read first time about Mahatma Gandhi some years before.

Martin Luther King Jr earned his reputation and success in his movements which were based on a unique model. What model is that? Understand the scope and linkages of the public issue one is concerned about and be cognizant of visible outcomes required for making a difference. Second, research the relationships and weightage of external factors and interrelated variables including perceptions of the people. Third, formulate a strategy for mass mobilisation, explore various routes like PIL, seminars, conferences, workshops, rallies, net-working, etc. (ICT and mobile phone had not yet become significant then). Fourth, find out other public figures, institutions and places with similar concerns, reach out and involve them. Fifth, arrive at a coalition of civil society groups with an understanding, without getting into role conflicts, and seeking cooperation from any quarter including corporates, cutting across party lines. Sixth, chalk out outcomes with milestones. Seventh, identify phases for visible results. Eighth, sustain whatsoever is gained thus far. Ninth, enlarge the coalition and seek news media involvement if not already done so by then. Never give up on a good cause. Pursue it. Strategize. Have patience. Make it research-based. Involve and rope in more people from more places. Get endorsements from new sources. Appeal to political parties, do not denigrate them, pursue with them but do not get identified with them. Mobilise youth and others who matter in judiciary and media, having responsibilities in the people movement. We now have mobile phones, new media and hotspots of citizen activism in most cities, which help in networking and scaling up.

Systems and Institutions Are Important

We need to remember and remind ourselves that the best bet for democracy and sustaining it are its systems and institutes. They are far more important than individuals to sustain, also because even legislations are not enough for bringing the desired change. India is unique in its too many laws and too little difference they make at the required levels. Also, things should get going not merely for the sake of individuals but also because of systems. Individuals, of course, make difference, make a mark, and help consolidate systems and procedures in such a way that the scope for individual discretionary decisions matters little and that too as an exception. To that extent, good governance stands a better chance, gets ground and is sustained. Good governance is not individual-centric or personality-specific; it is not even politics-centric. Contribution of individuals should be more to consolidate institutions, mechanisms, procedures and precedents in such a way that no matter which party wins an election or who becomes the head of the government, only policies, priorities and people in proactive roles should be able to change the course and destinies. And that is how leaders or parties should make their mark and distinguish themselves.

Such an understanding is critical for good governance and for it to take roots. People, voters and consumers or users of public services, all should have some sensitivity towards governance and should be able to differentiate government from governance and understand the rights and responsibilities as well as the linkage between development, democracy and good governance. Good governance cannot be achieved without the people realising the linkages or understanding the logic and processes involved in all that. This needs to be campaigned may be as a continuing theme and for a much longer period so that the next generation of citizens and voters in the upcoming elections could prefer better candidates. How is that possible? It is clear as of now that not all political parties and leaders are neither forthcoming nor will support the kind of changes needed for ensuring inclusive governance (as in the case of women reservation).

Good governance is a result of a range of interlinked initiatives taken together. Ten critical variables are indicated here as the ones through which good governance gets momentum. This list is only indicative, not inclusive. Unlike a Rubik cube, the alternatives and options available are far more and the optimisation manoeuvrability is several times more at a given time. But the puzzle in this remains eternal. The processes include or involve:

- Educational levels
- Legal route options
- ICT and Apps
- Social networks
- Administrative instruments and legal rights
- Demonstration of outcomes and differences
- Independent research data, training and sensitisation
- Self, third party and state regulations
- Public and private institutions with transparency
- Transparency/checks and balances practices and precedents

Education Route—A Sure Bet

Every child should be exposed to some of the basic ideas and concepts of good governance right from an early age. By the time, or before, one reaches the voting age, he or she should know about the republic, about the pillars of the state, what 'We, the People' mean, difference between government and governance, citizenship and rights and responsibilities and what checks and balances are all about. Four aspects should continue to be in the syllabus at senior secondary and secondary levels of school. These are:

1. Our Republic, our constitution, government, governance, pillars of the state, checks and balances
2. Rights regime of citizens, entitlements, significance of transparency and responsibilities
3. Instruments available to the citizens and communities to avail, and the procedure of electing a representative
4. The process of formulation of laws, passed and implemented

Including these aspects in the syllabus at those levels should be possible and that is what we should promote. There should not be any resistance for this from any quarter, including political parties, leaders and educators. Teachers thus have a special responsibility. It was a Hindi teacher (Krishna Reddy of Bollapadu village) in my eighth class in Mudunuru High School (1954), who, after meeting a childhood friend in New Delhi, explained to the class how Lok Sabha and Rajya Sabha function, drawing our Parliament building on the blackboard.

This had a profound influence on me and has even shaped my thinking and my priorities. And soon after my post-graduation, I landed in New Delhi, nearly 60 years ago (1962) with a self-generated interest in democratic processes. That was why I set up BREAD (Basic Research in Education and Development) 28 years ago and children libraries in government high schools (so far 1,020 libraries).

Schooling at these levels should also create sensitivities to distinguish what is desirable and what is not. That is how citizens should be able to differentiate good from bad or right–wrong, rights–responsibilities and the differentiators as the criteria for discrimination that matter in that process. Moreover, parents should also often engage with their children when they are at school.

Newer Technologies

ICT influences the practices, preferences and behaviours both at the individual and community level. Hence, the trends and tendencies in this respect matter for governance at a given time. ICT in India is changing much faster than perhaps anywhere else. Upgradation from one level to another level of technology is an issue. Only with such upgradation would one be able to avail online and real-time services. Interoperability of devices do matter, particularly because service providers are not enthusiastic to ensure such facility. A related issue is the speed of internet and usage charges. Some states may assure telephone as well as internet services and a number of television channels at a nominal cost, but the key variable would be the skill expected of the beneficiaries to avail the full potential of devices and their connectivity. In particular, to avail the crucial functions like banking transactions, basic services, and mobilising public opinion, familiarity of people with the potential of ICT is critical. At present, the percentage of people using the functions of a mobile phone is too low, and digitalisation has the ability to make all this a reality soon enough.

E-governance, on-line government, or real-time governance have been claimed recently by some leaders. E-governance initiatives should enable online facilitation of various services, which, in turn would make real-time governance feasible. This needs reliable infrastructure and inter-compatibility. The Central government has been extending the deadline for the completion of broadband and Wi-Fi connections to the remotest parts of the country. The new deadline is set at 2023. Video conferencing is limited to a handful of individuals though it is feasible at a larger level. Some leaders claim that a changeover has already happened with the availability of things on internet, access to cloud platforms and newer technologies and applications. Land records, MGNREGS and other massive schemes implemented by the government have been computerised. However, reciprocal outcome or experiences are not acknowledged yet.

Technology is a double-edged weapon. If one is not sensitive, there may be more negative effects than positive. Digital divide should not become a reality. Misuse of technology, interrupting or tampering of networks and intrusion into people's privacy call for some precautions at the user end also. What protection do we have for such situations? And as a safeguard from breakdown of devices or failure to service, there should be user end protection measures including insurance.

Delivery of Basic Public Services

A win–win opportunity for everyone is a key characteristic of a good governance. How such a situation could be expedited and made evident? Zero corruption in availing the basic public services required by most people is a key issue. Also, reliable public distribution system will go a long way in making people realise the difference.

My book, *Good Governance, Corruption-free Public Service* (SAGE, 2012), indicates how a dozen public services could be made corruption-free. The model I proposed suggests linkage analysis and field research among the users who could, as well as those who could not for some or other reason, avail the services. New initiatives and correctives, focusing on three or four of the critical functions based on such research among users, are required periodically. Such exercises help in sustaining and consolidating good governance. The bottom line is that majority sections of the people should not get trapped in situations as grave as corruption, as they do not exactly know how to get out fast.

Civil Society

Inclusive governance is the extent of the involvement and participation of citizens in the governance. Legislative committees, consultative forums and processes, public hearings, advisory councils, social audit, etc. are some of the parameters for inclusiveness. Also, various user groups should have a say in policy making. It makes a difference if the news media gives due coverage to what people do on their own, which is by no means insignificant in the overall productivity and governance of the country.

Society and democracy are not complete without freedom of speech and freedom to assemble. Good governance cannot be claimed without ensuring the citizens these freedoms and other rights mentioned in the Constitution. The local governments should facilitate their realisation by providing public spaces where citizens can assemble for some common cause. The society needs to assert, reassert, and modify its course whenever necessary, irrespective of the government of the day. Citizen activism should be encouraged in different ways. Their dependence on the government needs to be minimised as a policy and strategy for the development of democracy and governance. Success of government schemes or programmes depends on the involvement and interest of the local citizens.

Legal Literacy

Successive governments have been pushing legislations so fast of late that legislators themselves are not aware or sure of the provisions in the bills they pass. Then where are the efforts to familiarise the people, in general, and families, in particular, about their existence and their provisions? Only those who can afford or have knowledge could avail legal help. Laws on the rights of citizens or consumers are glaring examples where laws could not make much difference. The enforcement of already existing laws is yet another issue that is critical for governance.

Already Available Instruments

For an active or a concerned citizen, there are a number legal options available. These include PIL, public hearing, RTI, citizen charter, social audit and a series of rights including right to service delivery, right to redressal, etc. And there are a number of standing or parliamentary committees who could be approached or appealed to. However, only the users of the services know about the existence of such instruments and how to avail them in a given situation. Social audit has not made much of a difference where it is an affair within the department or by people in the system, without the involvement of subject experts or user activists or independent individuals from the academics. Citizen Charter is yet another example. Though they have been there for well over a decade for some public services, there is no evidence of a difference that they have made. RTI is yet without getting diluted because of the vigil kept by social activists and news media. But its potential is yet to be tapped.

Independent Research and Training

Both reliable data and training are a missing link in our public policy framework. Initiatives, interventions, and correctives for system adjustments will benefit only when backed by pre and post research. Research to understand and analyse issues in social systems and governance has to be based on reliable methodologies, both quantitative and qualitative. MS Swaminathan Research Foundation (MSSRF) in Chennai and Barefoot College in Tilonia, Rajasthan are two different examples that have made critical contributions to social research. Grassroots Research and Advocacy Movement (GRAAM) in Mysore is another such example. We need more of such independent research institutes.

I remember Prof. S.K. Goyal of Indian Institute of Public Administration in New Delhi (1975–1995) bringing to light, 50 years ago, how foreign investments into India were vitiating and how multinational corporations were penetrating into critical sectors of

India. That was much before the economic liberalisation of 1991. Those insights were responsible in sensitising the Parliament in taking certain initiatives. Another example of independent research is the one that I was able to conduct, initially from ORG in Baroda and later from CMS, where I could highlight the linkage between availability of toilets in schools and girls' dropout. Another example is my other research on the linkage between school children reading non-text books and its influence on better citizenship. Government took note of that research almost a decade later because UNICEF already recognised it beforehand.

Child labour is yet another example. It was an ORG report, which brought into light, for the first time, the magnitude of the problem (an estimated 42 million children being involved in child labour then), which the nation took notice of thereafter. Housing needs of the country was another aspect that ORG brought into light in the mid-1970s. I took up another research-based analysis of panchayats, and the outcomes of this research were instrumental in bringing about the correctives in the implementation of the landmark 73 and 74 amendments. The Institute of Social Sciences, New Delhi, is another institute that took to the training of elected women and sensitising elected members. We need more such efforts.

Training is an essential component, both to bring change and to scale up, with specially designed courses and programmes. Even after 15 years of RTI Act having been in effect, only half of the government functionaries could be sensitised about the provisions and only a fraction of activists could be oriented in that direction. For both research and training, the state agencies alone will not do. In fact, independent and professional agencies which take up these essential support services are better to make a difference. If research is not an objective and data is not reliable, it will be more misleading then helpful.

Regulatory Mechanisms

Self-regulation is better than the one from the government. But that is not always enough, particularly where the growth is in leaps and bounds, as in the case of mass media and ICT, for example. Where 'let lose competition' is prevalent, independent regulatory mechanisms should be preferred and research-based expert and user groups should be the active players.

Institutional Support

An individual or one-time committees or a movement or an institution, even independent and professional one, is not enough for a big change in systems and structures. When a big change is contemplated and engineered, institutional support is needed on several fronts. Such complex and gigantic efforts should not be left to one or more individuals, however dedicated and capable they may be. Power of one person is never enough to sustain or consolidate a change in a country the size and diversity of India.

NCAER, Staff College in Hyderabad Barefoot Institute in Tilonia, Rajasthan, Self Employed Women's Association (SEWA) in Ahmedabad, Deccan Development Society in Telangana, or Rayalaseema Seva Samithi in Tirupati, Gandhigram Rural Institute in Madurai, Deshmukh Institute of Development in Uttar Pradesh, GRAAM in Mysore, Area Development Institute in Ahmedabad, Trivandrum and Chennai, Indian Statistical Institute in Kolkata, PRIA, CMS and CSDS are some of the examples of research and training institutes fighting the cause of good governance. Wherever civil society supported institutes have come up, as in Pune, Ahmedabad or Bengaluru, for example, their impact, both locally and nationally, could be evident even after 50 years.

Transparency and Checks and Balances

No movement for change gains ground and could be sustained without transparency in its operations. Efforts for transparency makes an affirmative difference and helps speed up the process. Checks and balances works even better where there is transparency. Checks and balances also implies cross-sectional interactivity, periodical critical appraisals, concerns for the impact of initiatives by different institutes or agencies engaged in the overall process of development, democracy and governance.

Index

About the Author

N. Bhaskara Rao is the founder–chairman of Centre for Media Studies (CMS) and of Marketing and Development Research Associates (MDRA), which is a prestigious market research and forecasting outfit. He is also the founder of Basic Research in Education and Development (BREAD). He is a pioneer in applied social research in India and an eminent mass communication expert with over 50 years of experience.

An independent analyst and a strategic advisor on public policies, public opinion, reforms process, media trends within and across, he is also known as a pioneer in monitoring and evaluation and rating methodologies. Dr Rao has earned three post-graduate degrees and a PhD from the University of Iowa, USA (1970).

Dr Rao made a mark on future studies in India with his 'India 2001' series starting in 1975, sponsored by the Resources for Futures, USA. His work *India 2021* (1985) provided a perspective for the second millennium studies. He initiated and led the *Vision 2020* programme for the Andhra Pradesh government. His 1995 publication *Marketing Communication: Perspectives into Media Scene 2020* provided a basis for the convergence view of communication.

He has authored a number of books. Some of his prominent works are: *Politics of Leadership in an Indian State* (1967), *Controlled Mass Communication in Inter-state Conflicts* (1971), *India 2021* (1985), *Social Effects of Mass Media* (1997), *Good Governance: Delivering Corruption-free: Public Services* (2013), *Poll Surveys in Media—An Indian Perspective* (2012) and *Unleashing Power of News Channels* (2012).